Italian National Cinema 1896–1996

From such films as *Cinema Paradiso* and *Dear Diary*, this book presents a striking image of Italy as a nation and a people. In the first detailed study of Italian cinema from 1896 to the present, Pierre Sorlin explores the changing relationship of Italian cinema and Italian society, and asks whether the national cinema really does represent Italian interests and culture.

Sorlin discusses the work of major filmmakers such as de Sica, Visconti, Fellini, Antonioni and Moretti in the context of national film output, considering both films which became internationally acclaimed and those which, though popular with the domestic audience, were never released outside Italy. Beginning with the evolution of the cinema audience and the development of domestic production, Sorlin examines Italian cinema from the dark years of Fascism through to postwar Neorealism and big-budget commercial films. In the final section he discusses the place of cinema in the context of the rise of television, contemporary political crises in Italy, and Berlusconi's attempts to dominate the media landscape.

Italian National Cinema provides a challenging vision of national cinema, not just as a reflection of Italian culture but for the crucial part it played in the transformation of contemporary Italy. It includes a filmography and bibliography of Italian cinema.

Pierre Sorlin is Professor of Sociology of the Audiovisual Media at the Université Paris III and Fellow of the audiovisual department of the Institute of Contemporary History in Bologna. He is the author of *The Film in History*, *European Cinemas, European Societies* and *Mass-media*.

National Cinemas series
General Editor: Susan Hayward

Reflecting growing interest in cinema as a national cultural institution, the new Routledge *National Cinemas* series brings together the most recent developments in cultural studies and film history. Its purpose is to deepen our understanding of film directors and movements by placing them within the context of national cinematic production and global culture and exploring the traditions and cultural values expressed within each. Each book provides students with a thorough and accessible introduction to a different national cinema.

French National Cinema
Susan Hayward

Australian National Cinema
Tom O'Regan

Italian National Cinema
1896–1996

Pierre Sorlin

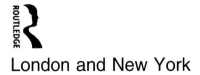

London and New York

First published 1996
by Routledge
11 New Fetter Lane, London EC4P 4EE

Simultaneously published in the USA and Canada
by Routledge
29 West 35th Street, New York, NY 10001

© 1996 Pierre Sorlin

Typeset in Times by BC Typesetting, Bristol

Printed and bound in Great Britain by
Biddles Ltd, Guildford and Kings Lynn

British Library Cataloguing in Publication Data
A catalogue record for this book is available from the British Library

Library of Congress Cataloguing in Publication Data
Sorlin, Pierre.
    Italian national cinema 1896–1996/Pierre Sorlin.
        p.   cm. – (National cinemas series)
    Filmography: p.
    Includes bibliographical references and index.
    (pbk. : alk. paper)
        1. Motion pictures—Italy—History. I. Title.   II. Series:
    National cinemas series (Routledge (Firm))
    PN1993.5.I88S66   1996
    791.43′0945–dc20   95-43288
                                                                                CIP

ISBN 0-415-11697-X (hbk)
ISBN 0-415-11698-8 (pbk)

Contents

Illustrations

PLATES

TABLES

Acknowledgements

It is my good fortune to be on very friendly terms with three leading experts in Italian film studies, namely Aldo Bernardini, Gian Piero Brunetta and Christopher Wagstaff. I was in touch with them while writing this book and their names are often mentioned throughout the volume, but their influence goes much beyond what can be acknowledged here.

I owe special thanks to Susan Hayward, an ideal series editor, scrupulous, helpful and sensitive; her corrections and suggestions have modified my initial text considerably.

I appreciate the help of many people who have commented on sections of this book in its various stages, notably Ronald Clark, Oliver Jenkins and Pippa Reid and I am grateful to them for their invaluable guidance in bringing the project to fruition.

This book would not have been completed were it not for the help and support of many friends, namely the researchers of the Istituto Ferruccio Parri in Bologna, Luca Alessandrini, Luisa Cigognetti and Lorenza Servetti, the members of the 'Trento Group', Lia Baltrami, Ilana Bet-El, Valeria Camporesi, Alon Confino, Kyoko Hirano and Jerry Kuehl, and, last but not least, Giovanna Grignafini, Pepino Ortoleva and Francesco Casetti.

Many media centres provided the access to films and magazines that is so essential to such research but I owe particular gratitude to the Mediateca Toscana and to the wonderful library of the Istituto Ferruccio Parri in Bologna and its librarian, Elena Tripodi.

The author and publishers would like to thank the following for furnishing pictures for the book: Museo civico del comune di Carpi and its curator, Luciana Nora, for the photographs of Carpi; Istituto Ferruccio Parri, Bologna, for stills from *The Last Days of Pompei* and *What Rascals Men Are*; Avant Scène du Cinéma for stills from *The Octopus* and *We Sinners*.

Introduction

In May 1915, Italy entered the First World War. The cinema was then twenty years old, like the young boys who, coming from the islands, from Campania or Tuscany, were sent to die on the dry, treacherous plateau of Carso. The cinema was born, it developed and reached its peak in a world divided by harsh national oppositions; a world where nations were often conceived of as living entities, collective bodies whose defence and expansion seemed worth sacrificing the individuals who made them up. History, be it political history or the history of the arts, had its share in diffusing the concept of national identities. It was responsible for the spread of a semi-mystical idea attached to blood, soil and language.

Images of the past, of a common, shared past, as they appear in history-books or films, are central to the basic, most common conception of a nation. Not surprisingly, when they began to study motion pictures, cinema specialists, following in the tracks of other historians, divided movie production and its history according to state borders. Films have long been taken to be part of a nation's culture, more complex than the institutions and companies which make and circulate them, but still fundamentally governed by national traditions. Politics, diplomacy and trade play an important part here too. Quite often, governments and political parties use what they call safeguarding of their national culture as a pretext to either bargain with other countries or reinforce local prejudices against foreign products. Conversely, producers, directors and technicians who feel threatened by imports lobby for protectionist laws. They say that they are fighting for the preservation of authentic local values but theirs is no more than the attempt of professionals to keep in business and continue to control the local market. Italian film producers never stop complaining about the impending crisis brought about by external competition. There is a powerful impression that little of their rhetoric has changed for a century during which there has been among them a continuing preoccupation with promoting the specificity of national films.

AN INTERNATIONAL BUSINESS

However, cinematography has always been a worldwide craft. Its history ought to be told from two different vantage-points, an international as well as a national one, and it is somehow depressing to see how often it remains narrowly parochial, confined by the limits of one country, in its sources and perspectives. Right from its beginning, the cinema grew as a cosmopolitan business. At the end of the nineteenth century, technologies of sound and picture reproduction were evolving very rapidly. Both scientists and industrialists were anxious to test innovations and adopt, or pirate, them when they were effective. Information was freely available to everyone in the world. Journals published article after article about new devices and data were exchanged back and forth so much that, despite patents, the latest movie-cameras and projectors were imitated by competing firms. People interested in the fashionable medium rushed to the main production centres, and technicians from these places were sent to work elsewhere. The development of cinema came about through permanent exchange. By about 1910, European firms had already set up in America, and American companies were established in Europe. Not only did films circulate, but actors, technicians and filmmakers also travelled from one country to another, diffusing their skills and learning other modes of working which they would later take back home. I do not intend, here, to retell a well-known story, merely to stress that already, before it was twenty years old, the cinema extended beyond national frontiers.

There is nothing original in what has just been said and it may be argued that, while financial or commercial practices, equipment and techniques (lighting, for instance, or special effects) were effectively more or less unified, huge differences persisted in other areas, such as plot construction or story lines, which were nationally determined, and that, with the coming of sound, languages erected barriers which could not be easily crossed. The issue of language is crucial to the debate and it will be dealt with later. But I must first clarify the question of narrative.

In the early years of film exhibition, there were no established conventions since producers were content with selling as much footage as possible. There were short stories but also long documentary pictures. The logic of most programmes was associative rather than sequential. Spectators did not object to jumping from one set to another, or from comedy to drama. As has been demonstrated by David Bordwell and other researchers,[1] a turning-point can be detected at the end of the 1910s, when the short pictures of the previous period became outdated and gave way to what has been called the 'classical cinema'. Taking Romantic and Victorian novels as their models, scriptwriters in all countries wrote continuous, coherent stories based on the social and personal identity of a small group of people. The events told in these fictions were generally not actual but hypothetical, they were neither necessarily involved in the realm of facts, nor necessarily withdrawn from it. In other words, classical films did not merely reproduce a fragment of our planet, they created an autonomous world which reflected aspects of daily life, while also being an original image. Despite its ability to capture the external universe, the mainstream cinematic production, at least till the 1960s, developed less as an 'imitation of life' than as a cultural form based on closed narration and selection of a small number of characters. It is no wonder that structuralist study of narrative, which scrutinizes the formal organization of stories, dominated film-studies for a few decades in the middle of the twentieth century. Such criticism, which defined movie protagonists by the actions they accomplished, retrieved exactly the formulas defined and disseminated by handbooks for screenwriters some fifty years earlier. If we consider the average cinematic production we cannot but acknowledge that the format of the stories, their length and their main components were standard for six or seven decades.

The diffusion of patterns mostly, but not exclusively, concocted in Hollywood, and the consequent standardization of cinematic narration is rather well documented. But the new art also introduced other innovations, especially in the industrial countries. It assembled new kinds of audiences, larger than those that gathered in theatres. It widened the boundaries of what could be shown or talked about. It was not common, before cinema, to reflect on motion in general terms. Film promoted motion in the abstract; together with its contemporary, the motor car, it made people ponder the importance of speed. Likewise, it brought into the public a sense of the collective, of masses evolving in urban spaces, of huge crowds. Perhaps more importantly, it disclosed previously unnoticed aspects of social life. Here I shall emphasize just two significant transformations linked to the propagation of the cinema.

The first transformation has to do with the eroticisation of the human body. In 1917, Antonio Gramsci wrote a short paper about a fashionable actress, Lyda Borelli.[2] 'She is,' he said, 'the actress *par excellence* of the film, in which the only language is the human body with its endlessly refreshed plasticity.' However critical he was of Borelli and her sex appeal, Gramsci made a good point when he stressed the status of bodies, especially of women's bodies in cinema. It is true that the meaning of sexual characteristics is socially constructed and evolves according to the times, signifying alternately innocence or wickedness, purity or shame, weakness or strength. Sexuality has always been a key component of art and literature, but no other form of entertainment had ever made its spectator watch so closely and lengthily openly sexualized bodies, bodies whose motion itself could be eroticized.

A second transformation, possibly more important than the first, is the diffusion of new models of social life. Most representational works, be they novels or plays, paintings or audiovisual creations, provide glimpses into the world in which they have been conceived. I am not speaking here of realism, but of symbols. By tackling problems as basic as life and death, conflict and passion, or even, more simply, food and housing, fictional productions stress simple facts of atmosphere which make up daily life. In the literary productions of the nineteenth and early twentieth centuries, even in those which did not attempt to describe class conflict or social distinctions, allusions to dietary tradition, clothes, furniture and so on ensured that urgent concerns lurked in the background.[3] In most cases, cinema is not as accurate as literature. It does not ignore conflicts but tends to locate them outside any concrete society, in a rather abstract world which could be everywhere. For instance it avoids the lengthy exploration of a house, the description of a meal which, in novels, are so revealing. Films generally come to their public proposing to feature nothing but the highest quality in furniture, clothes, cars. Even in populist dramas describing the situation of the poorest people, everything is perfectly decent. It is open to discussion whether this is some sort of indirect commercial advertisement, a way of promoting saleable goods by screening them, or whether films advertise themselves by providing viewers with the momentary personal pleasure of seeing beautiful objects and being introduced to the homes of the rich. Whatever the reasons, movies have long informed their spectators about up-to-date conventions or habits, they have promoted consumerism and introduced a sense of society as a source of pleasure. The culture that cinema advertises creates an image for the exporting country which redoubles export profits. It is in this way that, thanks to American but also British and French pictures, the Italians were soon informed of a life-style which was not yet theirs and became familiar with it at a time when the spectre of hunger had not yet vanished from Italy. In many parts of the peninsula, especially in the countryside, the old ways survived well into the twentieth century, but cinema contributed to estranging people from habits they themselves still observed.

SEEKING 'NATIONAL' CHARACTERS

Throughout the industrialized world, cinematic production relies on the same bases, tells the same stories with the same range of characters, and uses the same technical devices. However, we assume we can tell an Italian from an American or a German film. What makes us believe that we can distinguish them so easily? There is no clear-cut answer. There is the difficulty of agreeing a commonly accepted set of codes for describing, for instance, 'Italianness', and I guess that, in this respect, there is even a sense of collective self-doubt among Italians. But we must distinguish the way Italians conceive of themselves and the reasons why we bestow on a given film the label 'typically Italian'.

A first criterion might be the display of institutions, habits and values characteristic of the country. I feel uncomfortable with that kind of ill-defined form of measurement since no one can state what is quintessential of any nation. All nations are probably fractured, self-contradictory structures, they have always been better conceived as masses of interest groups than as single, unified entities and, in our days, many of them are tottering on the verge of dissolution. I shall nevertheless risk giving the main outlines of Italy. In my view, Roman Catholicism and communalism are the most significant features of the peninsula.

The Roman Church, with the pope as both sovereign of the Catholic world and bishop of Rome, is an unavoidable given of the country. Church attendance has declined so dramatically, in the second half of the twentieth century, that we tend to forget that, previously, religion was considered a sacred social force and the clergy the constant shadow of secular authority. Religion has long been a central component of communal practices as well as of the various discourses of political theory in which public relations are discussed. It has always had a powerful effect on the way in which national thinking developed.

Early in the Middle Ages, at a time when the feudal system dominated most of Europe, the peninsula witnessed the victory of the producers over the knights, in other words of middle-class over aristocratic values. Hereafter, the pursuit of personal interest prevailed over the pursuit of honour. The peninsula was divided into small urban or, less often, agricultural communities in which people developed fragmented cultures based on a local dialect and a dense network of associations. Italian communalism was defined within, and articulated by, the mosaic of regional and local entities which made up the 'Italian' world. Inward-looking diversity was by far the most salient characteristic of that whole. Each provincial denomination brought to the public arena long-rehearsed and still keenly debated beliefs about its origins, rights and specificities. Italian regions have developed a civilization of their own which makes them distinctive, perhaps as distinct as Belgium from Holland, Spain from Portugal. A good many cities can match Rome, not merely as an economic capital, as in the case of Milan and Turin, but as rival centres of culture.

In the battles they had to fight against centralising powers, domestic or external, the Italian cities found support in the Papacy which feared the bourgeois less than the warriors, and which, looking at the world from an ecumenical point of view, ignored the spread of national claims. This long-lasting alliance deepened the influence of the Catholic Church which, from the beginning, backed Italian communalism. While other territories were unified around a dynasty, the peninsula was known as 'the Italies'. It was not thought, by most of those who inhabited it, to be a country, let alone a nation, people conceived of themselves as heirs of complex of concordant cultures developed in small, limited territories. When the

House of Piedmont began to federate these provinces, in the middle of the nineteenth century, it had to fashion a nation-state before trying to create a nation, but it did not find a clear identity, for Italians have always been far from agreed on the forms a state should assume.[4]

In a long peninsula in which means of force were limited, orders from the centre carried little weight and effective authority derived out of a delicate process of negotiation in which the peripheries had a significant voice in determining what measures would be obeyed. Regions were not united by doctrines of sovereignty but by an unexpressed political process that rested on a general belief in the interest of an enlarged market and on a shared fear of social unrest. Italian elites attached greater importance to economic, and especially commercial, growth than to the development of a common law. Once the old system of independent principalities and towns was transformed into an unitarian realm, people were deprived of a past against which to measure or attach themselves. Unified Italy rested upon mythical foundations, her government imposed an official version of the recent past that bore little relation to history and, therefore, was unable to provide the sense of organic rootedness conveyed by such terms as nation or homeland. The constitutional structures and intermediate civil bodies being weak or lacking, Italian myths focused on either the Church above or the people below. Fascism attempted to create a consensus based on the uniform socialization achieved by concentrated power but, however important it was for the modernization of the country, it was too radically opposed to communalism to survive the defeat it suffered during the Second World War.

I have described at some length what I see as the most important of Italian traditions, only to stress the fact that it would be hard to track them in the country's cinematic production. Little room is left to religion in Italian films. There are priests, sometimes, but they often look ridiculous or old-fashioned and never reflect the lasting influence of the clergy. It is true that most pictures sound highly moralizing, if not edifying, given their way of rewarding loyalty and punishing the baddies. The cinema has often been presented as chiefly a capitalist device to make money while keeping the workers quiet. Of many films that is obviously true. But we know too little about the context in which they were seen and about the manner in which they were received to evaluate their impact. I would rather say that Italian films display a moralism common to the various cinemas of the western world, what was nicely called, in the 1960s, 'a mixture of the Ten Commandments and the common law',[5] that is to say, a mild moralism, neither deferential nor resentful, sometimes superficially subversive, which depends on limited competition, limited conflict and limited coercion. This is a far cry from the flaunting of symbols, habits and rules inherited from the Roman Catholic Church and deeply rooted in the public and private lives of Italians.

The core of Italian as well as other western films is the family. The cult of the household is far from alien to Italian traditions, since kinship remains the most important bridge to sociability. But families are not like the socially unattached, free-floating entities we see featured on the silver screen. In concrete life, they are never conceived of outside a local context which, conversely, is seldom evoked in mainstream cinema. What I am suggesting, here, is obviously much too approximate. We shall come across many films which do not square with the above statements. Nevertheless it remains the case that Italian films, however stereotyped they may be, are not suffused with the dominant trends of Italian culture.

BUILDING A CINEMATIC CULTURE

Instead of considering 'Italianness' a datum which can be hunted down in artistic works, we had better first explore the way foreigners meet the peninsula and its life-style. To begin with, what do foreigners know about its cinema? Out of the 2,405 films that Italy made in the heyday of its cinematic production, the decade 1960–69, 312 found commercial distribution in the United Kingdom, and 280 in the United States. Three titles sum up what attracted the Americans: *The Good, the Bad and the Ugly* (1966), *Constantine and the Cross* (1961), *To Bed . . . or Not To Bed* (1962), in other words spaghetti westerns, historical epics and soft pornos. The British were more eclectic, they took an interest in comedies and dramas, they were also keen on war stories that take place in the Mediterranean. Let us, very approximately, call 'genuinely Italian' those movies whose casts are entirely Italian and which stage Italian characters in typical Italian surroundings of such films. English-speaking audiences were merely offered Dino Risi's *Love and Larceny* (1960), Germi's *Divorce Italian Style* (1961), Vitorio de Seta's *Bandits at Orgosolo* (1961), Pasolini's *Accattone* (1961) and *Mamma Roma* (1962). De Sica's *Two Women* (1960), *The Condemned of Altona* (1962) and *Yesterday, Today and Tomorrow* (1963) were successes but only the first deals with an Italian situation and its cast is international. The biggest Italian hits were Zeffirelli's *The Taming of the Shrew* (1967) and *Romeo and Juliet* (1968) which, not surprisingly, were judged quintessentially Italian so that 'Italianness' was mostly exemplified by the Italian adaptation of Shakespeare! It is true that film buffs could see many more Italian pictures at the London film festival, in film societies, in cinema schools and universities. However, the sample was still limited and, more important, different in the United States and in Britain, which means that, when they talk about the Italian cinema, Americans and English do not refer to the same pictures. It is not necessary to recall that what we watch and how we watch depends in part on what we hear and how much we can understand. Many films (possibly the most characteristic ones) exploit cultural stereotypes (traditions,

Plate 1 Posters: the first step of a cinematic culture, Carpi, 1951. The films advertised, two melodramas, were among the year's biggest hits

regional pronunciation) that foreigners cannot understand and, for that reason, it is almost impossible to sell these pictures abroad. Most Italian films offered to American audiences draw attention to the visual, largely independently of what can be obtained from the accent, slips or even silences from which native speakers usually make sense of a production. The colourings and tonalities of emotion and perception that an actor's speech makes possible are differently, imprecisely and often mistakenly perceived when the actor's language is not that of the spectator or when it has been dubbed.

What has been said up to now does not imply that there are no national cinemas. On the contrary, one of the major aims of this book is to find out what was genuinely Italian or perfectly international in the movies that Italian studios produced. I have merely stressed here the fact that defining what can be labelled 'national' in a film is a problematic task because, unwittingly, most foreign spectators base their opinion on a narrow, inadequate selection of movies while native spectators do not care about 'typical features' since, for them, what they see is 'normal', consonant with their experience. Why then not resort to a simpler solution? A national cinema might be what is projected in the picture-houses of a nation, and defined by the different networks which organize the production of 'national' pictures but also the distribution and exhibition of all kinds of films, domestic or foreign. This implies neither the limitation of cinema to technicalities, nor ignoring what people care about most, the films. It is merely a matter of putting the films in the context in which spectators see and enjoy them. The importance of the system of distribution does need to be stressed. A nation is, among many other things, an area where the creation and transmission of merchandize is regulated according to given rules, in a monetary system and through specified channels. Habits, conventions and standards bring together those who observe them and one of the major problems which confront the European Community is the variety of laws and routines in operation among its members.

Films, which are goods manufactured to be sold, are not an exception. They are made and traded differently in different countries. What accounts for that diversity is what we could call the diversity of cinematic cultures. I take here the word 'culture' in its broad sense, which embraces the reasons why people go to the pictures, the way they attend cinemas, the pleasure they get from films. Giovanni Guareschi, who devised Don Camillo, one of the most famous cinematic and literary characters of Italy, talks in his chronicles[6] of country-people who, every Saturday afternoon, cycled to the town, miles away, and went to the cinema from opening until closing-time at midnight. They were mostly pleased by 'taking part in the story', which meant telling it again and again to other spectators or to people who had not attended. This is, I believe, an excellent example of cinematic culture. We are faced with a regular habit, involving an effort and some money. We note that there is no choice, something we must bear in mind when we are tempted to discourse upon the tastes or preferences of the public. Participation is the spur and the effort is rewarded by the pleasure of voicing shared impressions and memories.

A national cinema might therefore be the whole process of creation, distribution and consumption of films. The films themselves are of course central to the whole business. In the above-mentioned instance, people gather to see pictures and then endlessly talk about them. There would be no meeting without films. However, the making and circulation of movies would not be what it is if attendance was erratic instead of regular or if spectators were only keen to see westerns. Practice, itself determined by various factors such as environment, jobs and availability of other forms of entertainment, is what influences the programming of films. In this respect, the distinction often made between 'quality' and 'mainstream' cinema becomes less relevant. The distinction, based on aesthetic principle, does not provide decisive reasons for supposing that military comedies, melodramas or tear-jerkers are automatically seen by the uneducated and the poor, while highbrows prefer masterpieces. How and for what purpose people go to the cinema are the two questions which have to be answered first.

In my view, a national cinema is not a set of films which help to distinguish a nation from other nations, it is the chain of relations and exchanges which develop in connection with films, in a territory delineated by its economic and juridical policy. Historians will argue that, for them, a nation is a geographic entity where people are united by institutions, traditions and a language which, simultaneously, reflects and shapes the national character, and so my definition is akin to theirs, minus the reference to an idiom. Language plays a crucial part in conveying the sense of a movie but, oddly enough, it is not characteristic of its nationality. It is obvious that the English or the Spanish cinemas are not defined by their English or Spanish soundtrack and that Mexicans and Spaniards can understand the same dialogue without sharing the same ways of thinking or the same sense of what is precious.

It is different with Italian, which is scarcely spoken outside the peninsula. We must also take into account two other aspects of Italian cinematic culture. When sound films began, 'standard' Italian was not the dominant language of the country. It was used by the political or religious authorities, taught in universities and high schools and spoken by the elite, but most inhabitants continued to use local or regional dialects. Together with radio and later television, cinema helped introduce Italian to zones where, otherwise, it would not have been heard. Far from taking their identity from the language they use, filmmakers have actively co-operated in giving official Italian its present status of most common idiom in the peninsula.

Except in film societies, films are always released in Italy with Italian dialogue. However a good half of the pictures offered every year are of foreign, mostly American, origin. Dubbing has become a well paid job for actors and studios. A movie, once it has been dubbed, is a new product, akin to its master and at the same time significantly different from it. Every translation is an invention, the substitution of one sign for another, a new performance of a previous text which, as such, constitutes an original text. Let us consider a concrete case. Kubrick's *The Killing* (1956) has been titled, in its Italian version, *Rapina a mano armata* (*Armed Robbery*). A title is primarily a name which, like other names, when it is heard or seen, calls up images. *The Killing* announces something tragic; a routine hold-up turns into a disaster because someone has been murdered and, right from the beginning, spectators, while watching the quiet preparation of the raid, guess that some catastrophe is about to happen. *Armed Robbery* leads the public to expect a standard gangster story, so that the killing comes as a surprise. It can be argued that constructing and frustrating spectators' expectations is not a good strategy but what concerns us is another point: American and Italian distributors adopted two different techniques which resulted in two different ways of luring their respective audiences. For dubbing, an accurate translation of the dialogue would have been meaningless – the stifling and ultimately pointless task of finding exact equivalents between two incompatible cultures. But the conversational style adopted for the Italian version, the use of local slang, the unmistakably Roman accent of the actors, offer a highly specific view of the life and fate of the protagonists. Americans and Italians do not see the same Kubrick, which implies that cinematic studies must be concerned with both the process of translation, examining the ways in which translations work, as language and as art, and with the reception of the translation in its new culture. *Rapina a mano armata* is an acclimatized product that spectators easily put in the series of Rome-made, or Hollywood-made gangster movies. Language, in this instance, does a strange trick, it camouflages an object which belongs to the national cinema (people see it like any genuine Italian picture) while being alien to it (nobody thinks that the action takes place in Milan or Rome). For that reason, I feel very reluctant to define a national cinema according to the idiom spoken in films. Language is obviously a basic component of any culture but, unlike tools, or objects, it does not exist

Plate 2 Lobby of the cinema 'Corso', Carpi, 1948. Italian versions of American films

outside those who perform it. It signals the nationality of a film but, simultaneously, this film contributes to actualizing the language, to making it alive and accessible.

FIVE GENERATIONS OF CINEMA-GOERS

A nation is, at least as it is classically stated, a territory, a set of traditions and a language, but how far, and in what way, do works of art 'reflect' these basic features? We know so little about the effects of reading or cinema-going that we cannot refer the attitudes of readers or viewers to the hallmarks of the country in which they live. Understanding the function of cinema in a given area is not a matter of using predetermined criteria such as a so-called 'national characteristic'. In the last analysis it is a question about both the actual, purely material conditions of reception, and the impressions, the poetic, fanciful halo which surround all artistic creations. Viewing is first a social practice, depending on the context in which it occurs, and closely linked to the modes of consumption and enjoyment of the facilities of modern life. Viewing is also a largely imaginative activity, a way of taking pleasure in recorded pictures and sounds. These two processes, the tangible and the illusive ones, work towards shaping the reception of films within national boundaries, but they do not develop at the same pace. The former, caused by technical innovations as well as by competition between different producers and various means of entertainment, is a short-term transformation. The latter is a slow evolution, the gradual acclimatization of people to a new mode of representation. Since the end of the nineteenth century life has been reflected in pictures, and all those born since then have seen the world in which they live recreated for them on the screen, so that they have got used to having images tell them something about their own surroundings and play a pre-eminent part in defining what they are. The cinema of a nation, or rather the cinema consumed by the members of a nation, combines this long-lasting impregnation with short-term oscillations. Throughout the century that cinema has already covered, people have became more and more used to thinking in visual terms. But, simultaneously, the production and circulation of films, and the curiosity aroused by movies have not stopped changing. We must concern ourselves with the alternating rise and decrease in attendance and avoid a dynamic, continuous vision of an evolution which was never uniform. No simple factor can explain why people went to the cinemas or deserted them. A rush for the cinemas coincided with the relative prosperity of the 1920s and with the lack of it in the 1940s, It could be interpreted, sometimes, as a mark of social stability, but also as a response to social tension. What is more, practices were not uniform, either socially or geographically, during any period and it was encouraged or discouraged by patterns of family life and local traditions.

Any society is a blending of various generations, each of which has its own traditions and concerns. Let us imagine a cinema somewhere, in Rome or San Gimignano, at the end of the 1950s, when Antonioni's *The Cry* (1957), or Rossellini's *Il Generale della Rovere* (1959) were first released. The theatre was filled by at least three different groups. The oldest spectators were born shortly after the political unification of the peninsula, in a new, dynamic country; they belonged to one of the few generations to have an optimistic vision of their time which they thought superior to any other. Another group was made of people born with the movies who had participated, in their twenties, in a series of unparalleled catastrophes, the two world wars, the full retreat of liberal political ideals, the rise of Fascism. As for the last cohort, born between the wars, it had gone through hard times but had also benefited, when it reached its twenties, from a democratic style of politics, a booming economy and changes more profound than in any other comparable brief period. It seems unlikely that the historical experience of people of such dissimilar ages and backgrounds was comparable. Our imaginary spectators were looking at the same pictures but they could not interpret them in the same way and it would be unfair to generalize 'the response of the audience' from one generation to another. We need thus to take into account the increasing familiarity with pictures from period to period and the brutal changes imposed by momentary circumstances. The history of Italian cinema could then be conceived as follows:

– A first generation enthuses about the new art, the blossoming Italian production does not meet the demand, and foreign movies get a good reception.

– For the second generation, going to the pictures has become a habit. Local production, now less than that of Spain or Austria, is not sufficient, foreign films conquer the market. Radio creates new habits of collective hearing and triggers interest in sound films.

– Audiences of the third generation are recomposed by the arrival of suburban and rural viewers. National film production, which develops quickly, supplies more than a half of what is shown and is able to sell its products abroad; young filmmakers and technicians work at Cinecittà, equipped with some of the best studios in the world.

– The fourth generation, whose expectations have increased with prosperity are more interested in television than in films. Hollywood fights to maintain its position in the market while the local studios resist thanks to public subsidies.

– Countless commercial networks and video producers appeal to the fifth generation; producers need fiction films and boost the studios. Audiences decrease while filmmaking booms.

In this short outline, I have not alluded to the significance and valuation assigned to films. We cannot find, in any of the above-mentioned generations, a stable and coherent manner of understanding the cinema. In this respect, antagonistic readings are to be found within the same period. A study of the national Italian cinema cannot be based either on the interpretations proposed by the viewers themselves, or on our analysis of specificities expressed in pictures. It has to look first at practices and understand how people use cultural artefacts such as films to enjoy themselves and achieve a sense of the world they inhabit. What part cinema has played in Italian life should be our main concern.

Now, this is not an easy task. The sources for the study of social practices as seemingly simple as visiting cinemas pose enormous problems. About four-fifths of the films shown during the first decades of cinema have been lost. The limitation of the surviving records from before 1945 means that the prospects for not only a qualitative, but also a quantitative history of audiences are poor. There is an abundant supply of figures from 1945 onwards. But these statistics are not mere sources of evidence, they are statements of money owing, generated with a precise purpose: to monitor the circulation of films, in order to bring to the producers of Italian films their percentage of takings. It is better to have these documents than nothing, but accounts are not objective reports, they are influenced by the financial interest of those who use them. Figures do not 'photograph' national attendance, they tell producers how much money they may claim. I mention this to make it clear, once more, how a 'nation' is an aggregate of groupings pursuing their individual, divergent (producers' against exhibitors') aims within the framework of a shared practice (selling films).

Film critics and the many intellectuals who soon began writing about films were not as prejudiced or self-interested as the businessmen. However, their statements can never be taken uncritically, even when they look purely factual. The acceptance of cinema as an art was what could be called a construction of values. Defending Italian films was an expression of national dignity that can be traced from its beginning as a test of ability ('We do as well as the others') through its introduction in cultural events (the Venice festival, created to promote Italian films), down to the international fame won thanks to the triumph of Neorealism. Talking about movies was often a speech act, a recourse to a supposedly analytical discourse to do something else, namely to say that one was proud, or ashamed, to be Italian. The first feature-length film, *Dante's Inferno* (1911) got an enthusiastic response because journalists could say 'As an Italian, I am very pleased with it' or 'It is good for the development of a national culture.'[7] Conversely, exiles or opponents criticized Italian films in order to attack, indirectly, the country, its leaders and its life-style. Alberto Savinio, poet, playwright and film critic, never stopped lamenting the bad quality of the pictures made in the peninsula because he had a grudge against what he considered the parochialism of Italian culture.[8] Under Fascism, and also in the years of Christian-Democrat hegemony, the left overrated foreign productions in order to underrate what was made in Italy.[9] The so-called 'white telephones', the comedies of manners of the 1930s, exemplify this: critics unanimously condemned them and they were then considered infamous because they had been made under Fascism. It is only recently that researchers have looked at them rather than simply repeating that they were uninteresting.[10]

If the reader understands me as saying that there is little evidence available, I have not made myself clear. Statistics or newspapers and memoirs are invaluable for a history of cinematic production and audiences. However, while using them, we must recall that they convey impressions as much as information and that they were parts in the very process of creation and expansion of Italian cinema. There is always a critical gap between the subjective opinion of direct witnesses and the more distanced vision of historians but this does not mean that we cannot give a precise, substantiated presentation of subjective points of view – the points of view of those who, year after year, attended cinemas and created the Italian cinematic culture.

To give an account of the whole of Italian cinema in a book of this size is of course impossible. Panoramic studies often leave their readers short on details. I have chosen to mention few films, to concentrate on rather well known pictures and never to sacrifice the kind of close analysis needed to help evaluate the specific features and interest of a film.

The problem of film titles could only be solved according to the individual case. For some there is an English equivalent. When there was no English counterpart, titles have been translated literally but the Italian original can be found, with information on the production, in the Filmography. In some cases, the English substitute is inadequate: *Spivs*, for instance, does not convey the very peculiar significance of *Vitelloni*, a technical term for baby calves metaphorically bestowed on inadequate, emotionally immature adults. *Spivs* offers a different meaning, but it has acquired such power that a more accurate translation would fail to suggest the shade of meaning involved in the title commonly used in English-speaking countries. And this reminds us that, not being Italians, we do not see Italian films as Italians do.

First generation
The world in a dark room

The first Italian picture show took place in Rome on the 12 March 1896. It was staged by a travelling salesman of the Lumière brothers, two French industrialists who manufactured photographic and cinematic equipment, and presented moving pictures to advertise their cameras. A year later, the new art had already been tried out in all the big cities and had met everywhere with an enthusiastic response.

CINEMA-GOING AS A SOCIAL ACTIVITY

We know little about the first cinema-goers, which is a pity, because the end of the nineteenth century was one of those interesting moments when new ways of understanding public awareness become necessary. However, to isolate film-going from the context in which it developed would be misleading for various forms of cheap pictures, drawings printed in popular magazines, engraving and photography overlapped each other and influenced the newborn medium. Initially, the cinema was merely an extension of photography and there is no reason to marvel at its quick expansion, which occurred because photographers had accustomed people to concern themselves with analogous images. The close relationship between the two kinds of pictures must be born in mind where the origins of the cinema are concerned. In Rome, Milan and other cities, filmshows were organised in photo studios. The Lumières, who were anxious to distribute moving pictures that attracted the public, hired Italian photographers, who filmed what otherwise they would have photographed. These men were hampered by the very problems that the Lumières had previously faced. Their cumbersome and expensive equipment was burdensome and, in consequence, they tended to shoot scenes which did not present particular difficulties. This resulted in the emergence of a few recurring patterns such as street scenes, royal visits, military parades. Spectators did not get bored, mostly because they were fascinated by the moving things or people they were offered. Newspapers often presented the films as 'living photographs' (*fotografie viventi*) and expanded on the technical devices which permitted the production of an illusion of locomotion; they stressed the fact that the medium created permanent records of what human beings, animals, or trains looked like when they were in action.

But motion alone was not a sufficient spur to explain the public's interest, all the more so because audiences got quickly used to the novelty, and we must consider other motives. The cinema succeeded because exhibitors cleverly exploited its potential, because in moving picture-shows spectators found something which appealed to them, and because the medium, while it offered escape into a world of fantasy where distances no longer existed and where illusions could become reality, also opened a window on current issues and helped to understand the contemporary world. Films created a new form of culture, a culture in which the world could be observed from a darkened room. This, of course, was true in many parts of the world, and we must now emphasize the traits which distinguished Italy from other countries.

Theatre owners were quick to see the commercial value of the moving pictures and to exploit its money-making potential. It is often contended that, initially, the cinema was a cheap, popular form of entertainment. A close examination of the figures given on posters or in the papers establishes that, for low-priced seats, the charge was less than the cost of a half kilo of pasta. Going to the pictures was an inexpensive form of entertainment and was praised as such by its patrons. However, another side of the business must be considered. According to the comfort or the seat location, the cost could vary by a factor of up to eight, which suggests that affluent people were also used to frequenting picture houses[1]. The new art had various types of audiences at its disposal but, despite the many divisions between them, these audiences did not exist in isolation from each other, they all contributed in creating curiosity about the medium. For about a decade, pictures were seldom considered self-sufficient. They were more often part of a much longer spectacle and were used as interludes in musicals, reviews, vaudeville or variety shows. Cinema and live performance were thus closely linked in a country where theatre or opera and their stars were extremely popular with a broad range of the public. Travelling troups had an avid following not only among aristocrats, landowners and industrialists but among town and country people in general: they went all over the country playing to enthusiastic audiences in small cities and even villages. The boundaries between 'cultivated' and 'popular' entertainment, in terms of content and acting, were relatively blurred where theatre was concerned, so that different social strata were not surprised to frequent the same spectacle. This is not to say that cinema was latent in earlier theatrical forms but that the cinema made the most of pre-existing traditions. Some itinerant exhibitors of films went from funfair to funfair as conjurers used to do.

Other exhibitors came to an agreement with a pub or a *birreria* (tavern) and their films substituted for singers or pianists. Others for a few days, rented auditoriums or theatres; the inhabitants of Reggio Emilia were most impressed when, for the first and only time, their municipal theatre, which was strictly reserved for plays, accommodated a two-week moving-picture show in May 1902. The cinema was something to be enjoyed by everybody, advertisements stressed its universal appeal and perfect innocence. But the cleverest exhibitors also managed exceptional presentations. While families were expected to come on Saturdays and Sundays, other performances took place on weekdays. *Serate nere* (black evenings) were organized 'for adult men only'; special shows were aimed at amateurs interested in travelling, exploration or the news of the day. Newspapers even mention 'a presentation arranged for seminarists during which many ecclesiastics expressed their view'.[2]

In 1907, a journalist could write, using verbs in the past tense: 'the cinema had come to be part of people's ordinary life; saying that we were going to the pictures sounded as normal as saying that we were going to bed or to eat'.[3] Attending moving-picture houses was already a social habit and the importance of this fact must be kept in mind. Countless accounts prove that the performance was often of poor quality. We are told for instance that, in Rimini, 'advertisements induced people to expect an exciting event; a massive audience promised the management plenty of cash. Alas! Instead of wonders, obscurity. Nothing or, rather, an illumination of cries, shouts, screams, whistles coming from spectators who wanted to see something. Once more there was no honesty, the public was sent back to contemplate the stars and insult the stagehand'.[4] Viewing depends on the context in which it occurs. Spectators could simultaneously be angry about the quality of projection and happy to meet in an agreeable ambiance. A moving-picture house, again in Rimini, was praised because 'the daily shows are splendid, people enjoy a delicious cool, exquisite drink, and spend very little'.[5] The cinema promoted new opportunities for social contact. To take one simple fact: by looking at the films shot at the beginning of the century we can observe how quickly people got used to encountering a camera operator in the street and taking off their hat to his camera, in case some of their friends saw them on the screen. In the public mind the cinema was conceived as a means of communication.

This is not to say that programmes comprised just prosaic, uninspiring street scenes, only that we must not overrate their impact on viewers. Still, by watching early films, another interesting fact can be noted: captions grow in number, while posters give more and more detail about the content of the pictures. We may infer from this data that spectators, tired of seeing unidentified locations, asked for more precise information. The attention paid to the cinema by Italians was an expression of concern for the outer world as well as for their own country. We must recall that, in striking contrast to Britain or France, Italy had no national newspaper published in Rome. Most dailies were printed in regional capitals and dealt extensively with local concerns. With the cinema, for the first time Italians living in different regions could watch almost simultaneously the pope, the king and his family, floods in Venice, parishioners coming out after mass in Florence, Etna erupting and also events filmed in America or in Asia. The landscapes or scenes presented in the first films, the way they were framed, had such an impact on spectators that many of them provided patterns for subsequent productions.

For some ten or fifteen years, cinema presentations were strings of contrasting, interchangeable films each based on a distinct event or geographical situation. Momentary effect, and not consistency over the length of the projection, was a determining factor but, far from being disconcerting, this permanent shift of focus gave people the impression that there was always a surprise to come. Reviews and circus performances, relying on disconnected numbers, had proved a successful formula. In the first place, the cinema took the music-hall and fairground attractions as models, it sought to maintain variety.[6] Its shows, made up of small unrelated sequences, could be tailored to the taste of a particular audience; they were alternately instructive or dramatic, exotic and colourful or familiar, but they were always simply factual. As late as 1908, a journalist, pondering 'The Future of the Cinema', considered it merely 'an illustrated and animated newspaper, providing weekly graphic, moving information on all the most important events'.[7]

Moving-picture shows began in Italy as early as in any other European country. But the films that enthralled the Italians were shot by foreign companies and local film production did not start before 1905. By this time, an audience had already come into existence. The evolution of film-making, as of any form of industrial manufacturing, is a permanent dialectic between supply and demand. Now, in the peninsula demand took precedence.

FILMOPOLI: THE BIRTH OF AN INDUSTRY

Despite its long urban tradition, Italy in about 1880 was still a predominantly rural kingdom with four-fifths of her inhabitants living in small towns or in the country. A tremendous change occurred between 1895 and the First World War: the leading sectors, metalworking, engineering, and chemistry, developed very quickly, bringing capitalists and shareholders substantial profits; domestic trade boomed, banks, insurance companies and department stores were set up in regional capitals. Simultaneously, large numbers of country people moved to the North from the

South and central regions to work in the new factories. The population of Milan doubled during the last decades of the nineteenth century and other industrial cities witnessed a similar increase. The destruction of an old district of Florence, in order to lay out a monumental square lined with modern buildings, exemplifies the innovations which altered urban landscapes: town centres were no longer conceived as residential and commercial areas, they were meant to attract the city dwellers and provide them with pleasure and entertainment. Walter Benjamin, in various essays (although they cannot be considered a methodical study), has speculated that the building most typical of late nineteenth-century urbanism was the covered passage where people would endlessly gaze into the windows, musing quietly to themselves. His intuition is largely supported, in Italy, by architectural treatises and, more importantly, by arcades erected in most cities at the end of the nineteenth century. The covered ways allowed passers-by to go from one part of the city to another, onlookers could watch quietly, and bright lights induced them to glance at the shops and, hopefully, to enter them. Not surprisingly, when entrepreneurs decided to build permanent moving-picture houses, they located them in arcades, assuming that people circulating among stores, pubs and boutiques would be tempted to have a rest and would buy a ticket. In a few years, big cinemas opened in Naples, Florence, Rome and Milan. Most of them have been destroyed but photographs remain of the Moderno, a Roman palace inaugurated by Filoteo Alberini in 1904. The theatre was a long, high, impressive room, with a painted ceiling; its four hundred seats were all on the same level, while the screen, put at the top of the wall, dominated the audience. As journalists noted, there was something monumental and powerful in these temples of the new art.[8]

In the new cinemas, the shows were scheduled precisely. The public, which could no longer come and go, as it used to do in music-halls and pubs, demanded more coherent programmes. Filoteo Alberini soon became aware of the problem and tried to solve it by creating a production company. In 1905, his firm made what historians consider the first indigenous movie, *The Fall of Rome*, an evocation of the conquest of Rome by Italian troops in 1870. This unpretentious film[9] was a milestone in the evolution of Italian cinema. Alberini advertised it in a very clever way, he had it screened in the open air, in front of thousands of people. He invited society personalities, met with an extremely favourable response in the papers, and distributed his work in the best theatres in the country. In short, he created the promotion of national films in Italy. However, he was soon obliged to sell his firm, which became Cines, an anonymous company controlled by a big bank: capitalists were quick to get hold of the fledgling film production.[10]

The history of the Italian cinema industry is a complicated one which has been clarified by the detailed and careful research of Aldo Bernardini.[11] In the wake of Alberini's commercial attempt, numerous businessmen launched their own companies and there was an explosion in the number of small independent firms in the most important cities. From 126 in 1906, the output of films rose to 482 in 1908 and 867 in 1910, an increase of 700 per cent in five years. We must not be over-impressed by the figures: the longest films lasted no more than twenty minutes and most ran for five to eight minutes; they were generally prosaic, hurriedly made and were not easy to sell; film historians have long despised them but they are interesting today because they show the spread of film-making, a sudden growth which was purely speculative. Bernardini quotes a long series of small advertisements which read as follows: 'We are looking for financial partners likely to invest in cinematic undertaking heading for certain success'.[12] Most of these firms went bankrupt. The early years of the Italian motion picture industry was a history of young entrepreneurs who believed that they could jump in without spending money. However, at the same time capitalists attentive to the evolution of the international market, found that the motion picture industry was no longer a gamble but a good investment. Major companies and well known financiers got involved in the field. Bernardini, who has dug out the archives, lists industrialists, lawyers and landowners, often descended from aristocratic families, who united to monopolize the industry.[13] This is an intriguing story which deserves close scrutiny.[14] The northern provinces of Italy, Piedmont, Lombardy and Emilia, have long been integrated commercially and financially into the economies of Central Europe. They reacted early to the markets created by the industrial revolution, adapted their agriculture to changes in world demand, developed textile workshops which provided the peasants with a cash supplement to their subsistence incomes and integrated them into a monetary economy. In cities lived a rich, open-minded entrepreneurial class with worldwide financial and intellectual connections, which was interested in technical innovation and was ready to invest large amounts of money. Turin and Milan witnessed almost simultaneously the expansion of car factories, chemical plants and film production. If there is something typically Italian in the birth of the film industry, it is surely the sudden emergence of giant film studios. In 1911, three firms, Itala-Film and Società Anonima Ambrosio, both from Turin, and Cines, shot sixty per cent of the Italian films, including the only four movies which lasted more than an hour. Together with three less important companies, they made 80 per cent of the production. In the years leading up to the First World War, a group of entrepreneurs turned the industry into a large, busy operation bringing in very sizeable profits.

It must not be forgotten that the international market was then widely open. An historical phenomenon of major significance for the course of Italian history through the nineteenth and early twentieth centuries was the Diaspora. The United States notably, but also Argentina and Brazil, witnessed the formation, under the benign auspices of Catholic priests, of communities of dispossessed exiles who maintained a 'faith and father-land' ethos and created a communications network to keep in touch with the homeland. In some cities, in New Jersey for instance, up to a third of the population was of Italian origin, so Italian goods sold well there. For people who were usually poor and illiterate, film was a powerful medium by which traditions were kept alive, at least for one or two generations. The American exhibitors needed pictures not only for the immigrants but also for a booming native audience. Many of them, who did not want to abide by the rules of the Major American production houses, got in touch with European producers. Feature-length films were still few and far between at the beginning of the 1910s; the movie com-panies, fearing imitation, were used to making ten- to fifteen-minute films for short-term bookings, which put exhibitors in an awkward position since they were obliged to change their programmes every week or so. Buying Italian movies, which were not too expensive, was a good bargain for American distributors.[15] Conversely, the biggest Italian firms, once they had contracted with the United States, were in a position to develop their output: in 1914, they made ninety films lasting more than an hour, which were all sold abroad. The growth experienced after 1910 triggered expansion in all fields of the industry. Initially, the studios were relatively small so that filmmakers, when they wanted to shoot exterior scenes, went outdoors, on the city streets, and filmed what was happening there. This practice continued in Naples, where small firms went on making cheap films. But the most powerful companies settled in vast studio areas, larger than those generally used in America. Speaking of the few years immediately before the war, Gian Piero Brunetta reminds us that a journalist called Turin 'filmopoli': the city of films. It was not Turin which imitated Hollywood but the latter which emulated the former.[16]

'EXCELLING IN THE STAGE-HANDLING OF A GREAT NUMBER OF PEOPLE'

The Italian studios were then the biggest in Europe. We can explore them thanks to photographs but also, more importantly, thanks to *Mariute* (1918), a moving picture which illustrates the making of a film and which is one of the earliest examples of the 'film in a film' genre. The initiative was taken by a famous actress, Francesca Bertini, who had her

Plate 3 The quality of Italian lighting. *The Last Days of Pompei* (1913, director Eleuterio Rodolfi)

own company and wanted to make fun of the star system of which she was herself a part.

With regard to location, the main problems that filmmakers had to solve were lighting and scenery.[17] The film stock used during the early decades of the twentieth century, the orthochromatic film, was slow and sensitive only to the short wavelengths, from violet to green. Most companies counteracted the effect of these disadvantages by resorting to artificial illumination which, being both intense and stable, was sufficient to create an illusion of sunlight. The Italians were unconventional in showing a preference for natural light. Sunlight is free and provides a soft radiance, but it evolves during the day. Producers, except perhaps the smaller ones, did not bother about low costs but perceived the unique quality of skylight. The walls and ceiling of the workrooms were made of glass, the variations of sunshine were adjusted by curtains which filtered the sun's rays and oriented the light towards the most significant points. The illumination of the sets, as can still be observed today on the few available films, looks astonishingly plain and temperate; any kind of shadow, any trace of cloud have been removed, the background seems perfectly uniform. However the developing process imposed by the slow speed of the film was likely to create strong contrasts and the Italians were very clever in playing with oppositions. The simplest trick was to either blacken or whiten the environment and take the reverse colour for the actors, but there were many variants between the two extreme solutions. Carbon arc lamps were of course available but they were merely used to obtain special effects, for instance to emphasize dramatic moments and accentuate their dramatic impact, and their strength, limited though it was, was not negligible, as we shall see. The originality of the Italian lighting must not be overrated, as analogous devices were known elsewhere, notably in Denmark. However, for a decade there was undoubtedly an Italian skill in creating luminous compositions which vanished at the beginning of the 1920s, when a more sensitive film stock, the panchromatic, was universally adopted.

Even, regular lighting perfectly suited interior settings which were generally very simple. *Mariute* cleverly intercuts shots of Bertini's home and shots of the studio where fans and technicians are waiting for the star. The decor of both spaces and the arrangement of the objects are more or less similar, there is little furniture and the walls are uniformly white. This correspondence is intended to deprive the scenery of any dramatic function. Flat, colourless partitions do not relate to the characters, they do not become a significant part of the action; it is not the décor that matters, but the work of the actors.

However, in strong contrast with this radical plainness, the Italians often had recourse to an artificial depth-of-field which might be better called a duplication of the cinematic space. The technique derived from a practice common in theatres: while actors were performing front of stage, a distant character could be seen on a second stage at the back to suggest simultaneity of actions, or evoke some distant country. Filmmakers reworked and refined the procedure. In the foreground, they often managed a room kept in twilight, with a wide opening giving onto a brightly lit space; filmmakers composed scenes in which the main action took place in this extended background while secondary, more limited movement occupied the foreground. Such a construction permitted an interesting variety of relationships between the two planes; actions could be co-ordinated or disconnected; there was no principal space but a possibility to alternate indoor and outdoor scenes. Again, it is easy to demonstrate that the Italians were not the first to create this impression of depth of field, which seems to have appeared earlier in France. But, at that time, there was no question of competition; the same forms and constructions were experienced simultaneously in diverse areas. The point is that the Italians made clever use of the double stage over a long period.

The landscapes in Italian films were beautifully filmed. Even the Americans were obliged to admit their outstanding quality and sentences such as 'the settings are superb' or 'the settings are remarkable for

Plate 4 A soft, ill-defined background. *Malombra* (1947, Carmine Gallone)

picturesque effect', 'attractive stage-settings and out-door scenes' appeared frequently in their papers.[18] Italian cameramen were used to working out-doors and mastered easily the vagaries of the weather. Sometimes, when they had to shoot against a lake or a mountain, they focused on the foreground, thus delineating an ill-defined, soft background divided into various bands or patches of black and grey. But, most of the time, film-makers managed to obtain a perfect sharpness throughout the field, thus enabling the actors to move about freely, according to the development of the plot.[19] While emphasis was put on the actors in the indoor scenes, outdoor episodes attempted to establish a relationship between the characters and their surroundings. In many cases, landscapes were inserted at crucial moments, in order to create suspense or illustrate the state of mind of a protagonist. Elements of the scenery, notably architec-tural devices, might also divide the screen into smaller areas and contrast two or more actions. In *The Last Days of Pompei* (1913), for example, the urban architecture, luxuriously reconstructed, determined lanes where actors were obliged to walk, while a clever opposition between sunny and shadowy grounds opposed those who were smart and happy and those who were not. However, in general far more shots were taken merely to celebrate, capture and enhance the splendour and brightness of Italian nature – to give pleasure. In *Satanic Rhapsody* (1917), against the background of a gorgeous sunset over a lake, a group of people, filmed from slightly above, advances slowly, under an archway of trees, while a herd of oxen crosses the near foreground. The shot, which is rather long, has no psychological or narrative motivation; it has been made to play on various movements: ripples on the water, gusts of wind, gestures of the protagonists, the quiet passing of the cattle.

Italian panoramas were famous in the 1910s but what was unanimously considered exceptional was the mastery of crowds. Foreign critics celebrated the Italian excellence 'in the stage handling of a great number of people'.[20] In the mid-1910s, the Americans matched and even surpassed the Italian skill but for some five years previously the pre-eminence of Italian filmmakers was unquestionable. This was partly due to good command of the depth of field, excellent knowledge of the variations of sunlight, the quality of the settings and an amazing sense of graphic composition. But there was something else, an extreme ability to create a feeling of perfect liveliness, of delicacy and grace. The first part of *Satanic Rhapsody* begins with a long shot of a meadow taken from slightly above. Young women dance round in a ring while young men prance about in the circle. The camera then gets closer, it catches other young women who are dancing, playing on a swing in the middle of the field; couples arrive in batches from the background, cross the screen, whirl, frolic, play with other couples, slip away, the whole sequence is like a symphony of pure, refined, indefatigable motion. Sophisticated though it may look this extended scene is not uncommon. However, generally, the handling of crowds was more functional, more appropriate to the unfolding of the plot. Expectation, anxiety, doubt, which were the most traditional ingredients of dramas, were systematically replaced by the art of making extras move expressively. Let us briefly examine the screening of a classical situation, the last moments of an innocent person condemned to death in American and Italian films. The former tend to play on audience's fears and manage a last-minute rescue. The latter avoid any kind of suspense. In *Agnes Visconti* (1910), to take but one example, spectators had no time to be afraid. Once Agnes was condemned, there was no long, harrowing tension; the friends and foes of the poor woman entered her jail, thus creating a permanent, enjoyable excitement. Even the most famous movies of the period, *The Last Days of Pompei* (1913), *Quo Vadis?* (1913), *Cabiria* (1914), indulged in extensive sequences of pure movement. The earthquake which is the climax of *The Last Days of Pompei* is loosely edited; it is impossible to figure out either what is happening or why some people survive while others die. The great thrill of this episode resides in the fact that various groups, suddenly entering the field, running, briskly making an about-turn, finally breaking up, stir the hearts of the viewers. Dramatic action did not depend on bizarre accidents or chance, the thrill came in the controlled comings and goings, crossings, runnings, and departures of a great many, often hundreds, of people.

Plate 5 Quo Vadis? (1913, Enrico Guazzoni)

American critics honestly acknowledged the unquestioned merits of Italian cinematic art. But at the same time American studios developed another style which would soon supersede the European one. Having analysed on a moviola (editing table) an important sample of both cinematographies, Barry Salt has clearly summarized what he considers their most important differences.[21] He notes first that the average shot was briefer in Hollywood than in Italian films. Roughly speaking, for the same length of film, there were twice as many shots in American films. The scale of shot distribution showed a certain consistency in Italy, most films were made of medium shots, the editing was extremely simple, with no variations of scale, no reverse angle cuts, no parallel editing. In short, while the Americans alternated between different shots, took close-ups and constantly changed the location of the camera, the Italians preferred a small number of shots, concentrated several actions between the foreground and the background and developed their stories mostly through an excellent cast of characters perfectly lit and photographed.

Even if measurements or counts are arguable and prove very little,[22] the points made by Salt are important in helping a better appreciation of the work of Italian cinematographers. The predominance of medium shots in the handling of the narratives can be easily documented. In *Mariute*, a long shot of the whole studio, taken while Bertini is playing the 'film in the film' (the scene Bertini is supposed to play for another film, and which is supposed to be filmed like an ordinary sequence) shows the camera positioned about four metres from the actors and aimed at their chests. This sequence is made of just one prolonged short. Bertini has a heated argument with a man, they move to and fro, move closer or withdraw. In this sequence, and more generally in Italian films, actors have to portray, in gestures and attitudes, the whole gamut of emotions which, in an American picture, would partly be expressed by variations in the range of shots. The carelessness of the editing underlined by Salt was linked to the importance given to any individual scene. Provided the performance was good, filmmakers often did not bother to connect one shot artistically to the previous and following ones. A further example, taken from a very popular movie, *Sardinian Drummer Boy* (1915), will highlight some of the weaknesses spotted by Salt. As was often the case, the producers had decided to use a story which the audience already knew – in this instance the anecdote, common to many national folklores but particularly famous in Italy, thanks to a book read in all schools, of the heroic boy badly wounded while helping to rescue a group of soldiers.[23] Since the tale was familiar to everybody, it did not seem necessary to worry too much about linking one scene to the next. One image shows the boy, who has been sent to call for reinforcements, climbing down from a very high window; in the following image, he has reached the ground, and enemies start shooting at him: why did they not shoot while he was hanging on his rope? The two takes were probably made at different times and nobody thought that a few bullets were necessary in the first image. As the cameraman did not want to (or could not) make a panning shot, the boy, while under fire, was obliged to creep slowly on the ground, instead of trying to hide quickly behind a bush. Later, we find the boy in hospital; in a first shot, the commandant takes up the middle of the screen and the boy, left in the background, lies flat on his bed; but, since he was to occupy the centre of the following shot, pillows were added to make him higher; therefore, while the same dialogue goes on (in captions), we suddenly see the drummer seated. Clearly, spectators were not annoyed with such trifles; rather, they were horrified to see, in the shot just mentioned, a horrible, bleeding hole where the boy's leg once was (the boy goes on talking quietly and does not seem to bother).

In mainstream films like the one we have just mentioned, variations of scale and subtleties of editing were rare. But filmmakers had recourse to other tricks, not common in Hollywood, which were powerful and compelling. Lighting was exploited to signal what the Americans underlined with a close-up: a ray of sunshine, a lamp, a reflection on a wall isolated a segment of the screen and were sufficient to indicate what had to be noted. The editing was not uniformly slow; most films alternated sequences of dialogues and sequences of action or pure motion. Consider the outset of *Cabiria*: a Roman aristocrat returns home; two long shots show him greeted by his wife and servants, then two other shots are devoted to his daughter, Cabiria, who is playing in the garden; what we see here is the kind of lengthy scenes signalled by Salt. But, suddenly, nearby Etna erupts and we are offered one of these splendid successions of contrasting, brightly lit or almost dark, dramatic, very quick images characteristic of the Italian manner. After the drama, a few quiet scenes, then another crisis, and so on. It is easy to criticize: the first and the second shots of *Cabiria* are repetitive, the shift from the second to the third shot is artificial. However this is the point of view of a modern analyst used to a much more elaborate use of cinematic language. We must accept the fact, even if it does not square with our habits, that spectators liked narratives based on major events easily comprehended and remembered; gaps or elisions of minor incidents or even of explanations did not perturb them and they thoroughly enjoyed the magnificence of the outdoor pictures, the skill in staging massive scenes and the art of the actors.

TECHNICIANS AND STARS, FROM SERAFINO GUBBIO TO VALERIA NESTOROFF

Most films produced in the early 1910s sold well: we can infer from the prosperity of the market and from the good response of the papers that spectators appreciated what they saw in picture theatres, but we cannot prove it since we lack precise evidence. On the other hand, we have enough information to portray the small circle of those who made the pictures. In 1914, Luigi Pirandello, the famous Italian playwright, dashed off one of his few novels, *Shoot*. It is striking that a man mainly concerned with the evolution of the theatre found it necessary to describe the life of a big film studio, including its whole staff, from the cameraman, Serafino Gubbio, to the star, Valeria Nestoroff. In his novel, Pirandello's characters were recruited by the producer with the utmost urgency. This was perfectly consistent with what can be learnt from other, more factual documents. We have already seen how quickly film studios grew from 1910 onwards; in a few months, dozens of people were needed. Specialists were hired, at high cost, from foreign countries, but that was not enough. Since cinema-going was already a popular habit, it was not difficult to find inexperienced, ambitious volunteers. Young people rushed to the studios. Most of those involved in the business, from directors to technicians, had yet to reach thirty. They were cosmopolitan, enthusiastic, and their energy never flagged. Let us look briefly at some of them.

Roberto Omegna was twenty-five when he opened a picture theatre in Turin and began to make short films; he travelled through Africa, Russia and China, and came back with documentaries which he sold to various exhibitors. He was hired by the Società Anonima Ambrosio, which looked for expert cameramen, shot a first version of *The Last Days of Pompei*, and finally specialized in scientific films. Count Negroni, an authentic aristocrat who should have become a lawyer and would never have made much money, was only too happy to obtain engagement from Cines; like Serafino Gubbio he began as a cameraman but was soon entrusted with writing scripts and then directing films. His was a very common story – to list all the young men who, starting with unskilled jobs, quickly became famous would be tedious and I shall be content with one last example. Carmine Galone, who had no future as a stage actor, was asked, at the age of twenty-seven, to refurbish a script for Cines; he did it so well that he was called upon to adapt and direct several plays; twelve years after he started, he was a filmmaker of such reputation that he was invited to work in Germany and France.

Serafino Gubbio was content to put his camera where the director chose and turn the crank. Others were more industrious and, for a decade or so, since jobs were not clearly defined, keen people had a chance to produce varied, interesting things and to earn a good deal of money. The same person could alternately write, shoot, direct and act; there was a permanent competitive spirit, albeit marred by a lack of cohesion and continuity. All too often, improvization saved a film without totally masking its shortcomings. Amateurism was especially obvious in the preparation of the scripts. Clever schemes or fancy ideas, hastily written down, were circulated to a few people who added beautiful, gripping scenes, but did not care about the coherence of the whole story. Looking for money, Pirandello told a producer: 'I could prepare a project in a few days.'[24] There has been some romantic talk about the 'primitive' films which did not obey the 'classical' rules of cinema and are said to have educated the viewers' perception and ensure critical, aware audiences. Postmodern tastes feel at ease with fictions that are not firmly plotted, and instead of being organic narratives, develop a succession of saynètes, sketches and captions, with a disjointed time sequence. What we know demonstrates that Italian spectators were pleased with the films they saw. Is that enough to prove that audiences were more conscious, more discerning than spectators who are used to well-knit plots? At any rate, we must remember that most filmmakers were not especially keen on educating their clients and did not make linear stories simply because they did not have enough time to weave together several disparate anecdotes. This is not to find fault with the Italian studios but to understand better how they worked.

In 1911, Itala shot one film every three days, Ambrosio one every two days, Cines one every day. These were short works, remakes of previous movies, plagiarisms of foreign productions, documentaries, one-man shows, all aimed primarily at the domestic market. Most of them have been lost but their titles, *Colonial Romance, Love and Caprice,*

The Poisoned Barrel, True till Death, give us a clue as to what they looked like. The narrations were embedded in a sediment of cultural familiarity, they retold old stories with an iconography reminiscent of children's books and fairy tales. Although it was made a bit later, *Sardinian Drummer Boy* is typical of this traditional, nostalgic style, which was inappropriate for export. We have seen how the creation of big companies in the early 1910s was the beginning of a continuous expansion. Due to their agreements with foreign distributors, the Italian studios made 16 feature-length films in 1912, 90 in 1914, and 252 in 1916. A glance at these figures is enough to make us realize the speed with which script-writers were obliged to work!

Coming later to production than their counterparts in most European countries, Italian cinematographers looked for plays or texts which would please domestic audiences and propel Italy's productions into overseas markets. Classicism, understood as the recourse to literary master-pieces, was a very suitable frame of reference; it provided the studios with themes or characters that were usually already well known in the peninsula and abroad. But it forced filmmakers to redefine their work in a style close to that of the novel or theatre, with relatively homogenous accounts. *Dante's Inferno* (1911), generally considered the first Italian feature-length film, provides a good example of a careful, unpretentious adaptation. Dante's poem was divided into a series of scenes for which set designers made landscapes inspired by the most popular edition of the text. Children or spectators of little culture could follow an action which was simple and explained throughout by brief sentences borrowed from the poem itself. Even the cinematic devices, for instance the flash-backs in which a protagonist tells Dante his past story, or the limited panning shots, derive from indications given in the text. The Bible, Homer, Greek and Latin mythology, Shakespeare, the great Italian writers, Tasso, Leopardi, Manzoni, inspired numerous scripts, but failed to fill all the requirements of the firms, and it soon became necessary to accommodate more recent plays, popular stories and serialized novels which were padded out with subplots or news in brief when they looked too short.

American critics, who praised Italian movies for being thrilling and offering effective, impressive situations, blamed their plots which, too often, were of an improbable nature. A glance at the opening of *Cabiria* illustrates the point. As already mentioned, shortly after the beginning of the film Etna threatens to destroy everything. People run away in panic; but a gang of pirates camps placidly on the shore – simply because the filmmaker needs them to kidnap Cabiria. We shall analyse later the most significant of these films. However, given what has been said about making the scripts and the short time allotted for shooting, we can already guess that literary texts were treated in an off-hand way and that unnecessary characters, parallel stories and dramatic or even comic sketches were introduced into the film's general structure whenever it looked necessary to lengthen the film.

Pirandello's novel ends with the shooting of a film in which an English-woman, strolling in the jungle, is attacked by a tiger, but saved by a womaniser. The producer concocts this extravagant tale because a nearby zoo wants to get rid of a nasty wildcat: the climax of the film is the real killing of a real tiger and the riveting effect of this terrifying scene is to enhance the charm and beauty of the star.

Satirical though it is, the book provides a rather accurate description not of the studios, but of current preconceptions about cinema: the pro-ducer is only interested in money, actors indulge in absurd rivalries and the star is a whimsical woman entangled in unhappy, hopeless love affairs. It is true that a kind of star system played an important part in giving Italian cinema its reputation but this system has to be interpreted with reference to its specific context.[25] Being used to spoken parts, Italian theatre actors did not actively participate in the launching of cinema. The most famous of them, Eleonora Duse, waited till 1916 before making her first (and only) appearance on a screen and her colleagues were no more enthusiastic. Cinema actors, like technicians and directors, were mostly newcomers who jumped at the chance of working in the new medium. Francesca Bertini or Mario Bonnard, who would never have won a reputation on the stage, were international stars at the age of twenty-five. Francesca Bertini, who was born in 1888, explained clearly how she was enthralled by the show she attended in her youth, how she insisted, when she was 16, on getting a part in a Neapolitan film, and how quickly but painfully, she worked her way to stardom.[26]

In the 1910s, Italian studios contrived a myth, *divismo*, the cult of female stars (*dive*). This was, at first, a commercial bargain because only a very few female stars really hit the jackpot. At about 1910, actors were mostly extras who, every now and then, got a part in a movie for which they were badly paid. When actors were hired for leading parts, they had to fight hard to obtain good contracts and the best known of them stressed their own importance. Since big companies were reluctant to grant high salaries, small firms offered the best actors generous wages and advertised their productions thanks to the stars' name; *Celio Film*, for instance, was able to emulate the big companies in 1913–14 because it had engaged Mario Bonnard and Lyda Borelli. However, this is not sufficient to account for the early fortunes of stardom in Italy. The cele-bration of *dive* flourished in a country where there was no royalty. Italian kings had no pretension or vanity, they boasted about behaving like ordinary people and one of the first newsreels, dedicated to the royal family, featured a middle-class couple. *Dive* made up for what was lacking in public life, ostentation, magnificence, theatrical excess – in a word,

Plate 6 Lyda Borelli in *Malombra*

glamour. There were some ten *dive*, every firm anxiously exploiting its own star. But the two legendary ones were Lyda Borelli and Francesca Bertini. Performers of outstanding talent, they were clever enough to adopt different manners of performing. Borelli made use of her entire body; she was slim, graceful and supple; she could, in one little movement, turn round on herself, cross a room, jump on to a sofa; she tossed her head back briskly, then remained idle for a long moment, delicately quivering and finally vanished in some corner. Bertini, being more wooden, used her face to find endlessly renewed, unexpected, staggering expressions, she had an amazing capacity to express something by just slightly modifying her features. Later, when Italian studios surrendered to Hollywood, it became fashionable to make fun of the *dive*. It is true that, too often, they did their best to interpret poor, empty stories but, leaving aside the plots, we can still be impressed by the quality of their performance. Spectators were probably sensitive to their total, physical and moral involvement in the parts they played: they always looked convincing, their portrayal coming from inside themselves, that is to say spontaneously, beyond posturing and with a sense of how to put across what was needed. But there was something else: *dive* invented characters (which however did not survive the silent era). In a few films they portrayed working-class women, but in their most famous roles were iconic class-less, independent women, vulnerable and tough. The heroines they played rebelled against the constraints of family life but did not call forth a critical spirit, their choices had generally no psychological or social motivations, there was no revolt in their behaviour and they resolved the most explosive issues in purely private ways – usually by either marrying the male star or refusing to marry him. Despite, or maybe because of, their rigid moral and sexual routines, the Italians enthused about these pictures which sounded subversive but had nothing in common with any real situation.

There was no masculine equivalent to the *diva* and it is not by chance that Mario Bonnard, the leading man of the early 1910s, became a director: he knew that achieving success as a male comedian was too difficult. A few actors achieved fame, but on a different level. Film companies promoted men that Italians called *forzuti*, that is, bullies.[27] The way was opened by another one-man band, Emilio Ghione, producer, actor, director and scriptwriter who, by accentuating the lineaments of his strong-featured face, created an ambivalent characterization likely to make viewers feel uneasy. However, despite his strength and energy, his turbulent, sadistic treatment of themes borrowed from popular literature would not have created a long-lasting convention, had it not been for the intrusion of an outsider, Bartolomeo Pagano. A docker in the port of Genoa, Pagano was recruited by Itala-Films to play a minor part, the faithful freed slave in *Cabiria*. At once spectators enthused over

Plate 7 Francesca Bertini in *The Octopus* (1919, Eduardo Bencivegna)

his gigantic, ungainly body. He created a new character, the benevolent, unselfish giant, who would be the darling of the 1920s. And, for the time being, he had his share in the triumph of *Cabiria*.

CABIRIA, MASTERPIECE OF HISTORY FILMS

The release in 1914 of this film, already mentioned several times, was a milestone in the evolution of Italian cinematic production. The name Cabiria has become a familiar nickname, the one a candid prostitute adopts in Fellini's *Cabiria's Nights* (1957), a name which rings a bell even for those who are not interested in films. The picture was finished a few months before *The Birth of a Nation*, and Italian film specialists consider it the first great work in the history of cinema, comparing it with *Intolerance* which was made only two years later. Arguing about the respective qualities of different pictures would be a waste of time; *Cabiria* is indeed a remarkable achievement and the outcome of long, arduous effort.

Italian filmmakers were soon preoccupied by historical subjects. Taken in the broadest sense of the expression, chronicles of past times represented the exceptionally large proportion of one fourth of total Italian film production. It is obvious that many so-called history films were costume extravaganzas in which the re-staging of old days was no more than a reproduction of colourful settings, past periods being considered a source of compelling fictions with antiquity offering a good excuse to transform ordinary situations into wonderful tales. However, by having recourse to history, producers hoped that they would be able to gratify their potential audience. We must not forget that they were confronted with a difficult and peculiar situation; the number of viewers was booming but nobody was in a position to tell what these people needed or wanted. Classical drama, such as was staged in theatres, dealt with absolute ethical values, independent of time and location. For a new volatile public, likely to change its mood rapidly, such an approach was no longer pertinent. The conventions most appropriate had to be simultaneously flexible and easy to interpret, elitist and populist. It was quite acceptable, however, to substitute for the moral dilemmas of the theatre a film which dealt with clear-cut oppositions between good and bad people, such as when civilized Romans confronted cruel barbarian Carthaginians. Cinema embraced a kind of history accessible to everybody, it focused on well known epochs, the Roman empire, Venice and the Renaissance, the Napoleonic era, the Risorgimento, that is, the struggle for the unification of Italy. Seen from that angle, history could not be the rendering of some external, objective knowledge. Rather, it was intended to illustrate old-fashioned ideas about the past, furnish gripping anecdotes and evoke some of the problems of the time. Saying that history films dealt with current issues may sound a bit odd, but historical fictions, written or filmed, are not scientific accounts; they say more about the way in which a society admires its own roots than about the past itself. Italian films were no exception. They were ideological productions which evoked, indirectly, ideas or convictions that were expressed more plainly, in speeches or newspapers, by politicians or opinion leaders.

It is all the more remarkable that the most popular films were produced by Cines, a company whose only concern was with making money, and that the most famous director of history pictures, Enrico Guazzoni, had no political affiliation. Like others of his generation who got into film-making, Guazzoni was originally a set designer. He first got involved in film exhibitions, then wrote scripts, staged some of them, and was engaged by Cines, for whom he made some fifty movies (most of them in a few weeks), notably *Quo Vadis?* (1913), *Antony and Cleopatra* (1913), *Julius Caesar* (1914), and *Fabiola* (1918). Starting from an elementary script, he could develop a gripping two-hour story. Despite his lack of political concern, he often chose motives, compositions and illuminations loaded with ideology. This is best exemplified by two of his films made in 1914, when Italy had not yet entered the war: *Julius Caesar* and *How Heroes Are Made*, a fanciful evocation of Napoleon's campaigns. Although they are not warmongering and do not celebrate violence, both pictures expand on hostilities, bloodshed, and the role of great leaders. Fighting is described as a fact, an unavoidable fact, an ordeal in which everyone has to behave as decently as possible. It is striking to note that the battles are depicted from an individual, sometimes even from a subjective, point of view. In *Julius Caesar*, when the Romans first face the Gauls, the former are entrenched on a hill; we only see them throwing arrows or stones, it is their behaviour, and not a panorama of the battlefield, which tells the story. Then, once the Gauls have climbed up to the top, the camera seems to stick to the bodies, a few gestures, filmed in close-up, conjure up the ferocity of the encounter. Guazzoni was able to handle big crowds, as is clear later in the film, when the Romans cross the country, but for the fights, he preferred to show personalized actions.

The battle of Austerlitz, the main battle of *How Heroes Are Made*, is recounted in an extremely sophisticated way. A caption tells us that 'the drum is rolling' and we immediately see horsemen breaking into a gallop, as if the drum had made them move. A long shot of foot soldiers is followed by a medium-distance shot of a drummer (again a young boy, as in *Sardinian Drummer Boy*) whose forward movement seems to drag along the soldiers filmed in the background. And now we are on a hill; with Napoleon we see, through his telescope, the advancing troops as well as the wounded drummer falling down. Starting from the machine (the army), we go to its engine (the drum), then to the hand which operates it. Caesar and Napoleon are not only victorious generals, but they also care for everything, even the fate of a humble boy. Ideology, in these works, is as much in the form as in the content. The narrative is carried out thanks to technical devices (framing, lighting and editing) which help construct an explanatory model centred on the strength and ability of great leaders.

Political convictions are more openly expressed in *Cabiria*. After unification, successive Italian governments turned to colonial expansion. An attempt to conquer Ethiopia turned into disaster but, in 1911, the kingdom carried out a successful war on Turkey, which surrendered Tripoli (in today's Libya). Italian politicians then began to focus on their country's African mission. *Cabiria* takes place at the time of the Punic wars. Carthaginian pirates haunt the Italian coasts, kidnap Romans and sell them as slaves. Young Cabiria is bought by the high priest of Moloch, who wants to burn her alive in honour of his inhumane divinity. Twice in danger, Cabiria is twice saved by a gallant Roman and his freed slave Maciste, while the victorious Roman army destroys the nefarious Carthaginian Empire. The prevailing colonialist sensibility accounts largely for the triumph of a movie which denounced the barbarian Africans and extolled the civilizing vocation of ancient Italy.

Cabiria was not only a nationalist manifesto, but also an extraordinary film. Itala Film invested a great deal of money to produce and advertise it, and the director, Giovanni Pastrone made it skilfully and elegantly.[28] I have already described the clever succession of calm and conflicting sequences which structures the movie. Even in the former, new events continue. We see, for instance, the market in Carthage: exotic people in strange costumes, bizarre animals crossing the street. We witness this endless to-ing and fro-ing, together with the selling of Cabiria to the high priest. Pastrone was not too preoccupied with historical accuracy but was intent on pleasing and astonishing his audience, which he unexpectedly took from a crowded square to an empty beach, and from long shot to close-up. Camera movements were especially remarkable. Pastrone was not the first to make the camera move, but he was not content with just disclosing details, as most directors usually did: with the help of tracking shots he explored the cinematic space. An impressive sequence develops inside the temple of Moloch: while hundreds of Carthaginians pray, a slow tracking movement traverses the room for the sheer delight of revealing the immensity of the sanctuary. Of course, such a picture stressed the barbarity of Carthage, but it was also amazingly exciting. And it helped to emphasize the humanity of the Romans: two unarmed men did not hesitate to face the countless slaves of Moloch. The contrast was astutely accentuated by a touch of humour. Maciste's colossal strength enabled him to pulverize his foes; any encounter between him and the Carthaginians renewed the gratifying victory of the good giant over wicked dwarfs.

Cabiria is an anthology of cinematic tricks, of bright passages and wonderful images, of thrilling scenes and exciting pursuits, a brilliant, moving show which grants its spectators no pause for breath. However, while it was immensely successful at the time, it has never been ranked among the world's greatest films. Was this because it was eclipsed by Hollywood productions, as some commentators believe? I would rather say that it is damaged by the looseness of the script. There are too many plot lines, too many possible stories; the characters are flat and what lies beneath their actions is a shallow presentation of elementary psychic reactions. Angela dalle Vacche notes that the 'polymorphous textuality' of the film, its use of different materials, provides a glimpse of a composite, eclectic public, different from more modern audiences.[29] A kind of pluralism functioned, not only in emotional and intellectual depth but in overt bodily terms, as when Maciste's gesticulation enthused intellectuals and non-intellectuals alike. *Cabiria*'s triumph illuminates the taste of cinemagoers during the first generation. Its subsequent eclipse shows how much fashion changed with the following generations.

ASSUNTA SPINA, OR THE SPELL OF CONVENTIONS

In *Cabiria*, after Etna's eruption, servants steal the jewels of Cabiria's parents, but give the girl a ring by which she will be recognized when she comes back from Carthage. The main character of *How Heroes Are Made*, having been commissioned to deliver an urgent message, is kidnapped by a wicked woman; were it not for Napoleon's perspicacity, he would have been shot as a deserter. These incredible episodes belong to a classical literary genre, melodrama. We must not be misled by the label 'historical film': in the Italian cinema of the 1910s, even episodes taking place in a more or less fanciful past were blood-and-thunder dramatizations.

Defining melodrama is hard, since indeterminacy has always acted as a powerful drive in the evolution of this hybrid 'genre' composed of different conventions. Melodrama sought less to narrate a coherent story than to establish an open space in which spectators found predictable, standard stories but could also insert their own wishes and fantasies. The only stable pattern was the presence of women at the core of these fictions. Women, who could not act of their own volition, were permanently at risk since they were lacking in resolve and reliability, were easily fooled and subject to temptation. Like Cabiria, they needed protection. Beside the naive, innocent young women, films that were tear-jerkers featured libidinous, cunning and dangerous women, able to capture brave young men.[30] The biggest studios tried to produce elaborate films, in which male predominance was not too obvious. Smaller companies, like Elva

Notari's in Naples, were less smart. Their productions have been lost but such scripts as we can reconstruct, thanks to pamphlets or advertisements, were rather sexist. Women had to be faithful. When they cheated on their fiancés, the latter were supposed to kill them, and everybody, including the young women's families, helped the murderers escape punishment. Most pictures presented a small family, reduced to a couple and a child, which had little in common with the large households then common in Italy. These limited circles were powerful, sheltering and oppressive as well as weak and threatened. It was thus possible to play it in two different ways: a stranger aimed to intrude into a home which he or she would inevitably devastate, or an inhabitant wanted to leave, the departure hastening the end of the community.

Feminist critics have closely studied the identity assigned to cinematic women in the light of psychoanalysis. Their conclusions fit in very well with the prominent features of melodramas. On the one hand, a film character enacts what a female spectator is not allowed to do for herself, that is to desire a man; on the other hand, films present 'a kind of hallucinatory satisfaction' inasmuch as the same pleasure is repeated from film to film, never carried on up to physical completion and always acted through a proxy.[31] In the same way, it could be added that the anxieties of sexually immature men were reinforced by the depiction of histrionic women, and cast out by their final punishment. It is no accident that melodrama, filled with sex but never exhibiting it, fulfilling in images repressed impulses and at the same time warning against sexual drives, was immensely appreciated in Italy at a time when sexual issues could not be discussed publicly.

However, melodrama must not be reduced to this aspect alone. It was effective inasmuch as it alluded to more specific concerns. Cinematic families were imaginary, magical circles. They were also groups of relatives and this must be borne in mind if we want to understand why audiences took an interest in them. While telling extravagant anecdotes, these movies dealt, albeit obliquely, with problems like housing, violence and life in cities, with which spectators were directly concerned. Material goods and money were never totally hidden, seducers and wicked women were denounced because they attempted to appropriate the fortune of legitimate heirs. The charm of melodrama resulted partly from the overlapping of factual data and archetypal, endlessly repeated situations.

A look at the film titles is instructive: *An Adventurer's Love* (1912), *A Mother's Love* (1912), *The Redeeming Angel* (1911), *Love Is Stronger Than Gold* (1912), *Tempestuous Love* (1912). Reviewing them all would be tedious, and I shall be content with discussing what is probably the most famous of these films,[32] *Assunta Spina* (1915). Since the serial novel from which it was adapted turned out to be too short for a feature-length

film, the story was completed by additional scenes which in fact dupli-
cated the original plot. A young, beautiful working-class woman from
Naples, Assunta Spina, is engaged to Michele, who twice gets into trouble
with the police because her behaviour has made him jealous. The anecdote is dull and conventional but its cinematic treatment is remarkable.
In the initial sequences, hastily dashed off by an amateur scriptwriter,
Francesca Bertini, as Assunta, succeeds in being both sweet and dry; the
smile on her face shows that she would like to be cared for, but she is
not the kind of simple virgin who brings out the protective urge in
others, so that Michele's manifestations of love are alternately repaid or
undercut by a sardonic witticism. Michele's attack on an imaginary rival
is without foundation, but Assunta's conduct makes it look unavoidable.
Once the fiancé has been put in jail, Assunta, for absurd reasons, is
obliged to become the mistress of a clerk. In this section, Bertini's acting
changes, she gives a bitter note to her disintegrating relationship with
Michele, while displaying love, grief, hatred, and despair in a provocative,
unrestrained way. Clearly the film considers anger and violence legitimate
for men but not for women. Michele's fierceness is excusable as he
believes that he has been betrayed. On the other hand, even coquettish
smiles are forbidden for women and Assunta is punished. First she
becomes a prostitute, then, when Michele has killed her lover, she pre-
tends that she is the murderer. And yet, despite the very masculine flavour
which informs the story, Bertini is allowed to manifest emotions usually
considered unacceptable for her sex.

It is difficult to imagine how spectators reacted to this kind of film and
how they interpreted the importance given to emotion. Were these feelings
shared, or at least understood by large fractions of the audience? Or was
this picture used to denounce what was perceived as a destructive reality?
We cannot answer these queries. But we must not forget that, if viewers
participated in the characters' passions, they were also accustomed to the
genre with its rules and tricks. The flow of the narrative was interrupted
by incidents, trivial happenings or details too insignificant to qualify as
events but likely to trigger surprising mental associations as when, for
instance, the hidden past of a pirate ancestor made a wedding impossible.
An appreciation of the irony of a situation which was simultaneously
desperate and incredible was required to watch a melodrama. Enjoying
tear-jerkers was a cultural attitude.

FANTASIES

Melodrama was not only enthralling, it was also highly pleasurable since
it was conceived as a dramatic form of entertainment likely to turn into
a dream or a fantasy. A man encounters a woman, courts her, becomes

her lover; the husband challenges him to a duel and is killed: can you imagine anything more formulaic? But a convention acquires a new meaning when it is all told through a camera focused on the feet of the three protagonists, as in *Foot Love* (1914). The mere vision of moving shoes engenders a chain reaction which goes from the objects to the feelings or reveries that spectators can link to them. This movie, which depended on mystery (what do these people look like?), and the sexual connotations attached to the feet, was exceptionally enthralling but not unique since mainstream melodramas often played on allusions and double meaning.

Indeterminacy was a salient feature of films which mixed drama and history, adventures and sexual hints, thrills and laughter. Intricacy was especially developed in the comic strips, and that may be one of the reasons why they sold so well all around the world. The label 'comedy' usually bestowed on these pieces is not appropriate.[33] It is true that they set out to amuse but, choosing a form of humour which combined the mundane, the salacious and the unexpected, they revealed the oddities of everyday life, turning them into grotesque, dream-like fragments which, initially, looked like reality but, very soon, metamorphosed into pure fantasy. The best epithet would, I think, be crazy sketches, inasmuch as this refers to screwball comedies relying on irresponsibility, reciprocal destruction and topsyturvydom.[34]

There were plenty of comic actors since every company wanted to market its own farces, but the three best were Foolshead (Cretinetti in the Italian version), Polidor and Tweedledum (Robinet in Italian). Different though they were, these men had much in common. They were typical antiheroes but, unlike their American counterparts, they seldom experienced the frustrations of modern life, did not leave their home environment and were never dominated by strong women. Their stories, improvised on the basis of a rough sketch, were highly physical pieces of theatre briefly introduced, deprived of any kind of complexity and filled with purely visual gags. Tweedledum, in his short variety acts, took advantage of his awkward look: a little man came through a door in the middle of the screen, faced the audience, grimaced, and this form of controlled clowning was enough to make audiences giggle. Polidor was chiefly destructive. Once he had entered a room he managed to set everything into confusion; the best moments of his films developed on this common ground: he was guilty without being guilty. The climax, in which Polidor, seated on the floor, declared he had not planned to be a troublemaker was a perfect fusion of nonsense with devastation. Foolshead was more sophisticated than his colleagues. At times, he made use of his small stature, for instance when he lovingly carried his tall, plump wife in his arms. But he would rather lead his audience astray with false starts and unclear expectations, mock forebodings and misdirections. Capricious and unpredictable, constantly changing course in his absurd aims, switching from dazzling moments of humour to bitter-sweet irony, his pictures were hilariously funny. Fearing a blaze, Foolshead orders sandbags which, being delivered at lunch time, bury his family beneath a cloud of dust. Foolshead next opts for water; he fills buckets, washbasins, even baskets and bags with water – liquid streams into the house. The audience's laughter came from the contrast between the character's sheer application and the dramatic or surreal consequences of his efforts.

Polidor and Tweedledum, who had worked in variety shows, attempted to stage improbable, ridiculous events, Foolshead tried to create an individual who wants to think of something he cannot conceive. Their sketches were excellent but they could only be an overture, never the staple part of a cinematic programme. Furthermore, their plots were too loose, their characters too vague, to compete with American comedies. And yet, there was in their films a creativity, a sense of craziness which still appeals to present-day spectators. However short-lived they were, these screwball comedies played an important part in the wave of fantasy which developed in Italy's film studios during the 1910s.

*

These cinematic sketches were made in Italy but it would be impossible to label them as genuinely Italian since, out of the three above-mentioned comics, two were French and one was Spanish. Italian studios were largely open to foreign influences and hired many professionals from abroad. The first director recruited by Cines, Gaston Velle, was a Frenchman, and *Cabiria* was shot by a Spaniard, Segundo de Chomon. However, distributors and audiences did not care about these precise details. Films made in the peninsula, sold as Italian products, helped cover the commercial deficit of the country and in many instances, especially in Italian colonies abroad, were appreciated because of their origin. No other cinematography, in the early 1910s, was able to release historical pictures as impressive as *Quo Vadis?* or slapsticks as exciting as Foolshead's. Undoubtedly, there was an Italian cinema which reworked old patterns when it launched melodramas, and created new models with historical dramas and crazy sketches.

Given their international origin, these pictures were not likely to illustrate 'national values'. But we may suppose that the viewing of these (or similar) movies was a major integrating factor at a time when many people were losing their association with local communities and emigrating into towns. Going to the picture theatre became an act of consumption. Enjoying films implied a change of intellectual and moral standards, an interest in the past, however fanciful it was on the screen, an involvement in fantasy, an admiration for beautiful bodies and smart *dive*. We cannot know how cinematic culture originated and developed in the 1910s, but we must pay attention to the fact that an increasing number of Italians attended the cinema and took part, together, in a moving experience. *Cabiria* helped bring Rome closer to Turin or Naples, and to orientate the peninsula towards Africa, but nobody can ever assess what its real impact was.

Second generation
Their master's voice

Italy was quick to adopt the newly invented cinema and her studios developed so rapidly that, by 1914, the country was, together with Denmark, the third largest exporter of films in the world. Like most European countries, Italy lost its foreign markets during the second decade of the century and, after 1920, Italian production companies, unable to cope with the financial crisis, went out of business. In terms of film creation, the years which followed the end of the war were blank. But we must not confuse film production and cultural activity. By 1915, films were distributed in most parts of the peninsula. The children born twenty years earlier had learnt to watch the world in a darkened room, their experience was infused with a capacity to like and enjoy the pictures, and they had acquired what can be called a cinematic culture. Obviously the tastes and habits of the cinema-goers were modified by the European conflict and its aftermath. Warfare introduced the authorities to the business, and the cinema, which had previously developed freely, was obliged to take account of an outside master, the state. It had also to cope with a far-reaching innovation, often considered a revolution, the advent of sound cinema. From now on, voices were on the air, they could also be printed on films. Rather than seeing the second generation of film buffs as a lost generation, we shall try to define its place in the long-range evolution of the pleasure found in picture theatres.

WAR: BEYOND ANY REASONABLE EXPECTATION

In the early 1910s, cinema was attaining the 'age of reason'. For most individuals, the end of childhood is marked by a strengthening of official controls and this was true for the cinema. Censorship came first.[1] Everywhere justified as protecting 'the people', an ill-defined public-at-large, from moral corruption and bad influences, censorship is often advocated by the film trade itself, to counter foreign competition. Since 1896, various committees for the protection of innocent Italian souls had denounced the pernicious effect of films, but the first systematic campaign began in professional magazines and was aimed at 'the wave of immorality' which marred many Danish films, especially the most popular ones, starring Asta Nielsen. The board of film censors, established by the government in June 1913, suited the Italian film industry which could simultaneously criticize its decisions and take advantage of them, since the certificate guaranteed that their movies attacked neither the established authorities nor the Catholic faith. Censors were most punctilious on sexuality (*A Sister's Love* had to be altered to *The Sister*). They banned improper language but they were not very strict where the content of the scripts was concerned. Censorship was also convenient for the government which no longer had to face the demands of decency leagues but which had gained control over film production: taxes on exhibition, which were previously received by towns, were taken by the state from 1914 onwards. So, before the First World War broke out, the government had managed to regulate cinematic information.

Italy had no reason to enter a European battle which did not concern it directly. It was a haphazard coalition of politicians seeking an elusive grandeur and heterogeneous lobbies of jingoists which precipitated the country into the conflict. Its military staff being incompetent, its regular army only trained for colonial expeditions and its conscripts ill-equipped, the kingdom waged an exhausting, bloody war against Austria. Oddly enough, the government, which had been unable to prepare to fight, had long recognized the importance of propaganda and the role that the cinema could play to popularize its policy. For example, in the campaign in Libya (1911–12), cameramen were authorized to follow the action and forty newsreels made with their best takings were screened, week by week. In May 1915, a military film crew was quickly set up; it worked close behind the front line and did excellent work. The few reels which have survived show heavy guns pulled with difficulty by oxen, soldiers deprived of warm clothing in winter, attacks in open terrain against well entrenched positions. Of course, most of this material was never shown in cinemas. Instructions issued in July 1917 banned all theatre plays dealing with troop movements, armaments, operations, sanitation and losses. Furthermore, information regarding the war could never make up more than one fifth of any news bulletin.

Italian historians have long argued about the function played by the cinema during the hostilities. Some defend the idea that it was pure propaganda, a way of reassuring the civilians by showing them that everything was under control and perfectly normal.[2] These researchers point to considerable data. In 1915, money was offered to companies ready to make patriotic movies. Some sixty films, hastily completed, extolled the valiant Italian troops, always stronger than the Austrians. The archetype of these works was *Maciste, Mountain Infantryman* (1916). In this film, Maciste, the good giant revealed by *Cabiria* in 1915 and then re-employed in other comic films, has enlisted for the duration; he makes life hell for the Austrians, challenges whole squads on his own and takes them prisoner. He spies, discloses the traps, turns the enemy's weapons on themselves. Thanks to him, Italians have a lot of fun at war. This vein was exploited for a few months. Then, once it became obvious that hostilities would be long and murderous, the studios gave up producing bellicose pictures and went back to the previous series of melodramas, history films and comic sketches. While the Austrians were routing an Italian army at Caporetto, one of the bullies we have previously met, Emilio Ghione, was shooting an eight-part serial, *The Grey Rats* (1918), a fantastic, merciless duel between a formidable gang and a lonely justiciar, which provided civilians and even soldiers on leave with a short moment of escape. Not only did the cinema not respond to the experience of the war, but it resorted to the most traditional, escapist imagery.

So, on screen the war looked harmless, not to say lovely. Historians have not only commented on the deadening power of the films, they have also speculated as to whether spectators were cheated by these masquerades.[3] Most viewers were aware of the difference between a story, which has to be resolved at the end, and life. For them, Maciste and his foes were not real people but nice puppets. The comic vision of the fights given in cinemas even sounded subversive, since it was miles away from the official rhetoric about heroism and love for the country and did not comply with official pressure. Although wearing a uniform, Maciste was an irregular, he never followed the orders of his officer and acted on his own, in contradiction to the directives on joint effort and discipline. Despite its seeming reverence for the national cause, the cinema, some historians have argued, helped people to make fun of the official truth.

Interesting though they are, these two theses are, I think, too much inspired by present concerns. We have seen so many images of fights and war victims that, with hindsight, we find the movies which were shown in cinemas during the First World War ridiculous and unconvincing. But, at that time, people did not have the same visual experience. Most of them had never witnessed an actual conflict. A paradox of the conflict, especially in Italy, was that millions of men fought in a limited area, without affecting the majority of the population which went on leaving its ordinary life. Newsreels and documentary films captured something of the war. They offered images which could not be found in any other medium of information. We have little evidence of the reactions of audiences but in the few cases where enquiries were made after the screening we see that people attended in groups, veterans mixed with civilians, and that they all came away deeply moved. This happened because those who had not been mobilized, but who had had one of their dear ones killed, wounded or shell-shocked, wanted to 'see' what had happened, to understand and at the same time to 'participate'. To a large extent, the screenings were ways of mourning collectively.

Films undoubtedly lied, but representing this conflict fought in mud and snow by soldiers who did not move was not easy. The British authorities met the challenge by screening *The Battle of the Somme*, the world's first full-length war documentary, which was seen by over half the British population within three months of its release in 1916. In the same period, the Italians shot their own war picture, *The Italian War on the Adamello*. Unlike the battle of the Somme, the campaign on the Adamello was a limited operation which was never meant to put an end to the conflict. However, the purpose of the two films, made simultaneously, was identical. We do not have as much evidence about audience reaction for the Italian film as for the British one but we know that it was shown in many towns and met with a very favourable response. A comparison between the two films is very interesting. *The Battle of the Somme* uses impressive pictures and tries to account as explicitly as possible for the development of the battle. *The Italian War on the Adamello* does not follow any logical order. It deals mostly with the preparations for an attack against the Austrians, but the shots seem to have been edited at random. It is difficult to know why images of soldiers wearing a white battledress (and therefore ready to attack) mingle with images of soldiers in normal uniform, or with images of men carrying the parts of a gun. The operation seems less important than the way in which it develops. Emphasis is put on obstacles (snow, cold, slippery slopes) all of which are overcome by the men. Information is often sacrificed for the pure quality of the images, long files of small black soldiers filmed in backlighting trudge into an empty, snow-covered landscape. Silhouetted figures cross the screen and seem to vanish into the white expanse of snow. The attack itself is not shown but we are not spared some of its consequences. A commandant is told that his brother has been killed in action and sledges bring back a few dead corpses. It was a victory but one which was not gained without losses.

Historians who believe that films were only aimed at soothing war's pains will argue that, in The *Italian War on the Adamello*, the battle is set in the context of familiar motifs like human energy or the ability to fight against the forces of nature. But we must not forget that any film must be interpreted with reference to the institution of cinema as it existed at the time. We have seen how, in the early 1910s, historical pictures featured dynamic and spectacular military collisions, praised individual heroism, extolled violence and described wars in face-to-face clashes between huge groups of extras. Newsreels and documentaries of the war, which were not accurate reports, challenged this dominant imagery. They presented confused, repetitive actions conducted by characterless hordes of anonymous phantoms. The factual films were too few to destroy the conventional representations but they showed something which was not the official truth. How did spectators respond to the screening of such different visions of warfare? This is something we cannot evaluate. Would it be too much to suppose that, after the European conflict, audiences were less ready to trust all that was shown in picture theatres?

MACISTE IN POWER

On the silver screen, the real winner of the war was Maciste. A secondary character in *Cabiria*, he became a hero in the trenches and was given the leading role in pictures shot after the war. He was immensely popular not only because he protected the weak and the oppressed, punished the baddies, and resolved the narrative tension in the best possible manner, but also because his familiar face and his body were reassuring and made spectators cheer up when they saw him get a victim out of a danger-ous situation. He acted in, for Itala-Films, five films during the war, seven between 1919 and 1922, and then, for another studio, Fert Film, five pic-tures from 1924 to 1926. By about 1920, he was a famous figure; few Ita-lians had never set eyes on him, be it only on a poster. On reaching 40, Maciste was tall and strong; his broad shoulders and large forehead made him the perfect image of virility.

Plate 8 Maciste . . . (Bartolomeo Pagano in 1926) . . .

Plate 9 . . . or Mussolini? (The dictator addressing the crowd in 1938.)

Now, the same depiction applies perfectly to one of his contemporaries, Benito Mussolini. We must be very cautious when tackling the problem of representations, we must avoid far-fetched interpretations, and I admit that the relationship I will try to establish is hypothetical and is not backed by any piece of evidence. Fascists never used Maciste for their propaganda but the character perfectly fitted the kind of human being they wanted to promote. What is more striking is that Mussolini modified his look after the war. Previously a slim, nervous man with a meagre face and a moustache, he transformed himself into an athletic, heartening, protective fellow, keen on sport, alert, ready for action. Was there not an unconscious association, in the mind of lots of Italians, between the shielding hero and the vigilant leader? Did not Mussolini borrow a few features from the favourite actor? The post-war era, in Italy, was a time of considerable political unrest and of conflictual movements of bewildering complexity. The Italians were anxious about the status and future of their country and ashamed of their inability to allay them. Many of them supported Mussolini because they hoped that he would ease their torment. But the main question remains unanswered: why did they trust him?

Let us leave the realm of conjecture and go back to the firm ground of facts. After the heavy human losses endured during the conflict, the Russian Revolution had a powerful impact on Italian proletarians, both in the country and in industrial cities. After months spent fighting in the trenches, workers, craftsmen and even men from the country had grown increasingly restless and critical of the establishment. Simultaneously, those who had expected some reward for the country's entry into the war on the side of the Allies were bitterly disappointed by their departure from the ranks of the major powers – a descent reflected in Italy's eviction from the preparation of the peace treaties and in the limited compensation offered to the country for its intervention. Believing that they could take advantage of the situation, the unions and the newborn Communist Party attempted to mobilise the proletariat. Factories and estates were occupied by their workers and countless strikes paralysed the means of transport. Eighteen months of social unrest and the blurring of traditional values frightened the conservative forces (the Church, landowners, industrialists and businesmen, the upper middle class), which gave approval and financial support to Mussolini and his Fascist organization because they were able to oppose the Reds.

But the troubles did not last long. In 1920 the Left was already on the defensive and in 1922, when Mussolini was appointed prime minister by the king, people were no longer afraid of the revolution. The submission to Fascism was not merely a defence against Bolshevism, it was also an attempt to find a way out of the peninsula's greatest shortcomings. Italian businessmen were worried about the backwardness of their country: why was it less rich, less industrialized and militarily less effective than all its neighbours? Was it not because the impotent liberal monarchy was unable to promote a rapid development? Was it then unreasonable to believe that a dictatorship would be more efficient? Businessmen's expectations can be better undestood if we consider the case of radio broadcasting. Marconi, the engineer who had first used the atmosphere to send out messages, pestered the authorities to help him create a broadcasting network, but he could not get any support from the royal government. Immediately after Mussolini's appointment, Marconi visited the new prime minister and they soon came to an agreement. The industrialist had administrative obstacles cleared up and the political leader began to put out his speeches over the airwaves. As far as capitalists were concerned, adhesion to Fascism was an overt expression of a determination to modernize.[4]

At first, the problem of modernization and the endeavour to maintain social order were not clearly separated. Both implied giving greater power to the state which, on the one hand, meant securing the loyalty of a new bureaucracy but, on the other, tended to erode the power of employers. After a few years of collaboration, industrialists felt torn between submission to the regime and aversion to its authoritarianism. The Nazis had to face the same problem in Germany a few years later. They solved it by an institutionalization of their party, a process which was never well elaborated in Italy, where Fascism did not engender a body of unquestioning supporters. While industrialists were taking over the task of modernization, the men in power at best remained idle and sometimes got in the way of the manufacturers. In any case, the Fascist Party turned out to be such an empty organization that, when Mussolini was arrested much later, in 1943, the organization was immediately dismantled and could not even maintain itself in power.

This was the situation even in a field as limited as the cinema. Many producers and filmmakers backed Fascism because they thought it would save their declining industry. But Mussolini, *Il Duce*, imbued with free-trade principles, was not keen on interfering, except when an intervention could bring him political advantages. The nationalization, in 1926, of the Light Institute,[5] a firm which specialized in the production of didactic movies, was an acknowledgement of the importance of the cinema as an instrument of propaganda and education. The institute was entrusted with making newsreels that exhibitors were obliged to project during any film-show, and also documentaries likely to inform about the achievements of Fascism.

During the 1920s endless shorts illustrated the agricultural policy of Fascism, rural improvement, modern techniques of cultivation and, above all, the draining of marshland areas which were the principal economic success of the regime. Analogous themes were regularly treated in newsreels, which stressed the transformation of the country and the regeneration of youth through sport and open-air life, or lingered over Italian landscapes, praised folklore and traditions, and celebrated the hard work of country people and craftsmen. Politics interfered, of course, with meetings and street demonstrations, and references to the

'Revolution' but this was mostly background material; few slogans were included in captions and Fascist leaders seldom surfaced on the screen. The king appeared at times but the ubiquitous character was Mussolini, whose life, deeds and travels were regularly mentioned.

What was the nature of the response to cinematic propaganda by audiences of the day? This is a problematic issue since evidence is scant. All we can do is speculate about the films themselves, and the possible reaction of spectators. Looking at the documentaries made before 1926 and those shot by the Light Institute we must admit that the latter were, technically, much better, with sharp images, interesting contrasts and quick, vigorous editing. Spectators were probably more sceptical about the printed press than about the newsreels which, in their view, did not give information but showed colourful panoramas or surprising scenes. The few documents we have suggest that people were happy with the quality of the Light Institute's productions and with the presentation of Italy as a diligent community intent on adapting to the contemporary world. Newsreels were effective, as it were, not in advertising Fascism, but in reinforcing or articulating existing ideas and in convincing audiences that the country was on the right path. Did filmmakers deliberately avoid blatant publicity for the regime and deliver no slogans? Maybe, but I think we must take account of two other facts. The first is that, if Mussolini bestowed on the cinema the label of 'strongest weapon', if he and his fellows were keen on showing that they were more modern than the democrats, these men actually relied mostly on words or written texts and did not really care about images or combinations of moving pictures. The relative blandness of documentaries in Italy reveals how wide the gap was between speeches and practice, plans and execution. But there is more, and here is the second point. Most of the cinematographers who had joined the Fascists on opportunistic grounds had no political training, all they wanted was to use the facilities offered by the state to make films without facing heavy financial problems. Their stylistic experiments, which captivated the public and deeply influenced their colleagues, were not fitting as a political project. The creation of the Light Institute rallied several intellectuals to the regime but it did not provide Fascism with a tool likely to publicize its aims on the silver screen.

THE END OF FILMOPOLI

The Light Institute was the only governmental producer of movies. All feature films were made by private companies. The studios did not want to be nationalized but they would have liked to obtain some support from the state since their situation was dire: from 371 feature-length films shot in 1920 (which was the peak year), the number fell to 114 in

1923 and 8 in 1930. In that year, Italian production amounted to less than ten per cent of domestic cinema income.

This decline was blamed on war. It was said that, because of the conflict, most studios had been obliged to close, which reduced exports to America to nothing and gave Hollywood a chance to enlarge its market. All this is pure legend. Far from decreasing, Italian production boomed from 1914 to 1920 and turned out to be much too considerable for shrinking demand. The contradictions of Italian studios mirror those of the Italian economy. In the modern, expanding branches industrialists wanted to grow as quickly as possible, while they had to find money with long-term reimbursements. After 1910, Italian studios made a massive investment effort, spent a great deal of money on their plants and imported the best equipment from abroad; they were deep in debt and sales were not sufficient to cover their deficit. One of the structural weaknesses of the peninsula was its deficiency of short-term capital, especially in the post-war era when the banks, instead of lending money to the firms, bought up enormous quantities of government bonds.[6] The lack of resources undermined the studios' attempts to compete with the Americans. The producers thought that if they had more films on offer, they would find new clients, but this forced expansion was not a policy, it was merely a delusion serving to conceal the real problems – the fact that the difficulties were not new.

Before the war, Italian producers were already working in a limited national market and had to export as much as possible. In 1912, the three main customers were the United Kingdom, France and the United States which, together, absorbed 60 per cent of the film exports.[7] But, as early as 1913, when exports were still increasing, American importers began to prove reluctant; they bought as many films as previously, but they wanted fewer prints of them; an average of 30 prints each in 1911, fell to 20 for the comedies and documentaries, and 15 and sometimes 10 for the dramas. From 1912 to 1914, British imports were cut by a half, American imports by 80 per cent. In 1917, nothing was sold to English-speaking countries; the only customers were France and Spain.

As for the domestic market, it had been monopolized by American distributors. Selling directly to exhibitors would have implied the creation of a huge network of sellers, an effort far beyond the capabilities of the Italian producers. In 1912, Italian studios dealt exclusively with the commercial branch of the American Motion Picture Patents Company of America and did not care about the diffusion in Italy of their own films whose distribution was managed by Amercian offices.

Those production companies which had made too many films went bankrupt after 1920 or were integrated into other firms.[8] Directors, actors and technicians emigrated, even Maciste was hired by a German studio. The surviving companies attempted to destroy their rivals.

Giuliana Bruno has explained how small firms, like Elvira Notari's, were attacked by professional magazines (which were in the pay of the strongest competitors) on the pretext of immorality, and had their films refused by the censors, or cut by a half, or delayed in such manner that, eventually, they ceased production.[9] In a few years, the Turin and Milan studios, once the largest in Europe, fell into disrepair. Italian cinema, which had previously developed in Naples as well as in northern cities, shifted toward Rome. Fourteen out of the fifteen feature-length films made in 1931 were shot in the capital by Cines, the only studio which had managed to survive the disaster.

NOW THEY'RE TALKING

By this time, producers had to face a new challenge, the arrival of the sound film or 'talkie'.[10] The birth of broadcasting, the diffusion of the telephone and records had already triggered a shock to the Italian cultural system. No medium can be treated in isolation but this is especially true where cinema and the diffusion of sound are concerned. In some countries, and above all in the United States, the two were closely linked, and the same companies controlled radio broadcasting and manufactured sound equipment. In other countries, like Italy, radio and talkies were technically separated but their audiences developed at the same pace. This may seem a strange statement, as broadcasting began in 1923, while Italy did not produce any talkies before 1930. But, again, we are faced with a peculiarity of Italy.[11] The diffusion of broadcasting was limited by various factors, especially by the lack of implements. In 1931, a good radio set cost 3,000 lire when a small car cost but 10,000 lire: it was much too expensive for the poor and the rich would save for a car rather than buy a radio. It would have been easy to reduce the price to 500 lire but industrialists as well as retailers made more money with expensive models than with cheap fragile ones. The result was an expansion of collective listening: people gathered in places where they would find a set, a bar, a church hall, the house of a well-off neighbour. Fascism used the wireless very seldom. It is true that Mussolini's talks were all broadcast but, most of the time, radio was devoted to music, sport, and to fanciful variations on fictional topics, the most popular programmes being, in the early 1930s, an adaptation of Mickey Mouse and a whimsical version of the Three Musketeers.

The quality of broadcasting was hardly good, but the very act of transmiting the same programmes all over the country made its effect not only on what was performed but also on how it was perceived and accepted by listeners. Opera and symphonic music were too much for the primitive microphones. Small ensembles, groups of popular singers, chorus and light songs came over the air best. The radio stations were important in creating new ways of valuing and enjoying sounds. In this respect, radio and sound films evolved together, backed and advertised each other. Nothing has survived of the first programmes of the Italian radio. But reviews in newspapers often complained about the poor quality of the diction. Technicians, who lacked training, had to improvise, actors did not realize that a studio is not a stage. If things improved greatly in the 1930s, if actors were able to find a restrained and balanced performing style, if technicians learnt to make use of synchronized sound effects, this was beneficial for films and radio. By broadcasting songs popularized in films, radio recruited new listeners among film buffs and lured its listeners into going to the cinema. By putting radio sets in decor, by using them to inform or entertain the protagonists, the pictures invited spectators to buy their own set. Both Hollywood's musicals and radio were powerful agents of addiction to American tunes; they contributed equally to educating Italian audiences to jazz and modern dances. Sound films and radio, which enthused a large section of the population, stimulated resistance by the highbrows. Pirandello, who had adopted a hostile but fascinated attitude towards the cinema and had had several plays adapted to the silver screen, launched a campaign against the talkies, in his view an American contrivance likely to reduce a visual art to a bad theatre. The anger and revolt of the intellectuals betrays their fear: they proclaimed that recorded music was trash or that radio and sound films were contributing to the debasement of established cultural values because these media were tremendously appreciated by their listeners or viewers.[12]

The Jazz Singer was first released in Rome on 19 April 1929 (only eighteen months after its American première) and the sound revolution spread immediately to the rest of the peninsula, affecting all sectors of production and exhibition. Unlike Germany and the United States, Italy had not developed a sound system of her own, but she was forced into buying foreign equipment which was extremely expensive: in the inital years, up to a half of the takings on every sound film produced in Italy was paid as a royalty to foreign companies. Many film producers, believing that the talkies were a device contrived by American studios to kill off their competitors, assumed that sound would be short-lived because, unlike silent pictures, talkies could not be easily re-edited and adapted to different audiences and also because it would be difficult to export Hollywood's products in countries where English was not spoken. According to them, the Americans would soon return to silent film; it was not necessary to invest in the new, expensive technology. Only Cines installed recording equipment which allowed it to launch, in 1930, four talkies, the first Italian sound films.

Since the middle of the 1920s, attendance had been rising steadily in Italian cinemas and despite the economic crisis, which brought inflation and a high level of unemployment, it did not fall dramatically after 1929.

Unfortunately, before 1936, there was no estimate of the yearly number of cinema-goers; the only figures we have concern the takings and do not inform us about the public. In 1924, one third of the sums spent on entertainmment (including sport) went to the cinema; in 1936, the proportion was of 63 per cent and it remained at that level during the following years. The ravages of unemployment had a serious effect upon the number of people going to all kinds of entertainment, but the share of cinema remained the same. However, confronted with the demands of exhibitors, Italian production was negligible. In 1929, Pittaluga, one of the main distributors of the peninsula, rented 140 pictures, out of which 89 were American, 45 came from various European countries and 6 were Italian. Out of 1,700 talkies distributed in Italy between 1930 and 1935, only 128 – 7 per cent – were Italian. During the same period, American films earned 60–70 per cent of the cinemas' total income compared with 15–17 per cent for Italian films.[13]

We do not have precise figures but it is estimated that there were more than 3,000 picture theatres in Italy in 1929. In 1930–32, silent films continued to be shown in country cinemas but all the 2,500 theatres listed in 1933 were wired for sound, which means that 500–600 small independent theatres had been obliged to close in villages, provincial towns or suburban areas. This was surely one of the most important transformations that the cinema underwent between the wars. The takings were not affected since, in Italy as in most European countries, four-fifths of cinema income was obtained from first-run theatres. However, for at least one decade, going to the pictures became a typical form of urban entertainment. Following Pitaluga's example, a few capitalists organized their chains of cinemas, but exhibition remained mostly an individual business. Cinema owners who wanted to afford the new technology applied to a distributor for financial help, thus accepting in advance what the renter would impose on them. This was another substantial change brought about by the advent of sound. Distribution, which in the 1920s had been a primitive trade, divided between modest independent firms working at a regional or even at a provincial level, became, in the 1930s, a modern industry dominated by four American companies[14] and a few Italian ones, all firmly tied to their major suppliers,[15] working in the main regions of the peninsula, and therefore able to impose their will upon exhibitors.

Almost everywhere in Europe the American technological invasion provoked opposition. Governments claimed that they had to protect the culture inherited from their ancestors and progressively tightened their quota system. Italy was the country offering least resistance; its specific regulations were rather mild, the only strict one being that foreign films could not be shown in the peninsula if their soundtrack was not in Italian. Economic motivations account largely for that tolerance. The Italian studios, which were in direct competition with the American ones, were not strong enough effectively to oppose the distributors. Pittaluga as well as the American renters accepted no restriction on imports; they argued that, without Hollywood's productions, they could not supply the exhibitors with film. Fascism was ready neither to confront a powerful lobby, nor to displease public opinion. A policy of free trade suited it, it was content with taking limited measures and maintaining a high exchange rate for the lira, which hampered exports (though Italy had little to sell abroad), but reduced the cost of imported goods.

Fascism was also a one-man dictatorship. Its propaganda, unlike Nazism's, was randomly organized and Fascism was mostly advertised thanks to Mussolini's speeches. Il Duce, whose interview for the Fox Movietone News, in 1927, was the first political talk ever projected on a screen, had more confidence in documentaries or newsreels than in fiction for his publicity.[16] Under his direction, perceptible changes occurred in newsreels with the sound era. To begin with, Italy was regularly offered his endless harangues. The initial attempts, influenced by radio broadcasting, were awkward. The leader, glued to his microphone, did not dare move. But he soon learned how to deal with the equipment and the filmmakers improved their style. Mussolini alternately spoke, paused, nodded, and waved to the crowd, and long shots of enthusiastic supporters enlivened the films.

It has rightly been said that the ritual was typical of a system lacking a programme or well-defined aim, and thus obliged to create consensus around a charismatic chief, an actor ready to play a great many parts. If we do not look thoroughly at the celebrations, they seem boring and repetitive. But the new ceremonial introduced by sound had modified the scenery. A close examination of the films reveals a surprising environment behind the leader and helps discover unprecedented features. The rank and file have disappeared. More and more priests, young, smart people, Fascist bosses and officers fill the background. Moreover, the framework has changed, the countryside tends to be replaced by towns. The camera explores urban surroundings, which implies a different manner of composition. There are fewer slow pans of landscapes, more motion and a rapid editing process. Important though they were, technicalities do not fully account for the visible transformation. The decrease in information about the countryside in newsreels unwittingly documents the difficulties of the Fascist agrarian policy: the 'wheat battle' was won, but other production, including cattle breeding, declined, with one million workers leaving the countryside. Abandoning its rural supporters, Fascism turned towards the urban middle-class. It aimed less at teaching and convincing, and more at almost 'seducing' youth, Catholics and local opinion leaders. Documentaries and newsreels give an insight into the uneasy, contrasting evolution of the regime. Mussolini went on boasting in the foreground but close scrutiny shows that, around him, the scenery and the extras have varied greatly from the first years to the mid-1930s. Factual films convey something much more interesting than blatant publicity for the system, they exhibit the opportunism and the uncertainties of Fascism.

'THE TIMES WHEN WE WERE DISCOVERING AMERICA . . .'

Mussolini had another reason for letting American productions enter Italy. He could ignore neither the close family relationships developed between the peninsula and the United States nor the curiosity aroused, among various sectors of the population, by American culture. Techniques from across the Atlantic had widely penetrated the provinces. Exiled for political reasons in a far-away village of southern Italy, in 1935, Carlo Levi realized that, for practical matters, life was American to such an extent that 'the peasants spoke of pounds and inches rather than of kilogrammes and centimetres'.[17] Later, during the decade that followed the Second World War, the Italian Communists denounced what they called an 'Americanization of Italian life' characterized by hegemonic influence of the United States in the political and technological sphere, but also in the cultural field, thanks to a massive importation of films and records. Although a member of the Communist Party, Cesare Pavese, the poet and novelist, found it necessary to react against this campaign: 'The times when we were discovering America are over,' he wrote in 1948. In his view, these times were the inter-war period, not the middle of the century. Obviously, the modernization of Italian industry in line with the American example did not occur before the 1950s. But, where cultural life was concerned, Italy had long before proved receptive to the American influence.

The issue of the spell of America is not easily dealt with. If we focus on the rumours conveyed in books and magazines, many clues suggest that intellectuals were fascinated by the United States. Fascism had bestowed on Italian cultural activities an atmosphere of torpor and narrowness. Provided they were not suspected of Communism, artists or novelists could write, talk and exhibit at art galleries but they were denied any public recognition by a regime which favoured only its upholders. America supplied distressed intellectuals with a myth, a place to escape, it represented simultaneously devotion to freedom and human dignity, prosperity and social mobility – in a word, everything that was missing in the peninsula.[18] This unqualified enthusiasm helped belittle the local creations. The Italian films, confronted with Hollywood's, were claimed to be hackneyed, stage-bound and banal: 'The Italian cinema is a corpse in the hold of a sailing ship'.[19]

However the ordinary spectators, who did not voice their opinion, felt happy with 'their' movies. The figures given above show that Italian

Plate 10 A popular fiction, *The Sculptor of Human Flesh*. The American myth: skyscrapers, blood and mystery

productions, which amounted to less than 10 per cent of the films in exploitation, took up to 17 per cent of domestic cinema income; Italian films were fewer but any one of them was attended by more spectators than a foreign picture. If we want to get a general idea of common tastes, we must forget the literary reviews and open the 'popular' magazines. The attitude of the non-specialist press is revealing: most papers offered regular chronicles and gave to the cinema the same space as for fashion or theatre and more than for sport. Yet, the best sign of the favour enjoyed by the cinema was the proliferation of film magazines: in Milan alone, eleven new periodicals were launched in the 1930s. Printed in plain typography on bad paper under covers decorated with the photograph of an American star, these cheap weeklies were designed for easy consumption.

Unlike more specialized reviews, the magazines never talked economy or technique; their main topic was Hollywood and its inhabitants. The writers, who had a strong grasp of clichés, brought also a touch of the bizarre to their papers but never failed to arrive at a moral conclusion. The Italian Hollywood was not a wonderland, it was a world of harsh work and long-deserved gratifications. Let us visit Fred McMurray: he wakes up, every morning, at four thirty, as early as a wagoner who goes to his depot, he has a bath, a frugal breakfast and he starts working.[20] The Hollywood stars were anti-*dive* and never acted out of caprice. Take the case of Barbara Stanwyck: being an orphan, she was obliged to become a typist. But her neighbours were very helpful, and thanks to their support she succeeded, after many years, in making a name for herself.[21] The weeklies based their judgements on social morality. Their America was a dynamic country where people, threatened by modern, urban, industrial norms, learnt to struggle against the limitations imposed on their condition. It proposed an escape into an imagined society in which class distinction did not exist. At the same time, the United States was a continent where plenty of fun was on offer. The cinema, with its stars and images, was closely tied-in to other forms of entertainment which formed a vast network centred on America. When a film got an enthusiastic response, a gramophone record appeared with an anthology of the best tunes. A publisher, Mondadori, specialized in the diffusion of American-style detective stories[22] and of Italian versions of the Walt Disney comic strips. Italian youngsters were fond of Mickey Mouse and followed, week after week, the adventures of Mandrake and Jungle Jim.[23] Eugenio Montale, a poet who was not especially interested in film, admited that the cinema was 'an art for everyone, art for the crowd', and that, like 'popular songs and the fashionable Charleston', it was entirely timely.[24]

For the mass of the public, enjoying *Children's Hour* or *Flowers and Trees* did not imply any contempt of the Italian movies. Thanks to the weeklies, to the radio programmes, to talks in pubs and offices, cinema had entered the life of Italians who, without even being regular spectators, were aware of what was going on. Many magazines were sold with a supplement filled with bits of film dialogues or transcriptions of screen-plays illustrated by well chosen stills, which enabled people gathering in the streets or on the main square to comment on films they had not seen. Highbrows despised the cheap 'pulp' magazines but the periodicals were very effective in creating a cinematic culture. They gave information on films and events connected to the cinema such as festivals or prizes, they afforded their readers a basic film literacy by identifying and describing the main 'genres', their lists of attributions were even rather sophisticated. They singled out, for instance, beside classics such as 'drama' or 'comedy', less predictable categories like 'dance' or 'adventurous' films and, in doing so, they were a useful guide to the cultural outlook of potential audiences.

MAKING THEIR OWN FILMS

Fascism was itself a big show, an attempt to involve people by making them parade in the street and watch a performance they themselves were enacting. Through the systematic use of radio and posters, and through free screenings of propaganda films, Mussolini accustomed Italians to the consumption and enjoyment of modern media and made them the members of a 'public'. Making people participate was more important than persuading them, which, once more, accounts for the absence of overt cinematic propaganda. Fascism as such was pictured in only three films,[25] all of which were made in less than two and a half years (1933–5). How can we explain such a limited series? The assumption has been made that, after 1935, Fascists did not want people to recall they had seized power violently and, instead of emphasizing their long fight against Socialists and Communists, stressed their desire to unify all Italians. Evidence supporting this conclusion is found in the memoirs of a former Director General of Italian cinematography, Luigi Freddi, who states that when *Old Guard*, the last of the overtly Fascist pictures (1935) was released 'I should have forbidden it, for our regime did not need a reconstitution of the past which might turn out to be damaging to it.' This is a perfectly plain statement but Freddi was Director only briefly, was never an influential person and wrote his memoirs some fourteen years after the events.[26] We are faced here with a classical artefact: since Fascist cinematic policy is poorly documented historians are tempted to take Freddi's words at their face value.

Instead, let us look at what happened in 1932–5. In 1932 filmmakers were officially invited to celebrate the tenth anniversary of Mussolini's accession to power. An old Fascist playwright, Giovacchino Forzano, took advantage of the circumstances and made an overtly Fascist film, *Black Shirt* (1933), a theatrical chronicle of Italian history, from the First World War to Mussolini's 'March on Rome'. This film was actively promoted by the government and released, simultaneously, in the most important Italian towns and in several foreign capitals. As Forzano was described as *the only possible* director for Fascist films, younger directors reacted quickly. Simonelli's *Dawn over the Sea* (1935) did not win much praise with its moral vision of a redeeming Fascism, but Alessandro Blasetti's *Old Guard*, the chronicle of a provincial town during the weeks preceding the same 'March on Rome', was as successful as Forzano's. Clearly, there was no attempt to prevent directors from depicting the origins of Mussolini's dictatorship. We must find another explanation for the absence of films dealing with Fascism.

Black Shirt and *Old Guard* treated the same topic differently. Forzano intermingled archival material and invented characters, Blasetti created an imaginary situation. Both made awkward use of fictional devices. Forzano introduced artificially, in what seemed to be a historical evocation, a ruined, unhappy blacksmith who takes heart when Fascism begins. The presence of this protagonist was not necessary, his fate was a diversion between the initial depiction of old Italy and the final celebration of Mussolini's rural policy. Blasetti's main character is a twelve-year-old boy whose presence gives the film a refreshing hue; in the kid's footsteps, we observe various aspects of the rivalries and daily problems of a small city but we never get beyond the youngster's limited horizon. Forzano's initial confrontation between Nationalists and Socialists forced viewers to expect a gigantic struggle which never happened: the film comes to a sudden end with a documentary-like sequence on agricultural improvement. Blasetti, excellent in his description of a family, its friends and neighbours, did not try to bridge the gap between local disputes and the general upheaval caused by Mussolini's followers in 1922; using a weak narrative convention, he had the boy killed by the Reds, which justifies the rush of his father and brother toward Rome. Both directors, though not beginners, failed to depict the political side of their theme and made no effort to create a dynamic, persuasive image of Fascism.

What explains this disappointing outcome? Filmmakers were competing with one another. Forzano concocted his picture hurriedly to prove he could be a director as well as a playwright; Blasetti, who had already made seven films, was keen on working as fast as his rival. In 1933 both Forzano and Blasetti directed two pictures while a competitor, Palermi, completed five films. The same year cameramen Ubaldo Arata and Carlo Montuori each shot seven pictures: a small clique of influential people monopolized the studios and the limited means of production. Producers urged haste, most scripts were put together in a few days and then given to actors with no time for preliminary rehearsals. Freddi, a megalo-maniac, dreamed of introducing Hollywood's practices in Italy but nothing was more alien to Italian ways than the American methods. Improvisation which dominated the Italian studios up to the 1960s, never prevented the directors and technicians from making first-rate pic-tures but was inappropriate for thoughtful, sober-faced reflection on poli-tics. In addition, men like Forzano or Blasetti, enthusiastic supporters of Mussolini, did not care much about political problems. Since Fascism's main slogan was unconditional adherence to Mussolini, intellectuals were content with manifesting their allegiance, never deepening their knowledge of a constantly-changing programme. For Mussolini's supporters, films by Forzano or Blasetti were Fascist simply by depicting healthy, good-look-ing Fascists.

The duel between Forzano and Blasetti was also a conflict of genera-tions. Born in 1900, Alessandro Blasetti belonged to the age group which had grown up while the movies were spreading over Italy, had adopted them and had defined its place in the world by reference to the screen. After graduating, Blasetti worked in various film magazines where he developed a harsh criticism against the dominant cinema and its economy. Dreaming of an independent system of production, he founded a coopera-tive to shoot *Sun*, a silent movie which was considered a masterpiece but was not distributed and is lost. Intent on making other films, Blasetti had to bargain with Cines. The closure of many studios had led the most prominent directors and players to emigrate; newcomers were not excluded and could even direct older, well trained technicians who were only too glad to get a job. Although he had joined the Fascist Party (which required no more than a signature) Blasetti knew little about Mussolini's ideas. During the first period of his production, which lasted until 1935, he clumsily attempted to please Il Duce by glorifying the rural traditions of the country. His master-work, *1860*, which celebrated Garibaldi and the Sicilian coutrymen who had made Sicily enter the Italian kingdom, and was shot at a time (first release, 1934) when Musso-lini proved diffident about both the Garibaldian/republican tradition and spontaneous collective action, exemplifies Blasetti's awkard situation. However, the film is so brilliant that Fascist critics could not but praise it.

1860 does not tell the story of the liberation of Sicily from Bourbon domination, it tries to make its spectators feel what Italians could feel at the time and to imbue them with the (supposed) spirit of the Risorgi-mento. The film can be divided into three parts: a presentation of Sicily under Bourbon tyranny, the journey of a shepherd sent to call Garibaldi for help, and the final battle. But such a summary is misleading; it suggests a plot line, whereas, in fact, there are no sequences, identified by precise incidents, but only 'moments' and pathetic evocations which stir emotion by a clever combination of sounds, contrasts in lighting and movements of the camera. During his journey towards Genoa, the shepherd hears passionate political debates but, most of the time, the picture, almost without speech, is only punctuated by a few recurring sounds: blasts of wind, the crackling of a fire, a far-away drumming and a series of detonations. Every 'moment' is made up of a series of seemingly unrelated visual or sound details which take a meaning once the viewer organizes them into a coherent whole. A double opposition black/white and darkness/light interplays with an alternation of different groups (the Bourbon soldiers, the countrymen, the Garibaldians) and different places and succeeds in creating a permanent tension, without ever following up any episode to its end. The boundaries between evocations dissolve with the intrusion of images taken from another filmic space and with swift movements of the camera which link, or violently confront, the opposed camps.

Blasetti's film was a break in the tradition of Cines. An adherence to previous models can be noted in the lighting and in the fight which closes the picture. But, in contradiction with Cines' patterns, there is no rush of thousands of extras, no tumultuous crowd, no charismatic leader. More importantly, there is no priviledged point of view, subjective glances are few and attributed to secondary characters, and what spectators see is what the camera shows them, not what a protagonist observes. After the triumph of de Mille's *The King of Kings* (1927) and *The Sign of the Cross* (1932), Italians knew that they could no longer emulate Hollywood. They had to find original forms which would not compete against American productions. But de Mille avoided the debated issues, such as the Civil War, and he limited his vision to a fanciful antiquity. On the other hand, Blasetti tackled a tricky period and innovated in the field of cinematic expression. It is not by chance that *1860*, a striking, impressive film, is an exception, a special case in the history of world cinema.

However, Blasetti was not a loner, he involved many people in his effort, and helped other members of his generation to experiment new patterns. With the advent of sound, screwball comedy, made up of gags or familiar jests performed quickly and in quick succession, had lost its appeal. Hollywood propounded its musicals, filled with songs, dances and nonsense elements, but the genre required well-trained bands and dancers that Italian producers could not afford. Faced with the same problem, the Berlin studios were developing a German-bred slapstick based on a confrontation between the old and the new, tradition and industrialization, aged gentlemen and pretty working-class women. Italy tried to adapt the German model, sometimes with directors and technicians lured from beyond the frontier. None of these films were big hits but they contributed to give comedies a dominant position in Italian film production: out of 132 talkies made from 1930 to 1935, 76, nearly 60 per cent, were lightweight comedies.

Without Vittorio de Sica, would comedies have met with such a unanimous approval? I doubt it. Outstanding actor, great director, script-writer, de Sica was a legendary figure in his time, only to be compared to Charlie Chaplin or Orson Welles. The third generation of cinema-goers worshipped him but, being born in 1901, he pertained to the second generation. Like many of his contemporaries, he had soon given up school to perform in music-halls, theatres and studios; but silent films did not suit him well, he could neither establish a clumsy touching per-sonage comparable to Foolshead nor, before the advent of sound, sing, laugh and exploit the spell of his voice. *What Rascals Men Are!* (1932), the first talkie in which he had a part, was a success in the first weeks of its release.[27] A journalist noted that there was no story, no interesting image, no technical innovation, but that seeing the picture was an abso-lute delight[28] and this was almost entirely due to the main protagonist. Handsome, tall, slim, elegant, Vittorio de Sica bore a physical likeness to the kind of ideal man one would have expected to find in film magazines. His dress and manner were appealingly smart and formal, his attractive, well-spoken, inviting voice sounded at once promising and elusive. Although exceptionally gifted, he was not pretentious. He knew he could not do everything on his own and relied on his collaborators, his director, Mario Camerini, and his scriptwriter, Cesare Zavattini, who were both his contemporaries.

De Sica's originality is best exemplified by a comparison between Camerini's *What Rascals Men Are!* and Alessandrini's *The Private Secre-tary* (1931), a German-style slapstick.[29] *The Private Secretary* follows a traditional pattern: a young woman is courted by two men, an old under-manager she does not dare rebuff and a young clerk she does not trust. The film proclaims itself a studio production and reveals itself as such by the number of theatrical entrances and exits and by the way the characters' movements are organized symmetrically or in contrast. The casting is perfect, the speed and rhythm of dialogues superb, jests follow one another, but all we see is borrowed from previous forms of entertain-ment. Camerini and de Sica did not ignore their predecessors. Some gags in *What Rascals Men Are!*, for instance the sequence in which de Sica, cycling behind a tram, is soaked by a water cart, were adapted from exist-ing stock. However all the jokes, whether borrowed or invented, were filmed with an extreme swiftness, it was their suddenness which made them amusing, while on the other hand, the gags in *The Private Secretary* were all the more enjoyable in that they were expected. Camerini and de Sica's wisecracks were also developed for themselves, for the visual pleasure they provided, and were not meant to say anything about the characters. Interestingly, the two films present working women, a

Plate 11 Vittorio de Sica in *What Rascals Men Are!* (1932, Mario Camerini)

secretary and a shop assistant. Elaine Mancini rightly notes that the secretary 'unlike the real women of her age and skill', has easily found a job.[30] She does not type, her work is a mere contrivance which explains why she is courted by an old bore. De Sica and his partner are filmed in their respective functions; we are taken to a garage, a department store and a trade fair. Of course, the picture is not a documentary, we lack information about the places we visit and the camera focuses on the characters, not on their surroundings. However superficial it is, the relationship to a social context creates a different atmosphere and makes spectators feel that they are not in front of a stage. Although the protagonists talk a lot, it is difficult to say that it is 'dialogue'. There are no witty lines, no well-coined puns, words are a sound material used, together with noises, songs and musics, to go with the pictures, or modify their meaning. Throughout the projection, spectators are surprised and challenged in various ways, their deep involvement in the quick tempo of the editing and the actors' skill runs at curious odds with a desultory, frivolous plot. By preventing the full development of actions or effects, the film creates a sense of easiness and gaiety distinct from the wordiness of most comedies. It is not better than *The Private Secretary* but, at the time, it looked newer and fresher.

*

The first generation of cinema-goers had soon enthused over the moving pictures. The curiosity aroused by the films did not slacken during the second generation. Was there a big difference between the habits and vision of the two age-groups? Unfortunately, we lack precise information about the geography of picture theatres and the admission numbers, since statistics only begin in 1936. There were then 250 million spectators (compared with 900 million in Britain) which represented, theoretically, five viewings *per year* for every person over 15 years of age. Since we can make no comparison with the pre-war period, these figures do not tell us very much.

We must be content with inferences drawn from the press, from cinema programmes and from the films themselves. Despite a relative standardization, there were various kinds of picture shows in about 1915: some were shorter and made only of factual items, some were longer and included several fictions.[31] Twenty years later, the ritual had become fixed: a new feature-length film, short pictures (cartoons, documentaries, newsreels) and a live performance in the first-run houses, two old fictions in the suburban cinemas. Newsreels and documentaries existed before the war but, being shot and edited at random, they featured an odd, ill-defined world. A major change introduced by the war was a transformation of the factual films; they were no more trustworthy than their predecessors but they dealt with current issues, and centred on the universe that spectators knew. While, at the beginning of the century, newspapers and documentaries were far apart, after the war the cinema became a medium of information as important as the press and radio.

There was a large variety of cinematic fictions in 1915 and they came from many countries. Hollywood tended already to dominate the market but it was often difficult to tell its products apart. In the decade that followed the war, Italian production collapsed, but so slowly that its bankruptcy did not attract people's notice. Hollywood smoothly substituted for the Italian studios, and there was no gap in the evolution of film attendance. Despite this crisis, the second generation of cinema-goers went through two important modifications. The diffusion of recorded sound, on radio, on gramophone records and in cinemas, re-modelled spectators' expectations, created new habits, and introduced forms of social expression based on a combination of various aural and visual materials. In this respect, the experience of 1935 audiences was totally different from that of 1915 audiences. Sound films and American influence expanded together: it would be impossible to distinguish them, the technique came from the United States and brought with it the products. Unlike other European countries, Italy willingly accepted what was coming from beyond the seas. It did not feel threatened, even its strictly nationalist leaders proved tolerant. When a few young film enthusiasts exerted themselves and succeeded in making their own films, they did not pretend that they wanted to save the national cinema: for them, for everybody, genuine Italian production could survive beside a dominating American exploitation. And this, also, differentiated the second generation from its predecessor.

Third generation
The most popular form of entertainment

When the third generation of cinema-goers reached twenty, Fascism was in its heyday. A quick victory in Ethiopia (1936) had given Italy a colonial Empire which, according to its leaders, was all it needed to be a world power. Many European politicians considered Mussolini a 'reasonable' dictator, who had put an end to social unrest in his country and was likely to resist the dangerous, megalomaniac Hitler. Enthusiastic though they were, the Italians could not ignore that Mussolini's gesticulation was merely an attempt to camouflage a disastrous economic situation. The Great Depression imposed a devaluation of the lira in 1936: from 1931 to 1941, the cost of living increased by 60 per cent. The level of unemployment was probably abnormally high but we cannot evaluate it since, between 1933 and 1935, Italy did not publish the number of jobless, and the figures given for 1936–9 are not reliable.[1] Local studies reveal a poverty which, however, did not result in overt discontent. The Second World War soon broke out. The third generation of film-goers was mobilized and fought in Africa, in the Balkans and in Russia. It suffered twenty months of foreign occupation and, when it was only 30 years old, readjusted to civilian life in a ruined country. Ten years later, living in a democracy whose institutions appeared robust, it witnessed the transformation of the North of the peninsula into a modern industrial society of urban, middle-class consumers.

Few generations have ever experienced such staggering change. But this mutation would be of little importance for our study if it was not for the fact that the Italian population became more and more fascinated by movies, that Italian film production grew so quickly that, by 1942, it ranked fifth in the world, and finally, that Italy gave birth, in the wake of this sudden revival, to one of the most important currents of world cinema, Neorealism. We must avoid seeing any one-to-one relationship between the political or economic evolution and the boom of filmmaking. Things were certainly much more complicated and there is a paradox concealed behind the enormous success of the cinema that cannot be ignored: the years during which Italians ran to the movie theatres were characterized by a rapid increase in the cost of basic goods, a lasting shortage of jobs and, consequently, a significant reduction in the standard of living. An important cultural fact, perhaps the most important in the evolution of Italian cinema, namely the 'second take-off' of film production, at the time of the Second World War and the reconstruction, was an improbable occurrence.

GOD AND MAMMON

Until the middle of the 1930s, domestic feature films had been so few, and so hastily made, that the government contented itself with supervising the documentaries made by the *Light Institute*, and letting people watch an alien, half-mythical country, America. But, during the second half of the decade, Fascism progressively strengthened its grip over the cinema. Initially, the institution of the annual Venice Festival, in 1932, was merely an attempt to lure a few European and American intellectuals in the peninsula. But, by 1935, with the institution of awards reserved for Italian films only, the festival was used to promote Italian films. The same year, cinematic studies were reorganized, with the opening of an Experimental Centre for Cinema. Two years were necessary to train the first cohort of filmmakers, so that 1937 witnessed the official rebirth of Italian cinema, when Carmine Gallone's *Scipio the African* received the award for best Italian film. Other measures were intended to facilitate the renting of films and to help the studios,[2] but the most important innovation was sponsoring the huge studios of Cinecittà, in suburban Rome, at first privately owned (1937), but later transferred to the State (1938). With this giant plant in which half of the Italian films were soon shot, the country had the most modern cinema workshop in Europe and revived the tradition of Filmopoli.

How can we account for this sudden reversal of official policy? Money was surely a decisive factor. Foreign trade, exchange rates and prices defined guidelines for film importers. From 1920 on, Italy had spent enormous sums to acquire foreign films but, given the level of local production, it seemed difficult to adopt any other course. When Mussolini considered establishing a ban on imports, his son, Vittorio, who was a film buff, did not hesitate to publish an article which said: 'What is going to happen? Exhibitors will have to face a shortfall of some hundred films which, and let us say it with an open, Fascist frankness, were the bulk of our organization and lured the public.'[3] Despite the pressure of distributors, what Fascists called self-sufficiency began in 1936. But, although imports were strictly controlled, American films still entered Italy until the beginning of 1938, partly because exhibitors, backed by Vittorio Mussolini, were successful in opposing the ban, but, most importantly, because of the very nature of the Fascist autarky. In order to save an endangered economy, the Italian government aimed first at reducing expenditure by refusing loans to small firms. Almost all the film companies were very weak and needed public financing. Suddenly the ministry stopped helping them and told them to sell their products abroad. Simultaneously Italy tried to develop her exports by means of reciprocal agreements with foreign countries. For a few months it was hoped that bargaining with the Hollywood majors would rescue distribution from a difficult situation and revitalize the studios. But the United States was not interested in buying Italian movies; the dream was not fulfilled. In 1938 a total ban on American films, the worst possible solution, was reluctantly decreed, because the country could no longer afford to buy from Hollywood.

Oddly enough, the state did not content itself with closing its borders. In a period when the embargo deprived cinemas of the American films which represented two-thirds of the programmes, the government sponsored the creation of new picture theatres: about a thousand cinemas opened between 1937 and 1940. The key to this paradox is to be found in the difficult, conflicting relationship between Fascism and the Catholic Church. Before the First World War, Italy was parochial and badly administered. The monarchy was weak, and faced the overwhelming influence of a Catholic Church respected for its moral authority, to say nothing of its wealth. Unlike its Austrian, French or German counterparts, the Italian Church had never tried to create a national network of lay institutions. Understanding that it would have to compete with the newly created state, the Italian clergy, at the outset of the twentieth century, endeavoured to strengthen their control over the faithful and, for that purpose, cleverly used movies to give people 'healthy' ideas and to lure the young into the fold. Already in the 1920s, priests were advised to install light projectors in their parish hall, while 'good' pictures and even a few films made by religious societies were distributed at cheap prices. In 1934, the Church went a step further when it created a centralized organization, the Catholic Centre for Cinema, entrusted with reviewing the films and evaluating their moral value. The Centre's magazine, *Cinematic Information*, soon became very influential because it was the only journal which announced and analysed every film released in the country. Priests were then in a position to prevent their flock from attending certain movies. They were all the more persuasive in that, especially in towns, middle-class women helped them run the parish cinema and obliged their relatives or friends to see movies celebrating the virtues of traditional family life.[4]

Fascists, well aware of the situation, knew that the Church was taking the lead but, given its influence in the country, did not dare confront it openly. Their reaction was slow and indirect. In 1924, the government passed an Education Act (known as the Gentile Act, after the minister of education), which established, between primary and secondary education, modern schools intended, as Gentile admitted, 'to train the simple citizen and provide with the necessary skill those who will have practical jobs'. A limited syllabus made pupils take an active, direct interest in tools; cinema was especially well suited for such a programme. The creation of the *Light Institute*, two years later, was another step in the same direction. The Church could not neglect the resulting educational, well-made, entertaining documentaries; it was obliged to distribute them, at least partially. A treaty between Italy and the Vatican (1929) did not really ease the situation. In their competition for the control of public opinion, the Catholic Church and the state played an important part in expanding the cinema circuits by opening their own picture theatres. Cinema, which in the 1920s had tended to become an urban form of entertainment, began to re-enter small towns and even a few villages.

'I WENT TO THE PICTURES ALMOST EVERY DAY'

Was this a cause (more cinemas, hence more clients) or an effect (if more people ask for films, it is profitable to inaugurate other show-rooms) of the increase in film-show attendance? Probably both: the number of available seats and the number of spectators shot up at the same rate during the same period. The increasing curiosity of domestic spectators was a decisive factor in the evolution of Italian cinema: attendance jumped from 260 million film-show seats bought in 1936 to 470 million in 1942, 662 million in 1950, and reached its peak, 819 million, in 1955. The third generation, which was by far the most hooked on cinema, never slackened: the number of viewers expanded with an amazing regularity over two decades. There is no satisfactory explanation for such interest, which cannot be understood unless it is connected to a series of overlaping factors. It is often claimed that, when faced with a dramatic situation, an economic crisis, a war, a foreign occupation, people want to forget, be it only for a few hours, and try to have as much fun as possible. Maybe, but there is no way of measuring such a supposed desire and the contrary psychological argument could be advanced, that people, being hungry and frightened, do not fancy going out. Let us therefore rely on more concrete factors.

Victoria de Grazia has explained how the Fascist government was keen on creating a strong layer of employees and state agents likely to 'perform the social and political functions' of a non-existent middle class, ready to support its policies, to shake off the influence of the Church and to resist social unrest, in short capable of acting as a social intermediary 'between the political elite and the working population as a whole'.[5] Having first created modern schools, the state endeavoured, in the 1930s, to increase educational opportunities: in 1940 there were three times as many students in secondary schools and universities as in 1930. In order to provide the graduates with employment the government doubled the number of civil servants. There was thus, at the end of the 1930s, a significant proportion of Italians who received an academic training, conceived of themselves as intellectuals and were interested in literature and performing arts. Gian Piero Brunetta has explained beautifully how cinema was, to these people, a world apart, highly enjoyable, where the young could meet, without adult interference, and talk about art and life. University film societies developed from 1933, enabling their members to see, under official cover, subversive, or even simply rare films and to discuss them. Two first-rate cinematic magazines, *Bianco e nero* (*White and Black*)[6] and *Cinema* were launched in 1936 and met immediately with an enthusiastic response. Later, writing his *Autobiography of a Spectator* (1974), the novelist Italo Calvino (born 1923) confessed: 'There were years during which I went to the pictures almost every day and sometimes twice a day. That was between 1936 and the war, in short my youth. A time when, to my mind, cinema was the world itself.' In his small town, San Remo, there were three opening-run cinemas which changed their programmes twice a week, and two second-run cinemas which changed programmes three times: in other words, twelve films on offer each week.[7] All young people longed for films. Those who could not afford to go as frequently as Calvino were content to contemplate the posters and photographs, stuck on the walls or displayed in front of the theatres, which told a lot about the plot and main characters. 'We didn't go there that often,' a contemporary of Calvino, Fellini, admits, 'most of the time, we didn't have the money,' but cinema was, nevertheless, 'a gate into the impossible and unbelievable'. Brunetta is correct when he speaks of a 'mental cinema', of an imaginary, dreamlike entity antecedent to vision which could even be spared the direct contact of the picture house.[8]

College graduates or students were, of course, a small minority. Workers and peasants did not share the same experience but other factors helped entice them into picture theatres. Private savings, which amounted to $7\frac{1}{2}$ per cent of the gross national product between 1930 and 1936, rose to $13\frac{1}{2}$ per cent from 1937 to 1939. Italians were no more affluent, but, given the fact that the lira was no longer artificially protected, inflation increased at a time when industry offered fewer goods: people had more depreciated currency but could not spend it and were thus forced to increase either savings or unnecessary expenditure. At the same time, the price of cinema entrance, frozen by the government, remained low: in 1939 tickets cost 2 lire, the same price as a kilo of bread or a film-magazine, and less than a kilo of pasta. Table 1 compares the salary of a medium-rank civil servant, the evolution of household expenditure and the mean price of pasta and cinema seats in lire.

Table 1 Cost of a cinema seat, 1937–41

	1937	1938	1939	1940	1941
salaries (1930 = 100)	102	110	115	131	157
household expenditure					
(1930 = 100)	107	110	112	111	105
1 kg of pasta (lire)	2.52	2.43	2.62	2.78	3.20
cinema seat (lire)	2	2	2	2	2

The salary of civil servants followed the fall in the lira, its nominal value rising at the same rate as current food prices (see pasta). Many items were no longer available in shops: furniture, clothes, cars had vanished and private expenditure was declining. Most Italians, especially those who had a job with the state, could now treat themselves to the pictures.

The rate of inflation was dramatic during the Second World War and the Reconstruction era but the price of a cinema ticket, while rising after 1941, maintained its parity with foodstuffs. In 1948 inflation was curbed and between that year and 1955, wages increased by about 35 per cent. Unemployment persisted until 1955, but those who had a job earned relatively more money than before the war. However there were few commodities available, in particular there were 10 per cent fewer cars than in 1940. It is hardly surprising that, with more income and no opportunities to spend it, Italians went to the cinema on average thirty times a year, the third highest rate in the world after the Americans and the British.[9] The strong influence of family life must be taken into account: married couples went to the cinema with their children, parents and other relatives; no break occurred after the age of 25, as was the case in other European countries.

Another decisive factor was the permanent opening of new picture houses. The Church, still anxious to guard its flock against evil influences, had to compete, after the war, with the Communist Party but it was now backed by the Christian Democrats, who monopolized power from 1948 to the mid-1960s. An important aspect of Christian Democracy was its close relationship with women as voters and with priests as local supporters. This provided the basis for the superior national network which the party enjoyed. The Church expanded its influence through educational or cultural organizations. Knowing the importance of media, it created a popular radio slot, opened some three thousand parish cinemas during the period of the Reconstruction, and managed to show the most popular films, westerns and comedies, whose success was certain. Communist or Socialist regional and local authorities reacted whenever they could and established their own cinemas. Italy counted one cinema for 11,000 inhabitants in 1940, one for 6,000 in 1950, and one for 4,500 in 1955. Many of these theatres were poorly furnished, some of them were mere tents or open-air spaces but, thanks to their number, all classes were involved, even the workers and peasants.

For the third generation, cinemas became the most important centres of social life in Italy – all the more popular in that there were no other places where both sexes and all ages were admitted. Italy was a country where schools were sexually segregated, and where no woman, let alone a young woman, could enter a bar. In *A Violent Life* (1959),[10] Pasolini, a typical member of the generation, tells how, in suburban Rome, after the war, the only place where a boy and a girl could meet without running into a relative was a picture house. In Fellini's *Spivs* (1953) newly-weds who are obliged to live at the bride's parents home go to the cinema when they want to spend a few hours on their own and it is in cinemas that young men encounter women. Countless testimonies describe spectators arriving long in advance, settling comfortably, eating, drinking, commenting on the film. Other witnesses evoke the small country cinemas, with their balcony overcrowded, their clients standing, packed like sardines, in the aisle, the smell of sweat and salami, the crying babies and the elderly having a nap. Let us listen, among many voices, to the Sicilian Leonardo Sciascia:

> The show-room was an old theatre and we always went on the balcony. From there, we spent hours spitting at the stalls; the voices of the victims burst out. . . . At the beginning of the love-sequences, we started breathing loudly, as though from desire; even older people did it.[11]

The first opinion polls, organized by the Doxa Institute from 1946, show to what extent people were interested in the cinema.[12] In 1951, one third of the women said that they had been at least once a week to the cinema during the previous month, while another third boasted to be 'regular' cinema-goers. Of course, surveys deserve a critical look; all we can assume is that two-thirds of the interviewed women wanted to make known that they liked films. Doxa tried to define the social origins of the public; unfortunately, it had recourse to vague categories which are un-usable. The only divisions which can be made use of are the geographical ones, distinguishing the urban from the rural areas and the big towns from their outer suburbs. The urbanized, heavily industrialized provinces of the North showed a high level of attendance but the same was also true of Latium. Altogether, the North and Centre bought three-quarters of the tickets. A quarter of the viewers, who went to city-centre cinemas, were from various social strata but the other quarter which went to subur-ban cinemas was surely of 'popular' origin. We shall try, later, to account for people's taste but there is no doubt that many workers went to the

Plate 12 Advertising *Bitter Rice* (1949, Giuseppe de Santis). Carpi

pictures, especially in areas where the local social life was monotonous or where there were few public entertainments.

THE LIMITS OF CONSENSUS

We must bear in mind the fact that the cinemas were highly popular places of sociability if we want to understand what going to the movies meant for the third generation. Filmmakers made no mistake, they soon realized that a blossoming audience was ready to absorb more and more films. Once the market was closed to American imports, after 1938, the number of new pictures correlated with the number of spectators: 30 films in 1935; 78 in 1939; 87 in 1940; 98 in 1941.[13]

Film historians sometimes speak of 'the Fascist cinema'. What does that mean exactly? If we stamp as 'Fascist' all the 830 films made during Mussolini's dictatorship, between 1922 and 1943, we must add that 444 of them (54 per cent), were made between 1939 and 1943: the so-called 'Fascist cinema' did not develop that early! A few bureaucrats, for instance Freddi, whom we met in the previous chapter, dreamed of a concentrated, industrialized, Hollywood-like film production. The reality was something else. Approximately sixty small producers went on making two pictures a year; these men had no capital, they were all obliged to apply for state aid and, reluctantly, the government eventually granted the funds necessary to prevent bankruptcy. A wavering policy which cost the state a lot of money enabled the Italian studios to get over the embargo crisis and start, before the war, what would become the cinematic boom of the post-war period. This was perfectly consistent with the casual attitude of many Fascist leaders who, despite their declarations of ideological righteousness, did not really care about the political or ideological principles exposed in films and books. The label 'Fascist' was bestowed on all the pictures made before 1945 by young critics who hated the dictatorship and were keen on promoting a democratic, left-oriented cinema. In twenty years, Zavattini contended in 1945, Italian studios 'have not even produced one film, I insist: not even one'.[14] This was received wisdom, repeated from book to book, for three decades. But it must be recognized that the films were not available and that most analysts had recourse to written sources. It is only in the 1980s that Marcia Landy and James Hay, after a close examination of the films, introduced a more balanced view of the problem.[15]

When dealing with black-and-white films, we must take care not to be anachronistic: values have changed so drastically since the 1930s that we are not always able to tell what was a common belief of the period or what was typical of Fascism. We are tempted to ascribe to Fascism such features as the reverence for leaders, the importance of family life, the dependence of women and the overvalutation of nationalism. In fact, the same characteristics can be found in pictures made in Hollywood or in democratic European countries. The main slogans of Fascism, at the end of the 1930s, were: autarky, youth, and a fighting spirit. Only five pictures illustrated the first point and only indirectly at that, by showing Italian immigrants who feel homesick and return to the peninsula: at a time when America was virtually closed to Italians this was less propaganda than mere acceptance of reality. Where fighting spirit was concerned, things were much easier: it sufficed to show that the Italians were very brave and Cinecittà borrowed from Hollywood its standard genres for war stories.

These highly predictable films would not be worth mentioning if they did not share a common, unexpected feature: whereas the American war movies are optimistic and end up with their heroes triumphing over adversity, nearly all Italian versions turn out badly; pilots are killed or maimed for life; submarines cannot surface; guns jam. Let us take two examples, before and during the World War. Made in 1938, *Luciano Sera Pilot* was one of the few films dedicated to the conquest of Ethiopia. Its main character, an heroic pilot, half-destroyed, psychologically, by the First World War, died for a private cause, when he rescued his son wounded by the Ethiopians. Four years later, in 1942, *Giarabub* evoked the siege and surrender of an Italian fortress conquered by the English in Libya. Cinematic Italian soldiers fought heroically and, when wounded, suffered stoically; they were succoured by pretty nurses and ready to die but, militarily speaking, the outcome was usually disastrous. Only three of more than twenty films have a happy ending; two are 'colonial films' in which natives, naturally, are slaughtered, the third celebrates the heroism of the Spanish nationalists in Toledo.[16] Why did strict censors not ban sad stories suggesting to Italians that they had virtually lost the war? We are faced again with the inconsistency of the Fascist regime, so fussy over little things that it would make a director change two words in his script, but unaware of how devastating the depiction of defeat could be.

Flagrant propaganda does not exist in the Italian films of the 1930s, but historians often stress the importance of oblique publicity and note that two films released in 1937, *Condottieri* (in fifteenth-century Italy, *condottieri* were the leaders of independent military teams; the film was released in Britain with its Italian title) and *Scipio the African* featured great men: John of the Black Bands and Scipio, two charismatic leaders who, it is said, anticipated Italian nationalism inasmuch as Scipio conquered North Africa in 202 BC and John attempted to unify Italy in the sixteenth century.[17] Are these men presented, in films, as forerunners of Mussolini? A close examination of the pictures makes us doubt it. The two stars, slender, modest, silent, faithful husbands, have little in common with Il Duce. But there is more. In 1937 informed people began to wonder whether Mussolini should not retire: he was tired, lonely, and, since a military alliance had been signed with Germany, he tended to let his son-in-law and Foreign Minister, Galeazo Ciano, run Italian foreign policy. These two films offer two solutions for a leader who has fulfilled his mission. Scipio withdraws discreetly. We see him leading the Roman army during the final battle of Zama (the climax of the movie) but he does not go to Rome to receive public acclaim. After the Roman victory there is an unexpected cut. We suddenly see a close-up of hands spreading grain about: Scipio is back home amidst his farmers, he is again an ordinary landlord. In *Condottieri*, John confronts old Malatesta, whom he has first loyally served and criticized when necessary; before leaving, John challenges his former master to single combat and wounds him. Was the director conscious of the contradiction he was representing? I do not think so. It is then all the more unexpected that two *condottieri* (instead of one *condottiere*) are mentioned in the title and that the plot turns on the rivalry between the old and the young. The film foreshadows the dramatic fate of Mussolini and his son-in-law: during the final battle Malatesta is defeated and John is killed. In 1943 Ciano helped engineer Mussolini's abdication and was soon after executed as a traitor to him. The director could not know what was going to happen but Fascism was so contradictory that two inconsistent versions of the system, an apology and a sharp criticism of the chief could be presented in the same picture.

What is the apparent message of these films? *Scipio* is classically constructed. An establishing sequence informs us of the Carthaginian threat
and introduces Scipio. This opening and the battle of Zama frame the
story, suggesting that Africa is the core of the film. After the opening
scenes the film begins to alternate two sides, Rome/Carthage, Carthage/
Rome but, instead of following this simple line, development is interrupted
only to return to the depiction of alternate sides on the eve of the battle
of Zama. After the opening credits of *Condottieri* we are unexpectedly
presented with a wonderful, unreal and disturbing shot of Colleone's
equestrian statue in Venice. The picture is disconcerting since Colleone
lived one century before John, who never went to Venice. However, the
shot introduces two traits characteristic of the film. First, systematic ana-
chronism. The film keeps moving from one epoch to another, from one
location to another: it is, to a certain extent, an historical and geographical
exploration of Italy. Simultaneously the scene with Colleone anticipates a
recurring series of statues and horses which arbitrarily punctuate the film.
Colleone's statue is followed by a long sequence in which we do not hear
of John. A medieval castle is besieged, a frightening, black man succeeds
in kidnapping a baby: the whole scene is reminiscent of Italian contemporary melodramas and there are many other aspects, in *Condottieri* of
melodrama, notably fortuitous recognitions. The film associates loosely
four or five different images, John and Malatesta, John and his comrades,
John and his family, horsemen, statues, etc.

Scipio and *Condottieri* thus look totally different. The former's plot is
firmly constructed and sticks to a well-defined epoch; the latter is made
of various, poorly related episodes and mixes history, geography, melodrama and documentary. *Condottieri* helps us to throw some light on an
uncanny perturbation. Melodrama is also involved in *Scipio*: the honest
general and perfect husband is contrasted with the Carthaginian leader
whose vileness is revealed thanks to a long discussion of his dreadful
family. The film is torn between its main theme, history, and the tempta-
tions of melodrama but, instead of accepting and exploiting the distortion,
as *Condottieri* does, it tries to overcome it. Neither film is therefore able to
deliver a precise, coherent message. Scipio speaks of subjugating Africa
but we are provided with private intrigues or affairs unrelated to Rome's
foreign policy. Reviews of *Condottieri*, in film-magazines or in newspapers,
are revealing. Most critics were unable to say anything precise about the
film since they could not see whether they should applaud or condemn.
In the final analysis, neither film actually tried to promote a Fascist ideal,
they were simply good, exciting adventure films taking place in an historical context.

In the second post-war era, all films made under Fascism were considered devices to manipulate public opinion and make people forget
their real problems. The notion of 'consensus', developed by Antonio

Gramsci, the famous Communist thinker, was applied to Mussolini's cultural policy, with the implication that Il Duce sponsored film production to prevent social unrest. However, Gramsci was not content with assuming that the bourgeoisie, once it no longer needs to put down its opponents, tries to assimilate them to its own standards. His view was rather that consensus, far from being ever firmly established, had to be permanently renovated by the ruling class.[18] Statistics seem to confirm that the cinema, under Fascism, was mostly escapist. A good half of the 507 movies shot from 1935 to 1944 were comedies, one third were melodramas or family stories, and then came historical or sport pictures. With that list in mind, one can reasonably argue that cinema was a mere instrument which allowed Fascists to entertain the population during a difficult period. But figures are not sufficient, we must take a more precise look at the production of the film.

We have seen how Blasetti began his career in studios by making historical films – films dealing with precise events, the conquest of Sicily by Garibaldi or Mussolini's March on Rome. From 1936 onwards, Blasetti turned towards costume films and stories located in a vague, or even in a totally fanciful past. *1860* was remarkable, among other things, for its accuracy. The following films suggested that spectators might be much happier with a more relaxed vision of the past, where songs, bright clothes, anecdotes, even predictable tricks recreated the flavour of long-past events. While *1860* concentrated on ordinary people, *Ettore Fieramosca* (1938) and *An Adventure of Salvator Rosa* (1939) presented exceptional personalities likely to stir the interest of viewers. The former piled up duels, betrayals and pitfalls. The latter, more interestingly, created a double personality. In Naples, occupied by the Spaniards, in the seventeenth century, the same man, Rosa, was, openly, a famous painter who worked for the rich and the powerful, but also, secretly, a defender of the weak and of the oppressed, a kind of Robin Hood who fooled the exploiters. The ambiguity of the film has often been stressed. What, in the film, did Rosa fight for? He did not think of freeing the town from the occupiers and was not a 'national' hero; but, by serving the rich and helping the poor, he retained a hidden influence which made him stronger than the two opposing camps. Playing the weak against the strong and vice versa, he stressed the tensions created by inequality and denounced, indirectly, the ambivalence of consensus. Despite its costumes and luxurious scenery, the film was a comedy, but historical references give the story a depth that would not have been read into it at the time.

The kinship of *An Adventure of Salvator Rosa* with amusing films is all the more striking since Italian comedies, in the late 1930s and early 1940s, were based on two main patterns: one character was mistaken for another and the spectator, who knew who was who, enjoyed the confusion; or a character was totally maladjusted and constantly made blunders.

Social criticism seems to be excluded from such a simple scheme but it is necessary to go beyond the main lines of the plot and see how the story developed on the screen. A big hit of 1937 was Camerini's *Mr Max*, starring de Sica. The film tells the very predictable tale of two personalities: Max, whose modest job is to sell newspapers, gets an opportunity to go on a sea cruise where he courts, alternately, a rich heiress and her maid. Social consensus is at its best since Max feels at ease with both women and knows how to address them. But Camerini was too well aware of class distinction to show Max going through a Cinderella-like dream. His film slowly erased apparent differences (clothes, manners) to unveil the only actual criterion, money. Max, who was in love with both women, had no real choice; he was poor and bound to marry the maid. Artificial though they were, comedies often supplied a perceptive vision of social inequalities. James Hay has very aptly described the ambiguities of the genre; action took place mostly in pretentious, artificial locations, a liner or a dance-hall, where humble characters, parodying what was usually performed in these places, made fun of high society and highlighted 'the value of the common man'.[19] Critics rightly argued that, unlike de Sica, an ordinary newspaper-seller could not easily adapt to the upper-class life-style. But it must be noted that this way of life was also ridiculed by the film, that it was reduced to a series of conventions and gestures no more or no less significant than those observed in other groups. I am not pretending that Camerini or de Sica was trying to satirize the ruling class, they were much too respectful of authority for that. But they understood their public and, to please it, they alluded to social antagonisms, even though they lessened them or displaced them into an universe of gags and puns.

The issue is all the more complex in that Fascism was not a unified, coherent political force. Class conflict developed between rich and poor Fascists; the latter were not unhappy to applaud a mild criticism of the well-off. The second most important genre, beside comedy, was the social drama whose themes were akin to melodrama (natural children, seductresses, passion, crime and suicide) but set in contemporary surroundings. Social dramas never analysed the foundations of the social order but they criticized sharply the haves and the have-nots, describing the arrogance, the selfishness and the greed of the former, the submission of the latter. Scrutinizing all these dramas would be tedious but I must describe at least a few of them. *Yes Madam* (1941) follows an orphan, Christina, who, having been told that she must always say 'Yes Madam', finds a variety of domestic jobs in bourgeois families. Her first employers, a couple of old ladies, are incredibly harsh, never stop snapping at her, dig about in her things and forbid her to sing, read in her room or go out. She accepts this passively and the film makes it clear that, having no friends or family, she cannot do anything but obey. As soon as the ladies' nephew begins to court her, she is fired. The second employer, an industrialist, does not get the loan he needed and is obliged to sack Christina. Here, depression threatens and hits previously very rich people. In her last post, Christina contracts a fatal disease which helps close the film on a sad note. Clearly, the film was not a tract on injustice and inequality. However, it stressed tensions deriving from social differences. Its unhappy ending is important: Christina was not offered the classical solution of a wedding. In the film, she meets a few young men but the ones from the same background have no money and the rich are not serious.

An objection made to this film at the time was that such an approach provided a limited characterization and imposed a much too explicit narrative on an otherwise complicated, ambivalent state of things. It is true that films made for a large public were often simplistic. They were also, sometimes, rather sophisticated and, by exposing opposing points of view, could lead to mixed interpretations. Let us consider a successful movie, *Headlights in Fog* (1942). A bride, Wanda, leaves her husband, Cesare, a truck driver, because he does not want her to go on working; he has an affair with another woman and later starts afresh with Wanda. Two different readings are possible:

– (critical): truck drivers lead an exhausting life, operating night and day on terrible roads, live in out-of-the-way villages (where housing is less expensive) and have no family life. Many sequences support this version; or:

– (harmonious): a sensitive boss helps Cesare get over his anger; Wanda understands that women must stay at home when their husbands have hard jobs. There are images to back this version.

The blend of criticism and appeasement does not fully account for the popularity of dramas. Another significant factor was the lack of complexity apparent in *Yes Madam* as well as in *Headlights in Fog*: few events, no suspense or unexpected development. No psychological insight either: characters talk of ordinary, trite things, of their daily life and problems; it takes the viewer a long time to understand why Wanda has left her husband and when she drops the hint that she is unhappy she does not explain why. As for Cesare we do not know how he feels after Wanda has vanished. *Headlights in Fog* shows the two protagonists alternately in their new, lonely life and it is up to the spectator to systematize and interpret these short scenes in the light of their own situation. The camera work, which is excellent, explores the surroundings (trucks on the road, Wanda working in a shop, a pub, the various houses the characters visit) without ever trying to analyse them. If we go with the drivers during their long, exhausting night trips, we learn nothing about their wages, their working-hours, the freight they convey. The film begins with a eight-shot sequence: first, a landing, a staircase, a street, various noises (voices, banging doors, footsteps, cars) delineate a background; suddenly, we see a woman and a man who follows her: a fast, dramatic rhythm has introduced the viewers to a tense atmosphere without providing any real information. Cesare then goes to work and, in the third sequence, we see him on the road. The film interchanges first the cab and the road, then focuses on the misty, damp, crowded roadway. The sequence does not help to develop the plot: it is useless for the narrative, the journey is neither a flight nor a chase; but it is not a documentary either, merely a tight editing of contrasting shots which focus our attention on the wind-screen. It is exciting but not very thrilling and the grip loosens as soon as the sequence ends.

Most Italian spectators had to choose between comedies that featured well-known actors who re-enacted archetypal, paradigmatic stories, and dramas aimed at attracting audiences without expecting too much involvement. Of course, things were not that simple: on the one hand there were the foreign films (the prints bought before 1938 were still circulating), historical pictures, war and colonial films; on the other hand, distribution varied considerably from province to province. However, as a rule, the images offered to Italian spectators did not raise questions. They did not even create a world. Comedies, through the skill of actors, portrayed various types of personal relationships. Dramas conveyed the material importance of objects or locations and evoked a sense of place; they were escapist inasmuch as they did not 'denounce' anything but they also made viewers ponder their own condition, their way of life, which, from a political point of view, was not totally neutral. After the Liberation, Neorealism was much sharper and more systematic in its criticism of injustice or inequality but its techniques were those which had been tested in the late 1930s.

A STATE AFFAIR

The young critics and filmmakers who contended, in 1945, that nothing had been done during the two previous decades were driven by the desire to stamp out what was perceived as the Fascist threat; their hope was that it would be possible to start the whole business of cinema afresh. However, willingly or not, Fascism had reorganized and deeply influenced domestic production. The democratic government instituted after the Liberation could not ignore this reality. The 30 per cent tax imposed on total box-office receipts was the most important revenue that the state got from the leisure industry. Of course, this was not very important for the Treasury, but there were offices which managed the money, a large part of which was redistributed to the various parties involved in filmmaking: modifying the deal would have been difficult. Fascism had closed the market to Hollywood, instructed the National Bank for Labour to grant money to the producers, subsidized Cinecittà, kept the ticket prices at a low level and, in doing so, it had strongly favoured the renewal seen shortly before the war. Statistics suggest that something happened around 1937. The Italians who, previously, were no keener than other Europeans on visiting picture theatres, were not dragged along by the police and did not change their habits through happenstance. Theirs was a decisive choice which restructured their leisure time while giving the Italian cinema a second chance. We are faced, here, with individual motivations which, to a large extent, will always remain difficult to understand. Italians mostly watched comedies and social dramas but we do not know if this is what they preferred; all we can tell is that they understood these films which had defined styles, dealt with specific, limited issues and utilized recurring forms and conventions. The Republic, when it was established, had to take this new fashion into account.

The Americans offered a solution. In their view, there was no Italian cinema – an opinion easily understandable since they had lost contact with the peninsula for nearly a decade. They were also impressed by the fact that Italy enthused about Hollywood-made films. Umberto Eco, who was then under 20, has confessed that he became a film addict because of *Stagecoach* which, the first time he saw it, gave him the shock of his life, and his is not an exceptional case. The Italian distributors were keen on getting American hits, since there was no other way to fill their lists and since American movies, already paid for thanks to the national market, were cheaper than any others. Similarly, American companies wanted to sell their products and urged the State Department to back their efforts. Anxious to please Washington, Rome gave way to the pressure of Italian distributors. In October 1945, it abolished the ad valorem tax put on American movies by Mussolini to save dollars. Italian films were guaranteed one out of six days screening but the rule was never respected. Year after year, until 1954, the number of American films introduced into Italy remained at the figure of over 300. Statistics regarding the cinema business, which were established by trade associations (producers, distributors, exhibitors) whose objectives were often contradictory, are not reliable.[20] Still, it can be roughly estimated that, in 1949, 75 per cent of box-office receipts went to the Americans, 18 per cent to the Italians.

The exhibitors were the winners of the first round. Thanks to imports, some five hundred new pictures were on offer every year and, as has already been said, attendance doubled from 1946 to 1955. But the Italian producers, who had gone through a very brilliant period since 1938, were not ready to shut down. A few days after the liberation of Rome, in order to put pressure on the government, they founded the National Association for the Cinema and Similar Industries (ANICA).[21] At that time, purges against the most eminent Fascists had not begun; many people simply moved from the Fascist organizations to ANICA and were then maintained in their function. ANICA's task was to bargain with the Italian authorities and with the foreign – that is to say mostly American – producers. Italy had to face enormous currency problems and the government did not want to spend too many dollars on movies. As the Americans did not accept any limitation on their exports, the only solution was to help the Italian studios. In October 1945, a state subsidy equal to 10 per cent of earnings was granted to all producers of national films. Subsquent negotiations led to a series of co-production agreements with France, Spain and Germany. In 1949, new regulations instituted a tax on dubbing, raised the subsidy on national films and improved the conditions under which loans could be obtained from the National Bank for Labour. ANICA could soon boast that, in 1954, Italy produced 172 pictures, had imported, for the first time since the end of the war, fewer than 300 American movies, and that 39 per cent of the box-office takings had gone to Italian pictures compared with 53 per cent to Hollywood films. This was a big success but not a victory. In the early 1950s, Hollywood was going through a difficult period, its production was shrinking, and in fact it had sold all it could export.

Undoubtedly ANICA maintained the Italian studios very well but it could neither overcome the American dominance, nor firmly settle on foreign markets. The current justification is that Italy was too dependent on American financial and political help to confront Hollywood. This is surely true. But does the American competition explain why Italy was unable to build up a strong, coherent film industry provided with efficient financial support by the state? Foreign policy does not account for everything; many of the problems the Italian studios experienced in the post-war period can best be understood within the framework of domestic policy. Government funds were liberally given to crooks as well as to serious cinematographers so that, instead of strengthening the film business, the state weakened it. As Christopher Wagstaff says, most 'production companies were improvised, one-film affairs'[22] hastily set up to take advantage of public subsidies. It is not by chance, or because public controllers were inefficient, that redundant firms were supported by the government well into the 1950s. These companies were entirely dependent upon official help which enabled the authorities to control them closely and at the same time to satisfy, at least indirectly, the American studios.

The ambiguous attitude of the government must be put down to the political situation in the country. After the Liberation, while the Left was attempting to mobilize the masses, the Christian Democrats invested the state apparatus by either protecting ex-Fascist civil servants or occupying the managerial positions in all sectors of information.[23] Mussolini had insisted that cinematic propaganda should never be too intrusive. The Christian Democrats did not forget the lesson. They preserved the Light Institute, founded by Fascism, to make documentaries likely to advertise abroad. But newsreels, whose presentation was compulsory during film-show, were offered to private companies. Fourteen production companies seized the chance. Since exhibitors were obliged to have a newsreel in their programmes, the product was sold in advance, so that little, if any, investment was necessary. One of the companies, Settimana Incom, took the lead very quickly and its productions are worth a look. The tone, resolutely optimistic, was based on celebration of a changing Italy. Unlike Fascist documentaries, these films did not romanticise the traditional country. Beginning with a quick glimpse at the past, they stressed the improvements introduced by modern techniques and contrasted old ploughs with tractors or derelict farmhouses with hygienic, modern cowsheds. Emphasis was put on the diffusion of electrical power which made possible new light industries providing cleaner jobs and labour-saving consumer durables. There were also hints at employment for women and at the improvement of the female condition. In short, instead of advertising the government, Settimana Incom attempted to persuade its viewers that things were evolving rapidly and that the best they could do was to make the most of it.[24] The Communist Party tried to counter this hidden propaganda by making its own documentaries. Filming the gloomy multistorey buildings of Milan and the out-of-the-way villages of Sicily, they argued that the state had failed to carry out crucial reforms and that the price paid for a few economic advances had been dangerously high. These pictures were of course banned in right-wing constituencies but even in the districts that voted regularly for them, the Communist documentaries did not meet with an enthusiastic response because their vision was too critical. Spectators knew that the Communists were right and that Settimana Incom lied. However, being involved in an irreversible transformation from a country of sharecroppers and small shopkeepers into an industrial society, they did not want to ponder over what the cost of the changes would be.

This negative reaction highlights the importance of the cinema for the third generation and explains why exhibiting was a political problem, a state affair. Most Italians were anxious to give a positive image of their culture and life to foreigners, especially to the Americans, and were afraid of being criticized. Countless events and spoken comments document their uneasiness. In September 1946, the Under Secretary in charge of information warned the Chairman of ANICA: 'Not all the producers grasp and understand the grave moral and social responsibilities the cinema is charged with in this country'; there were, in their films, too many 'negative' scenes likely to deprecate Italy abroad so that the Ministry might be obliged to 'suspend the screening of a number of Italian films'.[25] In December 1949, adressing the Chamber, Prime Minister de Gasperi asserted that film was a most important tool in 'presenting Italianness to the world'. Shortly after, another Under Secretary, Giulio Andreotti, stated that the cinema had 'to make known abroad what is being done in our country' and show 'what is new where building, progress, work is concerned', this being 'a political necessity'. In February 1952, the same Andreotti castigated, in an open letter, Vittorio de Sica's newly released *Umberto D* which, by presenting an 'incorrect' picture of Italy, had 'rendered a very bad service to his country'.[26]

Andreotti's moralism has to be placed in its Italian context. Most opinion leaders, on the Left as well as on the Right, were obsessed by the idea that the cinema might be harmful; the notion of 'correctness' had not been coined then but it was deeply felt by clerks, priests, teachers and politicians. All these people may have feared a medium that was so universally appreciated and was beyond their control. Reading the publications of the Catholic Centre for Cinema, especially its magazine *Cinematic Information*, one is struck by the overwhelming number of condemnations 'likely to provoke feelings of hate', 'absence of human feelings', 'devoid of any appreciable moral aim' are a few amidst hundreds of negative opinions. A perfectly innocent comedy like Blasetti's *His Majesty Mr Jones* (1950), in which a loving father has a lot of trouble finding a Holy Communion dress for his daughter, was considered only fit for 'mature adults'.[27] Parish priests used fiction films to lure the young but the Church would have preferred to exhibit only documentaries, or even to have football matches instead of film-shows. This may sound exaggerated but the Catholic press often demonstrated a pathological phobia of the cinema: 'Nearly all mental patients are dedicated cinema-goers'; the cinema is 'the modern penal colony'; 'the dark well out of which flow the stinking sewers of criminality'.[28] The non-religious parties, republicans, radicals, Socialists and Communists made fun of this bigoted attitude but their opinion was not very different, they loathed all that was likely to lead people into temptation.

Given this premise, it comes as no surprise that the government, whose survival was largely dependent upon the support of the Church, was reluctant to help the cinema. A law passed in 1947, while proclaiming the freedom of producers and exhibitors, re-established a censorship more severe than that of Fascism, since the board of censors was exclusively composed of civil servants. No submission of script or casting was required but, of course, producers did not want to risk their money unless they were sure in advance that their film would be passed for exhibition. Unofficial though it was, this pre-production control was very effective. The censors, who were concerned with everything that might upset the Church or question the settled order of society, imposed changes which seriously altered the scenarios. Producers with little financial backing – and this was generally the case – selected insignificant, harmless scripts which would meet with approval. The power of the government was reinforced by another law, passed in 1949, which offered a bonus of 8 per cent of their box-office takings to films of 'artistic quality' – this quality being appreciated by a board of officials. The authorities had control over the films while they were being made; they could accept or refuse them and give the producers more or less money. There were thus many possibilities to reinforce the Italian companies, but politicians were too suspicious of films and filmmakers to take the chance.

The Christian Democrats were aware of the fact that stronger companies could be more independent and not easily accept the official line. De Santis's *Bitter Rice* (1949), which infuriated the Church, was produced by the leading company, Lux, whose chairman was a great industrialist and managed, as well as production, a distribution circuit. Out of 1,008 pictures made in Italy from 1945 to 1954, 75 bore the Lux label. The company was rich enough to project a critical point of view with satirical comedies (*How I Lost the War*, 1945), and fiction films based on surveys in the South (*In the Name of the Law*, 1948) and among farm workers or miners (*The Way to Hope*, 1950). Lux also pioneered the use of colour film and experimented with the aesthetics of cinema when it financed Visconti's *Senso* (1954). The next most important companies, *Titanus* and *Excelsa*, were less innovative; the former specialized in melodramas, the latter, which had initially produced Rosselini's *Open City* (1945), turned their hand to the comedy of manners genre. The few 'independent' films were funded by co-operative societies or, at least in the case of de Sica, who had created his own company, paid for by their director. But, again between 1945 and 1954, four-fifths of the films were made by 260 companies, most of which produced one film and then went bankrupt or vanished. The film industry was thus in a permanently unstable state. By discouraging the most creative scriptwriters, the selective generosity of government tax incentives debased the average production. Pictures were never more fashionable in Italy than in the middle of the twentieth century, when about five hundred new films, national or foreign, were released every year. This prompted speculators to try their luck at producing, believing it to be the key to a fortune. The best way of making a 'quickie' was to hire the set used for a previous film, find ill-paid, second-rate actors, and, while writing the script, opt for a well-tried formula. The popularity of the cinema began to decline at the end of the 1950s, when it was superseded by other forms of entertainment. One may wonder whether the unimaginative, rather anti-creative process promoted by the government did not contribute to this downturn.

NEOREALISM: THE MYTHS

The position of the cinema in Italian life was an important political issue and one word was at the core of the debates: Neorealism. When Under

Secretary Andreotti criticized *Umberto D*, his target, behind de Sica, was the cluster of productions on which that label had been bestowed. It was, Andreotti contended, the duty of the cinema to 'realistically conform to reality'; but it must be objective and avoid any exaggeration, it must commit itself to offer its public 'a healthy and constructive optimism'. In other words, the cinema had to demonstrate that everything is fine and everybody satisfied. There is nothing surprising in this text, except its date: in 1952, the promise of cinematic renewal that had followed the Liberation was long over and de Sica was the only filmmaker who attempted to maintain it. It has been contended that the death certificate of Neorealism had already been signed the previous year by Visconti's *Bellissima*. Visconti's first films, which will be analysed later, were Neorealist. But *Bellissima*, dispensing with ordinary people, dealt mostly with the studios of Cinecittà and with filmmaking. In this film, Blasetti, playing his real-life role of director, restored the rituals and conventions of the profession such as they had been established before the war and made it clear that cinema was not real life, that there was even a wide gap between them.

How can we account for Andreotti's tardy indignation? By understanding that, in the 1950s, the word 'Neorealism' had a political connotation. Roughly speaking, Neorealism was championed by the Left, by a good many writers, artists and film critics, by the most intellectual film magazines, while it was condemned by the Right and the Church. Harsh controversies, which developed even in the Chamber, led to the definition of an aesthetic concept. As David Forgacs once said, Neorealism was and still remains 'a descriptive category which was produced and developed in criticism'.[29] Gian Piero Brunetta was even more acute; according to him, it was 'a myth' which has now to be explored.[30]

The word 'Neorealism' was initially used at the beginning of the century by philosophers who maintained that there exist objective facts independent of human thoughts. It was then forgotten and resurfaced, at the end of the 1920s, chiefly in literary criticism. The first printed mention I have found is in the *Literary Almanac* for 1930. Drawing a caricature of the typical Italian intellectual, the *Almanac* assumes that he has 'a neorealist eye'. Such an ambiguous term could be used by the Fascists, who glorified the 'new' Fascist man, or by the anti-Fascists who looked for the 'real' man, behind Mussolini's puppets. When foreign critics saw, in various festivals, *Open City*, they tried to find a way of defining that skilful blend of traditional, melodramatic stories and a new manner of filming and acting. Neorealism was a vacant signifier and they adopted it. But their interpretations were at variance; some thought that it was the best description of the moral and physical destruction caused by the war, others maintained that it provided a metaphysical image of human beings faced with despair.

Italians were not enthusiastic about the term; it was seldom used in the late 1940s, or it was presented under another form, 'neo-verismo' (neo-veracity), which referred to a nineteenth century tradition of naturalism. This reluctance is not surprising, at least where the two dominant forces, the Church and the Communist Party were concerned. We have seen that the Church was used to condemning almost all films. *Bitter Rice* was classified as 'rigorously forbidden to the faithful'. But *Open City*, in which a priest plays a leading part, was pronounced 'harmful for children'. Sexual obsession had its share in these condemnations (there is an unmarried mother in *Open City*). Catholics were also suspicious of 'realist' pictures likely to give a 'deprecatory vision' of Italy. But, above all, the priests were upset by the negative image of the clergy presented in many films, with, for instance, those pious wealthy who, in *Bicycle Thieves* (1947), force beggars to attend a mass before granting them a piece of bread and some soup, or even with the parish priest of *Open City* who acts on his own initiative, without consulting his bishop, and gets involved in political matters.

The Communists should have appreciated pictures like *Bicycle Thieves* which, by depicting ordinary people, by showing their problems in the precise manner of documentaries, were likely to criticise capitalism and trigger class-consciousness. However, when *Bitter Rice* was released, the Communist Party were very disturbed. I mention this film because, after the Liberation, de Santis joined the Communist Party and forced himself into adopting the role of a committed intellectual even if he felt uncomfortable in it. *L'Unità*, the main Communist daily dared neither praise nor criticize the film; instead, it asked its readers to give their opinion, which enabled it to print a series of adverse criticisms: there was too much sex, too much American music in the film, the workers were not genuine, etc.[31] Communist puritanism matched that of the Catholics and the Communists, like the Catholics, were longing for happy, positive endings, not for ambiguous ones. Using different words, *L'Unità* could have said, like Andreotti, that there was a good and a bad realism. When it turned out that Visconti's *The Earth Quakes* (1948) would not be distributed, the Communist daily stood up for it with a paper which sounds like a manifesto:

> With that film we have got rid of the delusive label bestowed on our post-war films by foreign critics. It is absurd to refer to Neorealism where there has been no previous realism and there has never been any realism in Italy. *The Earth Quakes* is the Italian realist film'.[32]

It is not necessary to emphasize the nationalist tone in this proscription of the word 'Neorealism'. It is only much later, in the course of its polemics with the Christian Democrats, that the same *Unità* would praise 'that cinematic art known as Neorealism which has established the name and the triumph of the Italian cinema throughout the world.[33]

Once having emerged historically in the 1950s, Neorealism became for many people a relatively homogeneous phenomenon, something of a school. In fact, there were enormous variations among the cinematographers who were then grouped together. To begin with, Neorealism was not a 'genre'. There were domestic dramas, adventure films, even comedies which had neorealist qualities. This indeterminacy makes it tricky to give a definition. Intervening in the debate, the scriptwriter Zavattini wrote a short paper which is the only theoretical document ever produced by someone involved in that enterprise.[34] After having explained how difficult it might be to film a woman who was buying a pair of shoes, Zavattini became lost in generalities:

> There must be no gap between life and what is on the screen. . . . I want to meet the real protagonist of everyday life. . . . Neorealism has perceived that the most irreplaceable experience comes from things happening under our eyes, from natural necessity.

Ten years later, when the debate had become purely retrospective, Calvino answered Zavattini; he noted that the so-called Neorealists had been a loose federation rather than a closely knit group and that people had been bonded together more by common antipathies than by an informed understanding of one another's work. 'Neorealism was not a school. It was a collection of voices, largely marginal, a multiple discovery of the various Italies'.[35] The men who have been baptized 'the Neorealists' did share a few commitments and that is probably what Millicent Marcus has in mind when she assumes that Neorealism was 'first and foremost a moral statement'.[36] What these men had in common was largely an array of negative convictions; they repudiated the notion of films conceived as insights into the most artificial aspects of Italian life or as descriptions of formulaic relations between artificial characters. They thought also that cinema could be a source of knowledge and reality – but other Italian filmmakers had had the same ideas long before.

There were invectives against all the neorealist directors but the bitterest ones were addressed to de Sica, partly because an actor turned director disconcerted many people but mainly because, unlike Rossellini who was a fervent Catholic, or Visconti and de Santis who were left-oriented, de Sica rejected any political or religious affiliation. The theoretical debate was chiefly concentrated upon his films; they were credited with four innovations which were, by inference, extended to Neorealism as a whole.

A first novelty was that, in *Bicycle Thieves* and *Umberto D*, the main characters were not actors, they were, respectively, a worker and a professor, both 'real protagonists of everyday life'. But these men were surrounded by professionals and their part was entirely dubbed by actors. Most filmmakers had recourse to stars such as Anna Magnani, Silvana Mangano, Vittorio Gassman. Rossellini was especially clever when he chose, for *Open City*, Anna Magnani and Aldo Fabrizi, who had long been performing in comic plays and films, because their presence in a drama emphasized the horror of a war in which comic people had a tragic destiny. Other directors had already used the same sort of permutation which was not very adventurous. *The Earth Quakes* was the only film played entirely by people filmed in their own surroundings. Visconti chose, for that movie, a small Sicilian port, Arcitrezza, not far from Catania, and opted for the local dialect. The village gave him a landscape of sky and sea, with a community of fishermen. The language was so much an expression of the fisherman culture of which it was the voice that Visconti did not want it to be dubbed and was content with adding sub-titles without which most Italians on the mainland would not have understood. But soon after Visconti asked Magnani, that is to say a famous star, not an amateur, to play the main part in *Bellissima* (1951).

A second point which was considered typical of de Sica and the other neorealist directors was that they had taken small, banal events, and shown that they could be exploited 'like mines', to quote Zavattini. The plot of the majority of Neorealist films, including those of de Sica, is not different from the story told in previous melodramas such as *Yes Madam*. Melodramas often staged 'simple stories' and 'banal moments'. However, the Neorealist films did not ignore the most trite devices of traditional theatre. In *The Earth Quakes*, to take but one example, we have all the ingredients of a tear-jerker: the Good Man, who is poor, is doomed to failure, his sister becomes a whore, his girlfriend betrays him for the Bad Man, who is evil and humiliates the loser.

De Sica, it was said, had a gift for describing an atmosphere; he succeeded in exploring, and showing minute aspects of Rome, and Visconti was also very precise in his presentation of Arcitrezza. Undoubtedly, there was a documentary side in most Neorealist films but that was a cinematic inheritance of Fascism which had made Light Institute first-class school of short film making. Many documentary sequences in Neorealist films were borrowed or imitated from patterns long established by the Institute.

We have said that de Sica founded his own production company. Neorealism was interpreted as a reaction against the big producers, based on a small-scale, under-capitalized, decentralized industry in which groups of individuals formed themselves into production units for specific film projects. There are many anecdotes about that aspect of Neorealism. It is said that Rossellini had trouble finding money for *Open City* and was obliged to appeal to his friends, that he could not afford costumes for his extras, used out-of-date film stock and did not re-shoot the takes which did not please him. However, when one sees the films, one ca. but be struck by their professional quality. Then, when reading the cre one finds the names of outstanding technicians, all experts belonging to earlier generation who had, in the 1920s, founded the reputation of the Italian studios, people such as the camera operators Ubaldo Arata and Graziati Aldo, editors Mario Serandrei and Eraldo da Roma. One of the most enduring transformations that had occurred during the late 1930s and early 1940s was the arrival in the studios of sophisticated young people freshly issued from the newly established school, the famous Experimental Centre for Cinema. The older population of technicians trained on the job, who did not want to be displaced, willingly helped the most ambitious, imaginative directors. Graziati Aldo's work for *The Earth Quakes* was one example of a perfect combination of adaptation to the project of the filmmaker and personal inventiveness. Sharp, even crisp when it reveals the landscape, the light adapts then to the rhythm of the story. It never plays on dramatic contrasts but manages different zones of fluctuating intensity, thus distancing the scenery from the plot; the story takes place on the shore and in the bay of Arcitrezza but the countryside has no direct part in the story, it is filmed for its own sake, because it is worth a series of beautiful pictures.

Had it not been for the polemics which surrounded them, *The Earth Quakes* and other Neorealist films would have become, simply, 'the fabulous Italian films of the late 1940s'. But critics, intellectuals and politicians created a 'genre'. They created it since the films we still consider Neorealist are essentially theirs. It is worth noticing that, in a society where everybody was interested in cinema, and found it legitimate to talk about pictures, opinion leaders could not afford to appear unconcerned. Giving an opinion on cinema was their way of asserting their social influence, a kind of self-affirmation of their right to legislate.

NEOREALISM: THE FILMS

Neorealism has, in fact, not just one, but a variety of meanings. It is a tendency identified first by critics, then by spectators, finally turned into a series, or rather a generic field. 'Ism' categories are less artificial labels than traces of an historical experience out of which following generations have evolved. New analyses will change the references, stress differences, separate directors and films from each other. However, these people and their work all pertain to the same ill-defined, unescapable grouping: Neorealism.

Deciding whether a film should be classified as Neorealist is not easy: estimates of the total number of such productions vary, according to the author, from twenty to fifty. Even using the broadest definition, these films make up less than 4 per cent of the total Italian production, and less than one thousandth of the films circulating in the peninsula. Some of these films did very well, others did not. *The Earth Quakes* won a prize at the Venice Festival but did not find a distributor and was a financial disaster. De Sica's *Shoeshine* (1946) and Rossellini's *Germany, Year Zero* (1948) were also awarded prizes but did not cover their costs of production. The other works of Rossellini and de Sica had a limited success, while the biggest hits were *Bitter Rice* and Pietro Germi's *The Way to Hope* (1952) and *In the Name of the Law* (1948).

When *Open City* was released, in September 1945, spectators said that the film helped them to understand what they had gone through during the German occupation, what they had lived, without being able to measure what was happening. The première was, unwittingly, perfectly timed. Shot in Rome a few months after the Liberation, when many districts of the town still lay in ruins, the film mirrored the most dramatic aspects of the situation. The overall tone was pessimistic, the three main characters, all committed patriots, were killed, and the final image of the young boys going back to town after the execution of the parish priest was distressing. *Open City* testifies to a sadness common to many other Neorealist films. The mood of the time was downhearted. Silvio Lanaro notes that, in post-war Italy, there was a discrepancy between material losses, which were not catastrophic, and the impression, widely expressed in papers, talks and films, that the country had gone through the greatest disaster it had ever experienced.[37] In analysing Neorealism, it is necessary to distinguish what was typical of the contemporary atmosphere, and what goes much beyond the spirit of the time. We have already alluded to the documentary side of many films. As most of them unfold their plot against a rural or urban background, it would be simple to ascribe to them an almost complete picture of Rome, or Milan, or of some sectors of the countryside. But Neorealist films are not unique in this respect, *Yes Madam* explores Genoa rather extensively, *Headlights in Fog* documents both the same port and its hinterland. Landscapes, in Neorealist films, are not a simple backdrop, a collection of still photos, they are used to embody meanings, orchestrate formal themes, demonstrate or refer by analogy to other spheres of reality. The glimpses at the fishermen's work in *The Earth Quakes*, the houses destroyed by bombings in *Open City*, and the discovery of unexpected vistas of Rome in *Umberto D* are extremely suggestive but they attempt rather to move spectators than to describe the situation of the peninsula. It is true that *Open City* bore witness to its time but that was a lesser aspect of the movie and Neorealism cannot be reduced to perfect synchronization with the post-war era.

Besides, it would be artificial to say that Neorealism emerged in September 1945, for it had no precise origin. Three films made during the war, namely Blasetti's *Four Steps in the Clouds* (1942), Visconti's

Ossessione (1943) and de Sica's *The Little Martyr* (1944) can be considered either the forerunners of a new style to be, or the first manifestations of a different way of filming.

This group is all the more interesting in that the plots of the three films differ appreciably. Blasetti's is a bittersweet comedy, the story of an unmarried mother finally forgiven by her parents; the others end with the dramatic death of one of the protagonists. Based on *The Postman Always Rings Twice* (1946) the screenplay for *Ossessione* drastically changed James Cain's novel, while de Sica's film followed closely the book he adapted. What the films have in common is the fact that they incorporate considerable elements of Italian contemporary life into the narrative. Developing a multitude of secondary incidents in the margins of the action, they turn their plot into a series of sometimes poignant, more often unexpected, encounters between their protagonists and anonymous fugitive characters. There is a social context here but, instead of being explored for its own worth, it sets a background for unpredictable confrontations. In trains, in bars, on a square, people run into other people with whom they establish a passing relationship. Landing up, by chance, in a village, Blasetti's Roman travelling salesman spends a night with a family of country people and discovers a world he would never have imagined. Visconti's main character is a tramp who roams from place to place in northern Italy. Telling the everyday story of a young boy neglected by his adulterous mother and his jealous father, de Sica adopts the point of view of the child and leads us into the various houses where the kid is sent by his parents. Readers have surely noted affinities between *Yes Madam* and *The Little Martyr*. Both criticize the selfishness of the bourgeoisie, or of egoistic parents, towards innocent creatures, an orphan or a young boy. What is new, in the latter, and differentiates it from the former, is that attention shifts away from the main story to wander around. *Yes Madam* takes advantage of fiction to send a message, while de Sica's film leaves one disturbed and poses questions about a social practice hitherto totally accepted. Which formula is the best? There is, obviously, no answer. But there is no doubt that films that were pre-Neorealist, or unwittingly already Neorealist, introduced another standpoint into filmmaking.

Technically, they were also innovative. *Yes Madam*, like many contemporary films, is a succession of shots, each of them depicting a location or a character. On the other hand, being not entirely centred on the plot, the three films under review do not try to provide new information in every sequence. They all begin with an establishing sequence, but their prologue, instead of merely informing us, attracts spectators to the imaginary atmosphere of the picture. *Ossessione* opens on a long building, a shop, or a country inn, maybe an official building in some remote village, seen from above.[38] A slow tracking shot ends on a platform, in front of the house. It is an unmotivated shot which does not go with a motion inside the frame. Since we do not follow a human being, or a vehicle, we have enough time to perceive a few details, the sun, a curtain at the main door, a sign on the wall – but we might also be enthralled by the vibrations of the light or the clarity of the sky, in short by the ambiance. After the track, the film cuts to medium-distance shots; three men have a routine talk about petrol and viewers can be more interested by the sophistication of the editing, which has jumped from a general view to particulars, than by the dialogue. And yet, we must not be mistaken, these films are not experimental movies, they all tell a story. Visconti's tramp settles in the inn, becomes the proprietress's lover and, with her help, kills the husband. The police inquiry is loosely recounted but the flight of the murderers is extensively narrated, with dramatic use of the landscape and the soundtrack, as thrilling as the end of an American gangster story.

Visconti and de Sica's double orientation, towards both innovation and tradition, at least in the films mentioned above, cannot be over-rated. It accounts for many endless controversies over what films may, or may not, be called Neorealist. Film buffs have established a kernel of six films, which get a unanimous label of Neorealist authenticity, with a more or less wide circle of other movies. Even when it is limited, this ring is of paramount importance, it justifies the fact that, seen in retrospect, Neorealism does not consist of a small group of scattered masterpieces but of a whole batch of movies. To some extent, peripheral works are necessary to better understand what is in the centre. Thus looking first at de Santis and Germi will prepare us to meet the other directors.

We have seen that, for Zavattini, a good example of 'real life' was the story of a woman who buys shoes. Expanding on this case, Zavattini insisted that it was necessary to tell how hard the woman had worked to get the money. De Santis and Germi were realist in this sense. *Bitter Rice* takes place in a ricefield where women, coming from all over Italy, get an ill-paid temporary job. In *The Tragic Pursuit* (1947), de Santis accompanies the members of an agricultural co-operative in search of their funds stolen by gangsters and, in *Rome, Eleven O'clock* (1952), he investigates an accident which killed or injured several women queuing for a place as secretary. Through *In the Name of the Law*, Germi explores the social conflicts in a Sicilian village dominated by a rich landlord. He travels from Sicily to the Alps with the unemployed miners of *The Way to Hope* (1950) who will find work in France. These films are extremely precise in their description of the social context, much more than those of Rossellini or de Sica. Starting from a Marxist analysis, they explain how capitalism gives workers only what they need to maintain themselves and confiscates the 'surplus value'. *The Way to Hope* begins with a very impressive sequence of a strike; the owners of a mine have decided to close it, because it does not bring in enough profit; the miners attempt to occupy the shafts but are obliged to leave. Patterns of violence in working life and the problem of how to understand them are central to most films by de Santis and Germi.

Simultaneously, these committed movies have recourse to tricks and conventions borrowed directly from Hollywood; their plots are filled with dramatic, bloody episodes, their baddies, the worst possible guys, are always beaten by the goodies. By making the ending of their films not only provoke the kind of euphoria that is associated with the conclusion of a thriller, but also emphasize the triumph of their heroes, the film-makers open a gap between their documentary and their fictional sequences. It is in this gap that a good deal of the audience's pleasure is created. The characters, in gaining one thing they desire, ease the tension produced by their initial distress. On the other hand, as we shall see, de Sica does not resolve the problems, thus leaving the way open for different interpretations. Another device used by de Santis and Germi is a crude exploitation of sexuality. On the whole, Neorealism is puritanical, not to say misogynist, as can be deduced from the quantity of unmarried mothers or adulterous wives we have already met. Women always have secondary parts in de Sica's films. Important though they may be, they never take the lead in Visconti and Rossellini's, except in *Open City*. But they are essential in de Santis's and, to a lesser extent, in Germi's films. *Bitter Rice* takes full advantage of an element which is more cautiously used in his other films, the sexual attractivness of the female body. Teetering on the brink of womanhood, his main actress, Silvana Mangano, is a versatile pulp magazine pin-up, sarcastic one moment, especially with older men, flirtatious the next when a young man approaches her; making clever use of her perfect thighs, of her neck and bare shoulders she expresses girlish panic and womanly cunning with a controlled flightiness. The famous scene in which she crosses the screen, half naked, with the points of her breasts showing beneath her jumper, accounts largely for the worldwide triumph of the movie. Abject eroticism? In a country where the joint moralism of the Church and the Communist Party prohibited any allusion to sexuality, showing that capitalism alienates not only the arms but the entire body of the workers, was a form of social criticism. Neorealism was provocative in many ways but every film had its specific form of provocation.

Having explained that it is almost impossible to make an inventory of Neorealist films, Christopher Wagstaff confesses that he puts *Open City* on the list 'because tradition would not allow me to omit it' but that there are many reasons to exclude it.[39] As soon as one looks for precise criteria, Neorealism vanishes: its consistency resides in its ability to avoid definitions. Rossellini's movies should be counted out because of their strict narrative structure and because the main parts are given to famous actors, but who could conceive of a Neorealism deprived of Rossellini?

Plate 13 Bitter Rice (1949, Giuseppe de Santis). Silvana Mangano is fourth from the left

Many people would contend that it is his 'war trilogy' which encapsulates the very essence of the new reality.

Germany, Year Zero is a desperate picture. In a ruined Berlin, a young boy survives thanks to the black market; his thinking is so muddled by fear and hunger that he kills his disabled father and commits suicide. The dominant feeling is that the war has marked the end of previously respected human values and that Germany has gone to hell. Both *Open City* and *Paisa* (1946) stress the destructiveness of total war which, turning armed forces into machines for slaughter, has reduced the whole Italian population to the status of victims. At the same time, they show how these victims have realized that there is something to be done. Having somehow an idea of why they endure what they are enduring, they fight for the defence of a community instead of merely mourning a senseless slaughter. These two films must be analysed together, for they complement one another. *Open City* tells a homogeneous story; it is concerned with the life of a working-class district of Rome during the German occupation. *Paisa* is composed of six unrelated episodes made into a unit by way of a voice-over which recalls the stages of the Allied campaign throughout the peninsula. The sections are inseparable from their frame, there is a geographical progression from Sicily to the Po valley and a transformation of the relationship between Allies and Italians from one story to the next.

Open City is focused upon a fighting population. Its three main characters are a partisan leader, a priest who actively supports the partisans, and a woman whose lover is a partisan – in other words, a cross-section of the community. With the exception of a few crazy Fascists, all Romans resist the Germans, be it only by loathing and deceiving them. This general dedication to resistance is wonderfully conveyed by a combination of drama and comedy, of sobriety and deep involvement. Let us look at two examples. Late at night, in a working-class multi-storey block, parents worry about their children who have not come home. There is a bomb explosion, followed by two shots of boys running, then two shots of the boys congratulating themselves. After this quick introduction the sequence continues, at length, with the kids, who dare not go home because they will get a good dressing-down. Instead of emphasizing the deed, *Open City* shifts towards a more familiar, and more humorous episode. The second example comes at the end of the film with the execution of the priest. Again, rather than carefully describing the scene, the film lingers on minute details: a guard getting out of the prison van, the indifferent faces of two police inspectors, a German officer anxious to get a boring job over, the members of the Italian firing squad, nervous and pallid at being obliged to kill a priest. It is only when the members of the

Plate 14 Open City (1945, Roberto Rosselini)

parish youth club, hidden behind a fence, begin to whistle, and are heard by the priest, that the rhythm changes. While the previous shots were slightly chaotic, alternating the whistling boys and the listening man recreates a unity that is both stylistic (here, the succession of images is justified) and emotional.

The actor Aldo Fabrizi of course plays an important part in giving that scene, and the whole film, a gripping, impassioned quality. Taking advantage of his heavy-looking figure, he moves slowly, creating an image of determination and religious confidence appropriate to his part of parish priest. His association with Anna Magnani results in a perfect match. Her tormented face works hard for her. Alternately showing fixed despair, unbounded enthusiasm or intense concentration, she may appear unconcerned while undermining this with a look of profound anxiety and she has a way of standing as expressive as her face, a nervous twist of shoulders and chest that may suggest violent anger or, when performed with less speed, complicity. To a certain extent, she is pure motion, surprise and inventiveness, and every gesture is used to signify resistance.

The other actors are less impressive (they were also less famous at the time) but the whole cast symbolises the spirit of the Roman community crushed by the occupiers but still intent on surviving. There is no community in *Paisa*, or, if there is, the community is Italy itself. The film does not deal with resistance, even if the last episode is entirely centred

Plate 15 Paisa (1946, Roberto Rosselini)

on the action of partisans in Venetia. As in *Open City*, Rossellini inter-
sperses his film with dramatic and relaxing scenes. In Naples, a drunken
American takes marionettes for real soldiers and jumps onto the stage to
kill them; in a convent, the friars fast to obtain the conversion of a Jew
and a Protestant who are their guests. Most of the time, there is death,
wounds and ruins. Disembarking in Sicily, the Americans are considered
as enemies and they do not trust the Sicilians. Individual friendship might
be possible, were it not that war does not admit a moment's inattention.
When the Americans reach Naples, then Rome, they look so wealthy that
it is tempting to exploit them; reciprocal diffidence has replaced hostility.
Farther north, where the Italians have long waited for their Liberation,
partisans help to take Florence and in the Po valley fight side by side
with American parachutists. *Paisa* might be considered a history film –
but it is a history not told from without by a historian trying to clarify
the issue. It is the subjective, intuitive vision of an Italian who thanks the
Allies for their support and condemns them for having taken so much
time and let so many Italians be killed. *Open City* asserts the cohesion of
the Roman population, *Paisa* wonders what has been left of Italy after
two years of war.

Visconti's tramp, in *Ossessione*, goes through Italy without ever looking
at the country. The characters of *The Earth Quakes*[40] never leave the
shores of their village; when one of the fishermen says he is going to find
work on the mainland, his brother warns him not to run the risk of
leaving the village which is his shelter. However, the question that Visconti
raises here is not far from Rossellini's: what has become of Italy? Instead
of fishing for wholesalers who exploit them, four brothers buy a boat on
credit and work for themselves. They are unable to sell their catch and,
having lost all their belongings, much poorer than before, they go back
to their former situation.

Spectators who loved tear-jerkers should have enjoyed a film which,
however critical it is of wholesalers, is not more subversive than *Bitter
Rice*, or even *Yes Madam*. *The Earth Quakes* failed because of its style,
not because of its content. In the 1940s, the experience of a plot-empty
time was never pushed as far as it is in this movie where prolonged shots
of beautiful landscapes are moments of pure filmic pleasure; pictures and
sounds seem to develop for their own sake, outside the leading strand of
the story. Quite often, the village or its shore are seen in long shot, from
outside, with no relation to any of the inhabitants. Angles and framing
change with every shot, but the spectator is never provided with those
small clues which link each image to the last and give the sequence its
apparent necessity. When a boat enters the screen, we wonder whether it
is only part of the setting or an element of the plot, and the camera
follows it at length without answering the question. I have already stressed
the quality of Aldo's lighting; most of his pictures are of a striking

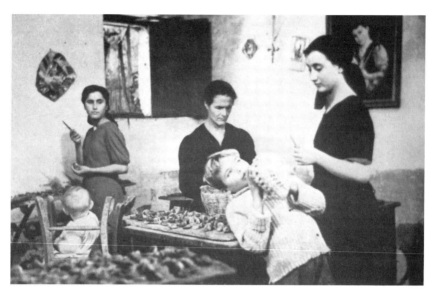

Plate 16 The Earth Quakes (1947, Luchino Visconti)

perfection and their beauty, their elegant slowness, make the debacle of the fishermen even more tragic. It is no wonder that producers used to selling stories of non-stop action did not promote the film: their public could easily cope with the despair of a poor worker, *provided* it was packaged in a non-stop succession of events.

Viewers may also have been disconcerted by the lack of personal emotion in the film. The fate of the fishermen is pathetic but, individually, they do not command sympathy. De Sica's stories are not much more full of details and new developments than Visconti's, but they are more gripping. De Sica may also have been cleverer, or more sensitive to spectators' habits. *Bicycle Thieves* and *Umberto D* do not end in disaster: we do not know what will happen to the characters, and viewers often argue for hours about the probable dénouement. De Sica's plots are simple and progress over a brief span of time. *Shoeshine* tells the story of two boys, an orphan and the youngest son of a large family, who get by on temporary work or petty larceny and are on the delinquent side of adolescence. The film focuses in detail on their lives, lies, miseries and thefts. Its subject matter might be depressing, or purely anecdotal, but the boys, their language, their sense of belonging to each other, eclipse the poverty and degradation of inner-city life. In *Bicycle Thieves*, an unemployed man finds a job which requires the use of a bicycle; he has his bike stolen and, helped by his twelve-year-old son, hunts for it all over Rome. Having recently come from some rural district, unfamiliar with the sub-culture of

Plate 17 Shoeshine (1946, Vittorio de Sica)

the Roman proletariat, the man is easily fooled by the thieves. However, he becomes closer to his son and the growing bond between them is sensitively charted, without excessive sentimentality. *Umberto D*, a retired state servant, can no longer afford lodging in central Rome; he ought to move to a suburb or to an old people's home, but he is too proud, or too stay-at-home for that.

   None of these movies has to be seen as a window on to Roman society – but rather as a glimpse of human suffering in a hostile environment taken with humour and sympathy. The tales are less complicated than Rossellini's, the style less sophisticated than Visconti's. De Sica avoids clichéd psychology. When the bicycle is stolen, in *Bicycle Thieves*, we get no hints as to the man's state of mind: we simply witness his immediate, erratic reactions. Peoples' actions are reduced to their functional aspect and are never separated from the surroundings; the man tracks his thief in the middle of the crowd, he disappears and reappears, we understand what he is doing without being able to follow it closely. The setting does not seem empty or uninteresting as is often the case with 'classical' films, its density compensates for the otherwise excessive presence of the characters. Instead of being a rectangle which frames the actors, the screen is treated as a surface open to various uses. People, objects and places irrelevant to the story are explored by the camera because they are part of the background; they are exploited for their visual and plastic potential. The three films are three itineraries through Rome. Yet the important thing is not the accurate description of various locations but the autonomy of these scenes in relation to the plot. Of course, the settings are not chosen at random, but the representation of streets, squares and houses does not help to develop the fiction, rather it intervenes like a break in the continuity of the narrative. This introduces, in the spectator's mind, an unfamiliar impression, the feeling that it is possible to represent the passing of time.

De Sica does not 'explain' his characters. However, they are not empty figures. This is one of the most intriguing and most enthralling aspects of his films, which is best exemplified by a look at *Umberto D*. In the first half of the movie, there is no precise point of view, that is to say we see Umberto *and* Rome, we do not look *with* him. With whom are we seeing? With an imprecise series of eyes we might be tempted to call 'the absent, indifferent look'. One day, when he comes back home, Umberto finds a couple making love in his room: taking advantage of his absence, his landlady has rented the room for two hours. The maid, who is peeping through a keyhole, offers to let Umberto look; he accepts. While the maid was peeping, we could see with her; but with Umberto we do not see anything because, in this section, he is, symbolically, blind. The point of view then shifts, in such a manner that many spectators fail to recognize the shift. Umberto is taken to a hospital for a few days. The hospital sequence

Plate 18 Umberto D (1952, Vittorio de Sica)

is filmed in symetrical medium-distance shots of different people, as if for an experiment in direct cinema, and its shots are bound by the logic of the action. When Umberto leaves, the style has changed, but the man has changed as well; he is able to look and we see what he sees, we go all over the town, we meet the people he knows behind him, as if his gaze were ours. A subtle device has got us to shift from an external perception to an admittedly subjective one. We could not side with an indifferent man but we are easily tempted to empathize with an old fellow who shows us that he has become a foreigner in his own city.

As can be inferred from this short analysis, Neorealism was basically an experiment, an attempt to promote another rhythm and to exploit the shape as well as the perspective depth of the screen, instead of limiting it to the figuration of a narrative. It had no follow-up and died away at the beginning of the 1950s, when new searches were already in progress. During the following decades, many filmmakers said they owed it a great deal: is there a link between them and the new cinemas, the various 'new waves' which appeared everywhere in Europe? Directly, none. But Neorealism obviously contributed to challenging the tradition of psychological, uninterrupted fiction which still prevailed in the middle of the twentieth century.

WHAT MADE SPECTATORS TICK?

Italian spectators did not spend a lot of time watching Neorealist films. But they neither ignored, nor despised them. We know how difficult it is to talk about tastes (and I shall come back to this problem later). However, it seems to me that the non-specialist press, which was not read by film buffs, can tell us something about the most widespread ideas regarding Neorealism. Italians were very fond of cheap illustrated weeklies, or, *rotocalchi*, magazines printed on a rotary press. I have systematically worked through three of them, *La Domenica del Corriere, Tempo*[41] and *Oggi*. Intellectuals disregarded the first because of its garish covers and its sensationalism. Every Sunday, this weekly presented on its front page a trivial event which was simultaneously tragic and amusing. For instance, a ceiling collapsed and the bed of two newly-weds fell on a family, killing some of its members; or a fellow, playing the fool in a church, caused a panic and several people were knocked down. None of these events were dated or localized; they were probably pure fantasies.

I shall return to these extravagant stories but I must first explain how cinema was treated in the magazines. Contrary to what one might have expected, the weeklies did not offer sentimental columns on the private lives of actors. They also avoided direct criticism. Announcing a limited number of films still showing, they gave an opinion which shows that they were well-informed. Short but interesting comments were given over to the products of usually neglected countries, such as Sweden or Mexico. *La Domenica del Corriere* (30 March 1947) praised Orson Welles as 'exceptionally gifted as scriptwriter, director and actor' at a time when even critics had forgotten that Welles was also a scriptwriter. *Tempo* indicated those it saw as hopefuls, James Mason for instance (23 March 1947). The magazines had a programme, or at least a line, which may be resumed in three points: youth, Italy, seriousness. They did not seem to worry about the effect they had on the public: the films they favoured rarely figured among the big screen successes, and, conversely, they paid much less attention to the films at the top of the bill. Their main concern was the image of Italy abroad, and for them that image had a name: Neorealism. They lamented the bad results of Neorealist films in Italy but delighted in observing their fame in other countries: 'Rossellini has not been successful in Italy with *Paisa* but we owe to him the fact that people talk about our cinema in foreign parts' (*Tempo*, 4 January 1947). After *Shoeshine*, that 'desperate cry of pain', it was assumed that Italy was 'the only country able to make intelligent and courageous movies' (*Tempo*, 15 November 1947). The magazines were not content with celebrating Neorealism, they imitated it. The influence of cinema on the popular press is well documented. The landscapes, shepherds, harvesting women which illustrated a report on Puglia (*Tempo*, 21 June 1947) were reminiscent of Germi's country people. The six pictures of young boys in a paper on war orphans (*Domenica del Corriere*, 9 March 1947) referred manifestly to *Shoeshine*. Not only the themes, but the framing, the composition, the arrangement of people and objects, the lighting, emulated Neorealist movies.

Were the weeklies, then, totally out of step with their readers? Or could it not be said that criticism fulfilled a particular function? It offered, under cover of the cinema, the means to reflect in depth on extremely varied problems at a time when political and economic change was happening quickly, while moral standards were being revised. When a magazine commented on war orphans with reference to *Shoeshine*, there was really no need to see the film, as the questions the film took up and examined were clearly set out in the article. However, the fact that this was connected to a film was not immaterial: cinema had a modern, living quality about it which justified lively controversy; it opened perspectives (on social injustice, sex, delinquency) which people would not have dared contemplate without the pretext of the film. *Shoeshine* was a flop but the debate it provoked lasted for months. Few Italians had not heard of the film and most of them were probably proud to learn that it had been acclaimed on Broadway and awarded prizes in various festivals.

Talking about a film and seeing it in a cinema are two different activities. The magazines I have quoted had a very large readership; many of their readers were interested in movies but did not care about film criticism. According to the inquiry carried out by the Doxa Institute mentioned above, spectators said that they based their choice of films on the names of the stars, the impressions of their friends, the chance to go to the cinema in a group, and transport facilities. Opinion surveys are never fully reliable. However, it is striking to see that neither the plot and the genre, nor the director were mentioned. Advertisements confirm the preponderance of the leading actors. It also shows the spell of Hollywood: an American label was the best publicity for a film, so Italian producers attempted to introduce a touch of America on their posters.

'For me, *the cinema* meant *American cinema*,' Calvino recalls.[42] Priests and Communists were equally worried by such infatuation. The position of the latter is easily understood: Hollywood was, for them, the Trojan Horse of capitalism.[43] For its part, the Church warned its flock against the dissoluteness of most US-made films. Oddly enough, different, sometimes opposing, discourses disclosed the same concern, Communists and Catholics considered the American way of life, as portrayed in films, to be a threat to Italian traditions But, in fact, what was 'the American cinema'? In Italy, Hollywood spoke a particular language, the language of radio. The actors who did the dubbing came from the radio: the voice-over, at the beginning of the film, or when the story was told by an invisible character, was that of a famous Italian radio announcer. American films were seen as products of Hollywood. However, the same musical variations, the same elaborations on boogie-woogie or samba rhythms, the same theatrical voices were heard in domestic and American films so that, from a cultural point of view, the latter did not sound unfamiliar to Italian ears – surely less than Swedish films.

And yet, there was a big difference. Hollywood, in its epics, its war films and its comedy of manners films, represented an abstract world, 'a world of terror' or 'life as a dream', as could be read on the posters. Spectators loved that universe of fantasy but they were also willing to see something of their own environment. Hence the increasing success of two series of films, melodramas and comedies, where middle-class people were substituted for American warriors and detectives or Italian bicycle thieves.

A ROSY NEOREALISM?

In the early 1950s, melodramas were the most popular films, second only to American blockbusters. The first big hit, *Chains*, released in 1949, was seen by six million people, one out of eight Italians. Not all melodramas were as successful, but few of them were flops.

Chains exemplifies the quality of a good melodrama. Here is a happy nuclear family, Rose, William and two children. Rose's former lover reappears to bid for her affection. She decides to visit the man and tell him that her past is over, but William, who has been informed of their date, kills the lover by accident. When he is on trial, an innocent Rose confesses adultery and he is acquitted. The barrister tells him the truth while Rose is about to commit suicide.

Mysterious encounters between Rose and her former lover or between the latter and William, long talks, innuendos, the despair expressed on Rose's face, the inquisitive gaze of her son, refer to the traditional patterns of melodramas. But, previously, these films were hastily shot and were 'anonymous' inasmuch as directors, producers and even actors were totally unknown. On the other hand, from a formal point of view *Chains* is extremely well made. The main lines of the plot, the function and status of each character are clear, dialogues are audible, new actions or parallel events are never introduced arbitrarily, all of which results in an easily understandable narrative. What is more, the images are perfect.

Technically speaking the best melodrama might possibly be *Nobody's Sons* (1951), in which strong contrasts are created between night scenes and bright sunlight, between the comfort of rich homesteads and the bareness of the hillside. The main female character of the film enters a convent and the camera plays cleverly on the typical features of an Italian nunnery, its white church, its trees, its long corridors. There is no sophistication in the scenery but a constant concern to give locations a highly symbolic and easily decipherable significance. Titanus, which produced these movies,[44] did not spend much money but always wanted its films to be neat and carefully prepared. The firm hired a director, Raffaello Matarazzo whose name became famous throughout Italy and has been rightly used as a label for a certain kind of conscientiously achieved film. With Matarazzo popular audiences no longer thought they were scorned by filmmakers and given any old rubbish.

More importantly, there were the actors. In the 1950s the odd couple Nazzari and Samson was synonymous with melodrama. They played either together or separately but one of their names, or photographs, on a poster was enough to inform the public about the genre of a movie. Amedeo Nazzari had been *the* great actor of the peninsula whom Italians used to compare to Errol Flynn but, in 1950, he realized that his moustache and his wavy hair made him look somewhat out of date. Instead of playing the ageing father in 'quality' films he preferred to be the main character in melodramas. For ten years he played 'the man who has been around'. Yvonne Samson was tall and wide-hipped, her features were regular but rather coarse with a wide forehead and full lips. Her vulgarity was sensual, she could look extremely rough but with appropriate make-up she would become either sweet or sexy. To put it differently, she was chaste but she could have so easily fallen. At times she would become an angel in a convent (she was, in 1954, the *White Angel*), but more often she would be redeemed by Nazzari's unfailing love.

Plate 19 Yvonne Samson in *We, Sinners* (1953, Guido Brignone)

The Nazzari–Samson match turned out to be entirely successful; a romantic star was the salvation of a sinner. Her rather common appearance prevented Samson from being a star. Matarazzo turned this shortcoming to his advantage. She was perfect as an ordinary woman, a housewife similar to those whom spectators encountered every day in the streets. Traditionally, melodramas took place in imprecise, more or less historical periods; men were busy at court and women idle, merely waiting for love or *coups de théâtre*. Matarazzo transferred his characters to contemporary surroundings, male protagonists were craftsmen, landowners, doctors or industrialists. In *Chains*, Nazzari has a small garage and Samson looks after their home, goes shopping or takes the children to school. On their free days they meet friends on the cliff and enjoy their time off drinking and singing. Nazzari understands he has reached a stage where he must widen his activities; he is looking out for money, and Samson's former lover offers him a loan. But this is not slapstick, Nazzari does not sell his wife, the bargain is serious and illustrates the difficulties of a garage-owner at a time when banks were reluctant to lend money to self-made men. Apra and Carabba have found an excellent definition for that kind of film. It is, they say, 'serialized Neorealism'.[45] Protagonists are purposely represented slightly above their actual condition; they are neither princes or gypsies but middle-class people. The fictional life of these prosaic characters is divided into two parts. On the one hand they try to improve their standard of living, on the other hand they are caught up in inextricable conflicts. Blood and mystery intermingle with daily concerns. Spectators enjoy the soppy stories which are so familiar to them and are able to contemplate a way of life far above the standard of their own, but which is nevertheless not just a pipe-dream.

That explains the terrific impact Matarazzo had on the Italian public: he did not change the plots but shifted the dream from terrible nightmares of sex and violence which had tormented audiences for years to concrete expectations. Fears were still there but softened by a reassuring background. Italy was becoming decisively industrialized, and could get rid of her old family concerns. But it is more than that. Melodramas succeeded because they were not a merely 'popular' form of entertainment. Doleful tales of crushed families were the common property of both cultivated and uneducated Italians during the first half of the twentieth century. The former enjoyed them when avant-garde novelists or poets used the tricks of melodrama to expound a philosophical or social thesis. The latter were content with seeing hastily constructed stories in theatres or cinemas. Working-class audiences were statistically stable but passive and, from a cultural point of view, melodrama, as a genre, was negligible. On the other hand something was set in motion with *Chains*. Audiences boomed and spectators became highly interested in what they were being offered. The innovations referred to above may be summed up in a simple way: there was an intrusion of 'quality' films into melodrama. I do not need to dwell again on the impact of Neorealism on films where the depiction of a social background is concerned, but I must emphasize another point. What intellectuals appreciated most, the subversion of predictable plots, was also introduced in melodrama. In *White Angel* Samson plays two parts. She is still the nun she was in *Nobody's Sons* (1951) and she is also a girl with whom Nazzari, who cannot have an affair with the previous Samson (the nun), falls in love. What are fictional characters? Are they not pure fantasy? How can spectators believe that they have anything to do with actual life? These questions, which Pirandello had asked a few decades before in his plays and novels, were central to Matarazzo's film. In other words, melodrama, which in the 1940s was an item of ordinary consumption, was made slightly uncanny and was thus viewed by popular audiences with a sharpened curiosity. Melodrama was popular inasmuch as the public responded to it very actively. Earlier, we skimmed a few front pages of *La Domenica del Corriere*, and looked at their strange, incredible, sad and diverting anecdotes. Both magazines and melodramas offered a glimpse of a fantastic kingdom, neither magical nor boringly everyday, and in so doing they matched each other.

The assumption may look paradoxical but I think that melodrama boomed in the 1950s because of, not despite, the expansion of a cinematic

culture. It is true that the difficulties of the post-war period distorted traditional frameworks of reference, debased the dominant images of mother
and family, obliged men to live on women's salary. Once out of the
house, women demanded good-quality films, they appreciated well-shot
films, they were intent on being offered familiar yet not too prosaic
fictions. The linearity of melodrama, the values it exposed, its insistence
on death, blood and family, were in many ways ideally suited to the expectations of popular audiences. Still, melodrama would never have flourished
as it did in the 1950s had it not been original in many ways and had not
spectators been able to make the best of its innovations.

SERIOUS JESTS

Macario and Totò, probably the most famous actors for film buffs of the
third generation, got no international or even domestic awards during
their long career. Comedy was immensly appreciated but never taken
seriously. Film festivals are concerned with meaning and signification,
their prizes reward artistic qualities. Comic films were often hurriedly
made and didn't try to say anything. When they conveyed a 'message',
they made it clear that it must not be taken seriously. More importantly,
they depended mostly on personal performances which were not easily
appreciated outside the cultural context in which they were produced.
Ignored outside the peninsula, comedies were of paramount importance
for the third generation of cinema-goers, inasmuch as they were a form of
protest with Macario, while, with the Neapolitans, especially with Totò,
they introduced to the screen the peculiarly Italian dilemma of regional
differences in language and traditions.

Shortly after *Open City*, Anna Magnani featured in *Down with Misery*
(1945), a naive farce showing that only rich black marketeers can succeed.
'Down with politicians, with talks, with inefficiency, etc.' was one slogan
of the time: it put into simple words an atavistic distrust of the state
together with an enduring resignation. Macario won a passing celebrity
by emphasising this latent frustration. Between ordinary situations, misunderstandings, frenzied chases, people losing their clothes, women
chattering, oblivious to the chaos around them, he attempted to introduce
a satirical glance at established ideas and standards. *How I Lost the War*
(1947) told the history of Italy, from the war in Ethiopia to 1945 from
the point of view of a poor man obliged to fight, successively, for all the
belligerents. In *The Hero of the Street* (1948) Macario was Lucky, the
perfect loser who failed in all his efforts. Nobody wanted to give him a
job, the girl he courted looked at him with scorn, his schemes to make
money were quickly scuppered. Uttered in the conversational, throw-
away style of a farce, short sentences, which now sound innocuous,

mocked judges, civil servants and politicians. One of his companions in *How I Lost the War* explained to him: 'Nobody has asked me whether I wanted to make war. They wanted it, they can make it. The loser will pay'. 'Well,' Macario answered, 'we shall be left with the bill.'

Macario was a stage actor, his films were dialogues in images. On the other hand, the Neapolitans, Totò and Eduardo De Filippo, attempted to prolong a tradition of puppet-shows and street theatre based on dreadful puns, verbal sleights and mime. To a large extent, they used the cinema against itself. We have noted that film and radio were then diffusing a standard Italian, understandable in all parts of the peninsula, which contributed to diminish regional idioms and deprived spectators of the ancestral jokes built on variations in accent, emphasis and word-games. This, the Neapolitans tried to counter, in what was probably the last encroachment of revue and slapstick on cinema. In their films, the characters, instead of exchanging pessimistic talk, as in Macario's, spent their time chattering. Prattling does not demand to be heard attentively and is always open to misinterpretation. Stressing the limitations of language, Totò destroyed words and switched them towards other interpretations. 'Armed robbery' became, for instance, 'shouldered robbery' (*Totò Third Man*, 1951).[46] Arm means weapon but designates also a part of the body. How do thieves break down a closed door? With their shoulders. Filling their scripts with double meanings, the Neapolitans denounced a tendency to have recourse to sophisticated, incomprehensible terms. But this did not end in some absurd jargon. There was something behind the words, a signification that viewers were invited to discover. In *Totò and Caroline* (1956), a policeman, on guard in a hospital, realized that he has slept in the bed of a woman who has just died. Has he caught her illness? 'Don't worry,' the doctor tells him, 'she died from inanition.' – 'Inanition? What kind of disease is that?' – 'Deficiency' – 'I feel deficient.' – 'She starved to death.' – 'Starvation! I'm relieved.' Complicated terms like inanition are easily misunderstood. Get rid of them and you see the truth: policemen do not starve.

However, Totò did not disappear in a cloud of puns, he was a physical presence. His bizarre clowning was the centre of the action and swamped the screen. He made full use of both his loose, rubbery body and a lightening-fast ability to switch moods from upset scepticism to naive enthusiasm and from affronted sulking to cheerful keeness. His sure grasp of the codes of the stage helped him to emphasize his own involvement and play on ambiguity, especially androgyny, with a tendency to draw on male feminity or maybe rather on the female weakness of an unsure man. Uncanny though he was, Totò was too sympathetic to be easily forgotten. When he showed up with a distressed gaze and trembling nostrils, spectators felt diverted by his comical expression and moved by his physical unfitness.

Plate 20 Fright and Arena (1948, Mario Mattòli). Totò (in the middle): an unlikely toreador

Macario and Totò offered a striking contrast. Macario's horizon was closed, his talks addressed those who conceived of themselves as resigned victims. Totò was much more complex. Coming from nowhere, being an alien in his own country, he lived in a nonsensical sphere akin to the preposterous universe of the *Domenica del Corriere*. Attached to traditional values, he made fun of them and, while stressing the validity of regional idioms, he ridiculed them. Caught between two worlds, past and future, unable to master events, he gave his spectators a sense of a suspension of time. His public delighted in listening to his strange speech, which represented a transition from the provinces where they were born, toward a new social and economic space which was in the making.

*

In the last part of this chapter, I have treated Neorealism and other aspects of the cinematic production separately. It would be wrong to believe that such a literary expedient mirrors a social division between a 'cultivated' and a 'popular' public. Intellectuals, who bought the fashionable film magazines, took part in the polemics about Neorealism, but theirs was merely a political, or theoretical interest. As far as we can see, for clues are scarce in this field, lowbrows and highbrows were equally fascinated by *Bitter Rice* or *The Way to Hope*, and equally reluctant to pay for a seat to see *Umberto D* or *Germany, Year Zero*. The case of *Shoeshine*, mentioned above, is typical. Italians distinguished what pleased them and what was likely to please others. It is true that the films of the late 1940s worked a new effect in the context of the 1970s because younger generations were more conscious of technical qualities and less concerned with coherent stories. This was not the case for the third generation, whose cinematic culture was shaped by a permanent contact with Hollywood and which was, therefore, sensitive to a logical unfolding towards a clear, if possibly optimistic, conclusion.

Cinema audiences boomed from the years of the Ethiopian war to the end of Reconstruction. The rise developed concentrically: the same people went to picture theatres more and more, they brought with them their relatives, their friends, all those who were like them, thus creating a social habit. In this respect, cinema played a fundamental part in the evolution of the peninsula. Opinion was then extremely divided, first for or against Fascism, later between conservatism and Communism. Cinema attendance was a unifying factor. Catholics or Communists, clerks, shopkeepers or workers, all Italians saw the same films, or rather the same kinds of films. For them, American actors were familiar figures, but de Sica, Nazarri, Totò were as familiar as the Hollywood stars. Cinema screens presented to everybody adventures and fantasy, glimpses of the American way of life and rosy images of Italian daily problems. During these two decades there was, undoubtedly, a 'national cinema' inasmuch as the whole nation felt concerned with films. But what spectators liked was neither genuinely 'national' nor totally foreign, only fully cinematic.

Fourth generation
The sweet life

There are a few films whose title encapsulates the very spirit of a period. Such was the case of Raoul Walsh's *The Roaring Twenties* (1939) and of *La dolce vita* (*The Sweet Life*, 1960). However, the legend of the fabulous twenties was contrived subsequently, during the Great Depression when, by comparison, the previous decade looked happy and prosperous. On the other hand, the members of the fourth generation of cinema-goers, those who reached 20 at the beginning of the 'economic miracle', were often convinced that theirs was a sweet life and bestowed on their own days the title of Fellini's film.

From the middle of the 1950s to the middle of the 1970s, structural trans-formations, namely greater applied scientific knowledge, a market-based industrial economy, and the rise of an urban society, triggered a sustained expansion in the retailing of consumer goods.[1] With modernization, the economic benefits of domestic self-sufficiency and the saving of money van-ished, but for people to recognize this and act accordingly required a radical change in attitudes. Family self-sufficiency, which was a necessity, especially on farms, was ideologically justified by traditional values supported by religion, the kinship system and gender roles. For this to evolve, a new cultural environment, dominated by secular, individualistic rationality, had to arise. To what extent did mental attitudes and expectations really alter? This is a question open to discussion. It has been argued, for instance, that the rapid decline in the birth rate, one of the most impressive features of Italian demography since the middle of the twentieth century, must be seen not as cultural 'modernization' but rather as the realization of traditional values of home and family in a world of new opportunities. The fact remains that people believed that a new era had begun. What part did the cinema play in the spread of that conviction?

FAITH IS THE MIRACLE

A miracle is something which mere man is not capable of bringing about, which is 'impossible', but which is nevertheless accepted as true. If there is no miracle without faith, faith is enough to give a miracle its identity. I am not disputing the fact that tremendous changes occurred from 1950 onwards. The growth, in the post-war period, of Italian industrial production in sectors as crucial as electricity, motor vehicles and chemicals, and the rate of this growth relative to that in other European countries, are statistical truths. But the process of calculating people's expectations by aggregating figures may be misleading. The numbers produced by such an exercise tell us nothing about how material progress was perceived at the time. There is probably a gap between the precise dates to which the figures refer and the dates on which perceptions were formed. What concerns us here is not economic growth itself but its social effects and its relationship to entertainment.

The classical interpretation of the advent of a consumer society was offered by Visconti whose film, *Rocco and His Brothers* (1960) attempts to show how the poorest were involved in the boom, how much it cost them and what benefits it brought them. A countrywoman from southern Italy who can no longer live in her village migrates to Milan with her sons. The family settles in the basement of a multi-storey building and the boys look for work. In a somewhat schematic manner, the film explores the four possible solutions: unskilled work, theft, technical studies leading to a specialized job, and boxing. Visconti puts particular emphasis on the last-named, which seems to him to be a metaphor for the alienation imposed by capitalism. A sporting activity has been turned into a brutal business that exploits young men, obliges them to sell their body and corrupts everyone associated with them. However, while one of the boys fails, the others get on very well. The family moves to a small flat, then to a large, well-furnished, light flat on the outskirts of Milan. The price is the division of the family. The boys have to work in different districts, they will soon become estranged from each other.

La dolce vita was released just a few months before *Rocco*. This was not mere coincidence; both films were concerned with the explosion of signs of prosperity in the late 1950s. Fellini's main character, Marcello (played by Marcello Mastroianni), a reporter for a gutter-press newspaper, is prying into rich people's business and is so involved in this circle that he is unable to stand aloof from it. The film is built upon a clever dichotomy between the protagonist, who has no opinion, no personal view, and the film itself which follows him from afar, as if there were always a veil, or a barrier between the characters and the public. 'This world, the world of the richest, is not yours,' spectators are told. Visconti developed the same idea in his film. At the beginning of *Rocco*, the family, who have landed in Milan late at night, cross the town by bus. Mother and sons marvel at the fantastic sight of brightly lit windows but they merely see them from a closed vehicle which will not stop before they reach their gloomy suburb. Later, one of the boys takes his girlfriend for a walk. They sit on

Plate 21 Anouk Aimée in *La dolce vita* (1960, Federico Fellini)

the low wall of a luxurious restaurant, just for the pleasure of watching, but a waiter orders them to go away: 'This is not for you, folks.'

The unprecedented outburst of economic and technological energy which occurred during the 'miracle' represented, for most Italians, simultaneously a palpable reality and a mirage. One of the brothers, in *Rocco*, works hard to get a degree. Some day this young man, born in an out-of-the-way village, will be a white-collar worker, maybe an engineer. His will be a serious life, that will stand no comparison with the existence of Fellini's main character. Marcello prefers to court women, pander to their obsessions, linger in pubs and saloons, anything rather than undertake serious work. In different, almost opposed ways, Visconti and Fellini tried to chart a generational sensitivity, they described the experiences, hopes and attempts of young men living with the stimulating prospects offered by an economy on the up. But the journalist, born into a well-off provincial family, has no need to commit himself to anything, he can live for ever on the margin of fashionable circles, while Rocco's younger brother is obliged to perform well if he does not want to end up like Rocco in the Alfa-Romeo car factory.

Depicting aspects of contemporary Italian society, Fellini and Visconti stressed a few highly significant points. They suggested firstly that there was a wide gap between the beliefs and desires of two generations. Rocco's mother and Marcello's father stuck to the values of a limited, well-knit community. Their sons insisted on a freedom in their work and behaviour which found its basis in a total involvement in economic progress. A second theme, developed mostly by Visconti, was the expansion of education which accompanied modernization and contributed to accelerate its pace. Between 1955 and 1965, the number of skilled technicians increased by 25 per cent, the number of university graduates by 33 per cent.[2] All these people found jobs even if, sometimes, they were obliged to take work which did not measure up to their qualifications. Wage-earners earned more money than they needed to keep their family but not enough to enable them to invest, so that, by the end of the 1950s, a surplus of money marked the shift from thrift to spending. A paradigmatic image of the period, reproduced in magazines and films, was that of the young shop-assistant who saved to buy a motorbike so he could take his girlfriend to the nearest beach. The emergence of new forms of deferred payment, the availability of ready-made clothes and motor cycles, profoundly altered people's conception of the domestic economy and exchanges. The theoretical respect for money and the habit of putting it away were debased by inflation or mere speculation and there was therefore no reason either to save it, or to make this debased currency the least cause for concern.

The question of wages and expenditure was closely linked to the evolution of the cinema. Both Fellini and Visconti demonstrated the spread of new forms of entertainment: music-hall, dance-hall and, above all, sporting competitions. Taking an interest in sport was the big fashion of the 'miracle' years, a passion common to all classes. Italians were extremely proud that the 1960 Olympic Games took place in Rome, and for a few weeks their capital city was the capital of the world. Experimental television was launched in 1952 with a talk on sports. Regular transmissions, which began in January 1954, included news and a weekly programme, *Sporting Sunday* (*Domenica sportiva*). Football, the most popular of all sports, became, in the 1960s, a source of permanent national interest. Sponsored by local industries which could 'buy' the best soccer players, the teams of Milan, Turin and other cities revived old rivalries between provinces. As can be seen in Table 2, money spent on sporting events increased slowly

Table 2 Cinema attendances, and spending on cinema and sport, 1955–75

	1955	1960	1965	1970	1975
sport (% of spending on entertainment)	5	5.5	6	8	10
cinema (% of spending on entertainment)	67	59	49	42	43
cinema attendances (millions)	819	745	680	530	513

but regularly. What does not appear in these figures is the growing importance of gambling. Totocalcio, a weekly wager on football, became a national activity in the 1960s and absorbed huge sums no longer available for spending on entertainment. Within the same decade, cinema takings declined rapidly, in correlation with the reduction in attendance.[3]

Many factors other than the interest aroused by football account for the decline of the cinema public. Contrary to what happened in Britain and Germany, television did not play a prominent part in the reduction of cinema attendance, at least until the mid 1960s, because TV programmes were of such poor quality. For a long time, people preferred to buy a vehicle rather than a television set, so that it took five years for the number of television sets to reach the million mark.[4] *Sporting Sunday* on television can be considered an excellent barometer of television viewing. On average, it was watched by fewer than 2 million spectators until 1965; then, it jumped to 5 million in 1970 and to 9 million in 1975.[5] Much more than television, it was the spread of labour-saving devices and electrical appliances which led people to save on entertainment. Oddly enough, films helped to legitimize the diminution in spending which would subsequently devalue them. They taught people how to live, how to occupy their empty hours. Cinema-goers tasted the life of the rich; they were introduced to an equality of consumption, which was not equality of status, but they were lured into believing that rich and poor could aspire to the same level of comfort and life-style. Let us take a very simple example. At the outset of Fellini's *8½* (1963), the protagonist is caught in a huge traffic jam. The same vision featured in many contemporary films. Now remember the car-free streets of many Neorealist films shot in big cities, Rome or Milan. Remember that the worker in *Bicycle Thieves* cycles quickly and easily from his distant block of flats to the city centre. The number of vehicles did increase enormously in the 1950s, but there is plenty of evidence of dramatic traffic congestion also in the late 1940s, as well as of the fluidity of road communication in the 1960s. The crowding of vehicles making any movement impossible is an everlasting commonplace which had already been exploited by Roman satirists. We must not forget that films are not sociological surveys but rather images based on factual observation, and that they cannot be taken at face value. Fellini revealed and exploited an obsession common to many people. However caustic it was, his opening scene sanctioned a general conviction: ours is the era of individual means of transport, for better or worse we have to use cars.

Fellini's irony is typical of the disenchanted criticism which developed at the time in Italian comedies and which we shall explore shortly. Understanding that kind of irony required a modicum of attention, which some spectators did not accord because, for them, cinema should be purely and simply entertainment. Up to the mid-1950s, all Italians saw more or less the same sort of movies. There were obviously differences of taste between the more and the less educated but all films, American and Italian, circulated throughout the peninsula. The disruption of this shaky community was another aspect of the generation gap mentioned above. Two factors, one financial, the other ideological, account for that transformation.

Faced with an erosion of their audience, exhibitors reacted either by closing down (two thousand cinemas disappeared between 1955 and 1975) or by modifying their operation. Peripheral and rural cinemas, where tickets were still cheap, were left to fall to pieces. On the other hand, first-run cinemas were refurbished. While, in the early 1950s, the price of a seat could vary by a factor of one to six, fifteen years later, it varied by a factor of one to twelve. Consequently, a film shown to few people in a central picture theatre brought in more money than a film offered to many in a village. In 1975, first-run cinemas, which made up only one eighth of the total, received half the total box-office takings. Christopher Wagstaff has given an excellent explanation of how this logic of exploitation led the producers to make two types of film, 'quality films', booked to national distributors at high prices, and 'quickies' booked to regional distributors.[6] The theme of a film or its category were less important than the quality or otherwise of its script, its acting and shooting, and its sophistication. A very significant aspect of this division was the reluctance of 'quality' directors to shoot in colour, at a time when Hollywood had long been converted to this medium, only because black and white looked smarter. Visconti, who had experimented with colour in *Senso* (1954), went back to black and white with *Rocco* and waited until 1967 before opting definitely for colour. Antonioni and Fellini shot in black and white up to 1964 and 1965 respectively.

Another important element of this evolution was the spread of education. University students, who often went to the movies, created film societies to hire films which were no longer distributed. Some priests jumped at the opportunity to reinforce their influence among the youth. The Catholic Church was then going through what was called its 'updating'. Film-shows and debates about the moral or aesthetic value of movies was seen as a good way of attracting large audiences. Created by Catholics, Communists or atheists, Cine-forums were a big fashion in the 1960s and flourished even in small cities. One of their aims being to describe, analyse and discuss the films, they looked perfectly repulsive to spectators who were merely keen to enjoy amusing or thrilling images.

Intellectuals had long contrived to distinguish between 'mass' and 'elite' cultures, but a new term, the adjective 'popular', surfaced in the 1960s. The most sophisticated films, those which could be commented upon in film societies, were introduced into the realm of 'high' culture, together with classical music, opera and literature, while the 'quickies' were relegated to the realm of pulp fiction or rock 'n roll. 'Popular' cannot be a

category of analysis, for this was merely speculation on the part of producers who, after calculating the chances of return on their investment, spent
more or less money on shooting. In doing so, they contributed to creating
a wide gap between two kinds of public. Christopher Wagstaff assumes
that in suburban areas and small towns, spectators, confronted with
loosely constructed stories full of thrills and excitement, let their attention
fluctuate, carefully following the fights or chases but beginning to chat as
soon as there was a pause in the action. If there were any truth in this
idea, we could say that the cinema initiated Italians to channel-hopping.[7]

Paradoxically, while the inhabitants of the peninsula were increasingly
bound together by economic and technological changes, while they
looked and dressed increasingly alike, managed their money and affairs in
ever more comparable ways, cultural practices and entertainment tended
to estrange them from each other. In the nineteenth century, opera could
temporarily unite all classes. In the 1960s, the managements of picture
theatres divided them into fans of entertaining films and amateurs of intellectual movies. But, of course, the rupture must not be overstated. Strong
links between individuals were perpetuated by family ties and regional
activities which remained essential building-blocks of social life.

COMEDY ITALIAN STYLE

It also took a long time for the partition into two different publics to come
into effect, especially in the most traditional sectors of Italian cinema.
Up to now, I have avoided the word 'genre'. Genres never exist as pure
types. For instance comedies and kindred forms, such as farce or slapstick,
fall into the category of humour and it is hard to tell them apart.
However, the triumph, at the time of the so-called 'economic miracle', of
new patterns of comedy forces me to recall that, usually, a comedy is a
temporary disruption of order which ends when routine is restored.
Comedies are enjoyable because they pretend to question authority and
rules. They are also harmless since they never threaten the law seriously.

Camerini's and de Sica's films, which provisionally blurred class distinctions and then reinstated them thanks to that most common trick, a
wedding, exemplify a formula which was highly appreciated in Italy,
although it was by no means specifically Italian. The model survived in
the 1950s and 1960s, notably with two famous series, the *Don Camillo*
and the *Bread, Love and* . . . films. The *Don Camillo* films were constructed
around an imaginary conflict between the parish priest and the mayor in a
village of the Po valley. Generated by an ideological opposition between
these two men, disorder was tempered by their mutual friendship but the
third film of the cycle, *Don Camillo's Last Round* (1955), departed from
this scheme. In this story, the mayor, a married man, who has fallen for
a seductive young lady, is brought to his senses by Don Camillo. This

shift from public affairs to private concerns was decided by the producer because, in comedies, the main source of confusion is sexuality.
The four *Bread, Love and . . .* films (1952–8) illustrated perfectly this
theme, defined by the first in the series, *Bread, Love and Dreams*. The
pretty Maria (whose part was played by Gina Lollobrigida) is courted by
all the men of her village, bringing about jealousy and discord. Luckily,
concord is re-established as soon as she gets married.

The last *Bread, Love and . . .* film was a flop, not because it was a
repetition of the previous films but because, between 1952 and 1958,
Italian studios had contrived a new style of dark comedy tales. These, the
only comedies which can be genuinely labelled 'Italian style', since they
look like no others, owed their success to showing unexpected moves in a
game whose rules were dictated by the generic expectations of the public.
While exploiting stocks of characters and plot ingredients, notably disorder, familiar to most viewers, the new trend excluded the morality that
ran through preceding movies. A few decades later, in the mid-1990s
during operation Clean Hands (*Mani pulite*) aimed at erradicating public
corruption, Mirco Melanco could assume that the bribery revealed by the
magistrates had long existed: it was first revealed by the 'Italian style'
comedies.[8]

Released in 1958, the same year as the last *Bread, Love and . . .* film,
Persons Unknown made fun of hold-ups and carefully planned robberies.
Why should people run a serious risk when it is simpler to take advantage
of a system which tolerates fraud? Many films reveal the circuits of bribery
and corruption by dragging them into the foreground, exposing them to
the full view of spectators. In these films, not only politicians but also the
average Italian were supposed to use bribery and to be unscrupulous.
Coming from all quarters, Italians invaded Rome to suborn politicians or
civil servants likely to give them a share in public funds.

Comedies Italian style sold very well, not only in Italy but all throughout Europe and even in the United States. Their success cannot be attributed solely to their cynicism: they were also of excellent quality. Unlike
the comedies of the 1930s, adapted from theatre plays, they were based
on original texts written by professional scriptwriters including Furio
Scarpelli, Age, Rodolfo Sonego. They were not content merely with
imagining amusing puns, but also created visually interesting situations.
The main parts were given to a cohort of young actors, Vittorio
Gassmann, Marcello Mastroianni, Alberto Sordi, Ugo Tognazzi, all born
in the 1920s, who entered the studios after the war. Against the romanti-
cism of Amedeo Nazzari and the elegance of de Sica, the newcomers
imposed a casual, witty style more adapted to sarcasm and scepticism
than to moralism. It is always dangerous to look for a relationship
between the larger movements and tendencies of an epoch and the
making of art works. However, when watching these comedies, I cannot

help noting correspondences with contemporary society. Let us take the example of *A Hard Life* (1961), shot by Dino Risi after a script supplied by Rodolfo Sonego. Alberto Sordi plays the part of an idealistic young man, Silvio, imbued with feelings of altruism, who cannot find a decent job. Having married an ambitious woman, and being obliged to make money for her, he begins to compromise. Being lucid, he sees everything with a critical eye, which enables the director to set out for us, in meticulous detail, the misdemeanours of the ruling class. Employed by a businessman, Silvio despises his uneducated, dishonest boss, while admiring him for his ability to con everybody and make money. The manager makes the best of the 'miracle'. Disgusted but impressed, Silvio is unable either to imitate his chief or to leave him.[9]

It is now clear that, far from being a consequence only of the boom, corruption was an inherited feature of Italian public life going back centuries. However, until the middle of the twentieth century, only the richest and most powerful profited from bribery. In his study on daily bribery, Franco Cazzola has explained how, during the decades which followed the war, more and more ordinary people obtained little perks like pensions, commercial licenses, success in exams, avoidance of taxes or fines.[10] Of course, small traders or industrialists, place-seekers and clerks did not need films to know how to use the resources of their commune or province. The cinema was not a cause but a symptom of a general tendency to seek personal interest at the expense of the community.

And yet, there is something in these comedies which goes beyond the spirit of the time. The disorder in these stories is purely individual. Some protagonists, like Silvio, feel ill at ease, but their doubts do not lead them to warn their fellow citizens against the rules of clientelistic competition. What is more, the classical happy ending, marriage, is totally debased. Let us look at another film, *Divorce Italian Style*, released at the same time as *A Hard Life*. Baron Cefalù (Marcello Mastroianni), bored with his uninspiring wife, would like to marry his pretty cousin Angela, twenty years his junior. As divorce is not possible in Italy, Cefalù manoeuvres his wife into leaving with a lover and kills her. Deceived husbands being morally obliged to take revenge in Sicily, Cefalù can quietly marry Angela. The film has been interpreted as a plea for divorce – a reform which would be passed a few years later, in 1972. But the whole affair is told as if the crime were a mere trifle. The film is hilariously, scabrously funny throughout. Cefalù is not a hero, he is a selfish, decadent dabbler whose fussiness makes him prepare a murder like a business deal. The final wedding is not an end. The last image makes it obvious that Cefalù will soon be cuckolded – maybe eliminated by his second wife. Far from making for a happy ending, cinematic marriages were a source of disarray. Sordi was destroyed by his wife in *The Widower* (1959), again a film of Risi with a script by Sonego, while Ugo Tognazzi, twice eliminated by his spouse, in *The Conjugal Bed* (1963) and *The Man Who Came for Coffee* (1970), became a complete wreck.

It can be argued that these films offered an image of the betrayal that men feared with independent women moving freely in an unconstrained social space – a space over which men had no longer control and where they could leave behind the sense of their manhood. I shall return to the problem later. What I want to stress here is the eclipse of a set of rules and tricks which, borrowed from the stage, had sustained amusing films for five decades. The portrayal of married life suggests the gap between the beliefs and desires of the third and fourth generations. The difference must not be taken at face value since, far from being destroyed, in Italy the family was still ranked above all other associations in terms of importance during the 1960s and 1970s. The previous generation used the household to express, symbolically, its wartime togetherness, its parochialism and its fear of foreign intrusions. The disintegration of kinship that runs through most of the comedies in the 1960s had nothing to do with the boredom of home life. It was comic, and gained its effect, by the simple fact that it was unexplained. And it was possibly a manifestation of bewilderment in front of galloping social upheaval.

BIG MONEY, GREAT FILMS?

Comedies proved to be very successful. They helped to ameliorate the position of Italian movies in the domestic market. During the first half of the 1950s, American films took 60 per cent of box-office receipts, while Italian films were reduced to 33 per cent. By the mid-1970s, the figures had totally changed: only 25 per cent went to Hollywood, and Italian movies took 65 per cent.

This explains why, despite a diminution in cinema audience, the Italians studios made more films in the 1960s and 1970s than in the 1950s. The peak year, 1972, witnessed 291 new releases compared with 114 in 1955, which was the best year for attendances. On the whole, the ten top money-makers, which were comedies and 'spaghetti westerns' received 20 per cent of the total receipts but a good half of the new films were flops. As in most periods, the financially most rewarding element of the film industry was exhibition, while production was not operating at a significant enough profit to be a worthwhile venture. Titanus gave up filmmaking in 1964 and concentrated on distribution, Lux closed down two years later. However, production did not decrease because, since the mid-1960s, Italy was involved in a programme of co-productions with France, Spain, Germany and with several Latin American countries. Once two companies, an Italian and a Spanish one for instance, had agreed on a project, both would invest money, tax refunds, when obtainable, would come from two governments, and the film would be distributed in two markets. In 1972, 142 'Italian' films, about half of the total, were co-productions. The idea that a film should be tailored to suit the programming requirements of non-Italian audiences was a novelty. For a long time foreign investors had had to be content with co-investing rather than co-producing. An agreement with a foreign company meant that Italian studios were obliged to accept editorial and economic control over their products. The producers had to bargain at length over the script, crew, and casting before reaching a compromise. The financial aspect of the deals was extremely complicated. In many cases, three countries were involved. But many firms benefited from investment by American distributors operating in Europe so that defining the nationality of a film on the basis of the money invested was impossible. In a few cases, when the director could control the whole project, the co-operation of two companies helped make difficult films: Antonioni's *L'avventura* (*The Adventure*, 1960), *La notte* (*The Night*, 1961), and *The Eclipse* (1962) were all co-produced. But, most of the time, greater commercial appeal was the spur, and companies decided to shoot commercial products likely to interest cosmopolitan audiences. Two series of films, the historical or mythological epics[11] and the 'spaghetti westerns', are the most characteristic products of international collaboration. Oddly enough, these films have often been called 'popular'. If 'popular' signifies a film which cannot please intellectuals, the label is not appropriate for the epics or westerns, which did very well in various social sectors and were watched, on their opening run, by upper- and middle-class audiences. If 'popular' means artless, the label is again ill-suited for there was much sophistication in several of these films. There was no homogeneity in these so-called series. Far from being 'mass produced' they were shot in different circumstances, by different crews and aimed a different audiences. Trying to analyse their themes and formulas to specify what is 'popular' would be totally misleading.

The first epics, released in 1958, *Hercules* and *The Rebellion of the Gladiators*, illustrate themes, mythological or historical, which, thanks to the development of secondary education, were familiar to many young people. However linear it was, the story could only be enjoyed by spectators able to pick out the references spread throughout the dialogues. The battles, well filmed and involving a large number of extras, were gripping, and the depiction of landscapes was excellent, but there was no attempt to create sensational effects. In the wake of these films, which were greatly appreciated, other companies tried to lure a larger public by reducing the plot to a mere pretext and multiplying the visual and sound tricks. But the most rewarding device was the introduction of a touch of eroticism. The male hero was caught between two female characters, a brunette and a blonde, both comely young women in short white skirts. Lips half-open, shoulders naked, short hair fluttering about, the actresses cast a seductive glance alternately at their male counterpart and at the viewer and, at times, came to blows.

It must be recalled, here, that the fourth generation of cinema-goers was submerged by a wave of pornography. Female nudes and overt representations of sexual intercourse were offered in magazines, journals, books and films.[12] The top money-makers of the early 1970s are typical in this respect. *Malicious* (1973) explained how the bare thighs of a pretty maid could stir up the male section of a right-thinking family, Pasolini's *The Decameron* (1971) illustrated, in the most explicit way, some of Boccacio's tales, while the main characters of Bertolucci's *Last Tango in Paris* (1972) spent their time making love, practising sodomy or masturbating. In comparison, the soft eroticism of the epics looked childish. A few of them sold well abroad and were even praised by foreign critics but in the peninsula their fame was short-lived.

The 'spaghetti westerns' were of much more relevance than the epics.[13] They made more money to begin with. The takings of the biggest hit, *For a Few Dollars More* (1965) were five times those of the most successful epic. These Eurowesterns were often featureless, badly shot and badly edited. In a few instances they were also original. Parodying what Italo Calvino called 'a puerile cinematic convention',[14] the fanciful, heroic wild West, they distorted it, thus creating an abstract space, a boundless wasteland which could not be likened to any existing country and was only fit for extravagant stories. The dialogues, which were dubbed in four or five languages, were laconic, the characters acted instead of talking, but noise or music were effectively substituted for the words. Up to the 1960s, the soundtrack was mostly used to supplement and decorate the images. With westerns, it stopped being a mere accompaniment of emotion. Working in close collaboration with their composers and sound engineers, directors made their drama emerge from the music, thrilling notes flooded empty landscapes, and accentuated their spell. Enio Morricone's haunting scores, endlessly broadcast on radio and sold by the hundred in record stores, created an aura of mystery which incited people to be at the next film-show.

But 'spaghetti westerns' were particularly important for the atmosphere of brute force that they introduced on the screens. The violence was not celebrated, it was reported in cold blood, as when Henry Fonda, in *Once Upon a Time in the West* (1968) resolutely killed a young boy who looked him straight in the face. Lost dare-devils enjoyed the fear that they caused and were themselves exploited by clever, wicked leaders. Even the most elaborate westerns indulged in a fantasy of sadism and brutishness. Women had almost no part in the stories which featured only tough guys. Parallels or oppositions are often dangerous in cultural studies but I find it necessary to contrast the Italian westerns with the

Italian style comedies. Both depict a corrupt world. But bribery, which was soft, almost legal in the latter, became overtly ferocious in the former. Comedies took place in comfortable, urban surroundings, westerns in a lawless no-man's land. Above all, there was a striking difference in the representation of women. Would it be exaggeration to say that, in contrast to comedies which mourned masculine weakness and impotence, the Euro-westerns glorified male strength?

A SEASON FOR AWARDS

Westerns obtained their best results in first-run cinemas. The same spectators enjoyed, alternately, the films of Sergio Leone and those of Fellini and Antonioni. However, unlike the latter, Leone was given no award. In this way, critics and experts succeeded in creating a dividing-line between 'cultured' and 'popular' movies. The number of film festivals rose dramatically, throughout the world, in the 1960s and Italian cinema benefited greatly from their development. Fellini's *La dolce vita* and *8½* were both awarded eight international prizes, Antonioni's *L'avventura* won seven film awards, while five prizes went to Visconti's *Rocco*. I could fill a whole book with honours of that kind since Italian movies got an impressive proportion of film awards in the 1960s.[15] Italian spectators had always been proud of the prizes won by Italian films. But, in this respect, there was a significant difference between the third and the fourth generation. The former, while satisfied at Italy's achievements, did not go to see a film simply because it had won an award, while the latter, at least in its most informed sector, selected its programmes according to the verdict of panels of judges.

Festivals created a category, the 'quality film', and told film buffs what they ought to see. The selection established by critics and journalists was part of film culture. It was also a guarantee offered to a public disconcerted by the changes that were affecting the very making of films. The fourth generation witnessed, sometimes in bewilderment, the advent of what was then called 'modernism'. This is an obscure term which can only be understood in relation to its opposite, classicism. A film was considered classical when its main aim was to tell a story, and when all its elements – dialogues, images and sounds – helped to develop the plot. On the other hand, modern films were meant to give their consumers an awareness of their process of construction. Spectators were required to pay attention to the components of the film, at the same time as enjoying the exaltation that following an interesting work of fiction can bring. Careful work on form allowed many unrelated sub-plots to blossom alongside the main story so that the fiction was not driven towards a predictable ending and, in some cases, had no conclusion. As was suggested by Gian Piero Brunetta, modern cinema compelled its public to 'complete its meaning'[16] so that, without the help of critics, many spectators might have been put off by films that were engaging one moment and disruptive the next. The most remarkable thing is that lots of viewers, not just a small group of fans, welcomed the 'modernist' films. This was due, in no small measure, to the work of the critics.

From a purely formal point of view, several Eurowesterns, Sergio Leone's for instance, could be called 'modern'. But they made no reference whatsoever to any specific context and their insistence on fanciful, extraordinary situations made them look more extravagant than modern. 'Modernist' films hinted at precise, often contemporary problems and were filled with details familiar to most viewers. In many cases, it would have been possible to choose the social context and read the films in this light. Let us look at Antonioni's *The Red Desert* (1964). The film begins with the visit of Corrado to his friend Ugo whom he has not seen for a long time. This might be an excellent opening for a confrontation between two worlds and two males. We are in the mid-1960s. Ugo is an engineer in one of the most promising industrial sectors, oil. Corrado's father once had a big estate, but land is no longer a good investment, the estate has been sold, and Corrado is obliged to emigrate to Argentina. Land against industry, a distressed man against a successful manager: even the following episodes, mostly centred upon Ugo's wife, could be analysed at that level. As emerges from this example, modernity was a matter of drawing out complex cinematic structures from simple initial motifs. It was also, as will appear later, an attempt to produce an effect of complexity by arduous work on temporality.

The late 1950s witnessed an outburst of cinematic inventiveness in most European countries. But while France, Germany, Greece and Spain had their 'new waves', nobody ever spoke of an 'Italian school', although there was as much innovation in the peninsula as elsewhere. This was partly due to the fact that several filmmakers – Visconti, Antonioni, Fellini – had made 'classical' films before opting for modernity. It must also be noted that the coherence of the story, however simple it was, and the emphasis on the part played by the leading actors were much more important for the Italians than for their European counterparts.

The case of Visconti, the most 'classical' of the directors, illustrates what changed around the year 1960. *Senso*, released in 1954, is about how a woman remembers her past and how she tells it to herself and to others. It is enclosed within a traditional framework of beginning (Countess Serpieri, who lives in Venice, then occupied by the Austrians, encounters Lieutenant Franz Mahler, an Austrian officer), middle (their love affair) and end (their mutual betrayal, which results in the execution of Mahler). Here history (the war between Austria and Italy) and individual story matched perfectly. On the other hand, they seemed to be loosely connected in Visconti's successive 'historical' movies, *The Leopard* (1963), *The*

Plate 22 The Red Desert (1964, Michelangelo Antonioni)

Damned (1969) and *Ludwig* (1971). The first and the third of them could have been titled *A Chronicle of Empty Seasons*, for there are very few events. As they have long done before, the Leopard, Prince Salina, and his family spend the spring on their estate near Palermo, leave the torrid plain for another palace, somewhere in the hills, in summer, and come back to Palermo in winter. Ludwig, King of Bavaria, goes hunting, courts his cousin, feasts with handsome young men. However, these time-less rituals develop against crucial historical backgrounds: in *The Leopard* it is early 1860s, from Garibaldi's disembarcation in Sicily to the defeat of the great leader by the royal army, the months during which the Bourbons lose their kingdom and Sicily becomes Italian; in *Ludwig* it is the time of the creation of the unified German Reich. These facts seem of little relevance for people more preoccupied with trifles than with political issues. Side stories, such as the affair between Salina's nephew and a pretty young lady, or Ludwig's failed engagement, are important parts of the films, as was the depiction of social pleasures or obligations. *The Damned* takes place during the first months of Hitler's rise to power. Nazism provides a gloomy atmosphere for the depiction of a series of perversions or misdemeanours. Here, as in the two other films, the picture is structured to culminate in a brilliant sequence of happenings, which are, respectively, in *The Leopard*, the ball in which Salina dazzles Sicilian high society; Ludwig's drinking orgy with his friends; and, in *The Damned*, the massacre of Hitler's opponents during a wild homosexual party.

Visconti's 'modernism' was not far from Sergio Leone's since both directors aimed more at giving their spectators visual and aural gratification than at offering the pleasure of understanding. Leone's *For a Few Dollars More* features a man from nowhere who wants neither money nor power and gets involved in an obscure quarrel which is no concern of his. Visconti and Leone centred their films round an actor, Burt Lancaster and Helmut Berger for the former, Clint Eastwood for the latter, whose ability to give a spirited performance was fully exploited, and whose gestures and show of feelings were widely exposed, for their own sake. The details of the plot and its progression were not the most important aspect of the films; rather, the public was asked to enjoy the quality of the shooting, the clever matching or images and sounds and, above all, the perfect production of the most impressive scenes.

Actors, considered as figures, as bodies liable to be endlessly photographed, were central to modernism. This peculiarity often went unnoticed at the time because actors no longer personified well-defined characters, as was the case previously. And yet, the actors did not play empty, ill-defined roles, the social status of the protagonists was perfectly clear, as has been explained for *The Red Desert*, the characters were meant to have a job and were even portrayed carrying out their activities. Daily life was not forgotten but its impact on the fate of the characters was never clear. More importantly, these fictional people were deprived of conscience, spectators did not watch the world through their eyes and were not informed of their state of mind. It must be added that there was relatively little action in most movies. Fellini's *Cabiria's Nights* and *La dolce vita* were made up of different episodes which could have been edited in a different order without modifying the general trend of the movie. At the outset of the former film, Cabiria, a Roman prostitute, has just been cheated by a crook; when the film ends, she has again been deceived and she is all set to be abused many more times. Trying to 'understand' her would be useless since she is nothing but actress Giulietta Masina performing with various supporting actors in different sets. Antonioni's films were also modulations round a woman (usually Monica Vitti) and her relation to a man, another woman or even to herself. The characters were inserted in precise surroundings (an area of land devastated by industrial plants in *The Red Desert*) but it was up to the viewer to decide to what extent they were affected by their milieu. Long sequences of uncertainty, where 'nothing happened', appealed to the attention of the public because they seemed to contradict the strongly marked poles of exposition and social description which were always treated with care.

Plate 23 Monica Vitti in *The Eclipse* (1962, Michelangelo Antonioni)

Contemporary audiences were interested and puzzled, they wondered what these works were about. There was no answer to the query. However, it could have been argued that the films were about time, about cinema and about spectators. The stories often covered only a few days and the brief time span accentuated the dramatic tension. Antonioni's *La notte* (1961) begins one afternoon and ends at dawn. Its two leading characters are involved in different sub-plots and meet various people. Their life looks like that of Milan socialites. But the constant shifting from one to the other made it impossible to find continuity in their actions and the sudden introduction of long shots, which seem to alienate the protagonists from the scenery, create a distance between actors and spectators. What is depicted is not the routines of an ordinary night but the impossibility of showing that night, of making sense of even such a short period. Time is also abolished in Pasolini's *The Hawks and the Sparrows* (1966). It is questioned in *8½* where past, present and possibly future are muddled. Relaxing for a few days in a spa, that is, spending long empty hours in a dead city where people have landed up by chance and have nothing to do but wait for their departure, the protagonist of *8½* mixes up his activities, his dreams, his memories and his fantasies. This is not a trip into the past, a man's attempt to go over his life again. There is no chronological progression, various periods intermingle as if, time being frozen, the same person could be simultaneously adult and child. The exciting final parade, in which everyone in the protagonist's life, the living and the dead, form a circle and start to dance around him, represented as a young boy, could be considered a promise of rebirth, or a definitive confinement to childhood.

By refusing to adopt a consecutive order in which events follow regularly one after the other, the modern films offered their characters a wide range of options and trajectories. This is what Pasolini explored with *The Hawks and the Sparrows* when he made Totò, the comic actor, travel in a timeless space where different periods coexisted and where Totò, both a merciless landlord and a pitiful tenant, spoke the language of birds in medieval times and witnessed the expansion of cheap air travel. The three examples mentioned here show that there was no concerted effort to investigate the very nature of duration. Some directors were more interested in the significance of the moment, of any moment. Others pondered the weight of immobility. Still others fought against historical determinism. There were also personal inflections: Fellini's *Juliet of the Spirits* (1965) showed how a woman could free herself from her past. Pasolini's *Theorem* (1968) is a fable in which an emissary from nowhere metamorphoses, one after the other, the members of a family. What was at the core of these meditations was an interrogation on the function of rhythm in films. Narration was suspect because it offered a single-minded, logical view of things. But nobody was in a position to suggest an alternative solution, which explains why the same filmmakers could, successively, disturb and then re-establish a chronological order.

Modernism was therefore an inquiry on the potentialities of cinema, not a struggle to describe the world. The stories told in the films, the characters, the actors were used to scrutinize the mode of operation of the cinema. Marcello Mastroianni had the leading part in *La dolce vita*, *La notte* and *8½* in which he was respectively a journalist, a writer and a film director. Sociologists could say that, after depicting workers (*Rocco and His Brothers*, Antonioni's *The Cry*, 1957) and drop-outs (Fellini's *La Strada* (*The Road*), *The Swindlers* and *Cabiria's Nights*), modern filmmakers turned towards their own social group, middle-class intellectuals. This would be perfectly true but would merely explore the external appearance of the films. Mastroianni played the role of filmmaker Guido Anselmi in *8½*. But Anselmi himself, being unable to make a new film, plays the part of a creative director, ready to shoot again, in front of his producer, technicians, actors and friends. Bombarded with questions, he has to find the right way of answering without giving an answer – in other words of pretending. This was not very different from the role Mastroianni played in *La notte*. There, he was a novelist invited to parties where he had to behave as a novelist. Role-playing in ordinary life (the part we 'play' to give others an image of ourselves) has often been studied by sociologists. This is not what was at stake in the films mentioned here since Mastroianni was first and foremost an actor. The point was rather to illuminate the ficticious nature of theatrical or cinematic performances. Wittingly or not, modern cinema took the opposite course to Neorealism and warned its public that any film was a fabrication whose only reference was not life itself, but cinema. Fellini's title was itself a warning: having already completed seven feature length films and three shorts, the director was shooting his 'eighth and a half' movie. In contrast to offering an illusion of transparency, modern films stressed the importance of technical devices and practicalities. Instead of effortlessly operating his mental film of memories and fantasies, Guido Anselmi was brought back to reality by cinema itself, he was obliged to care about sets, script and actors, and to make it clear that filmmaking is a job, not a pastime.

Modern films were appreciated because they obliged their public to be very attentive, and they were criticized because they appeared too demanding. Following them demanded a deep involvement. Usually, they exposed a situation, but they seldom raised a precise, well-defined problem, and they never advanced a solution. We have noted that *8½* can reasonably be interpreted in totally opposed ways. Antonioni's films often portrayed a couple on the verge of breaking up, but the film ended before anything has been decided. Corrado, in *The Red Desert*, makes love to Ugo's wife and then leaves. What will happen to him and to the woman? Maybe nothing, because, after all, fictional heroes do not survive the fiction of which they are part. The characters in these films were not given an appearance of existence, they were kept aloof, silent, deprived of evident feelings, as if they only existed for and by way of the film camera. In some cases, it was even difficult to decide what was taking place on the screen. Who is the visitor who disturbs a quiet family in *Theorem*? An angel, a devil or a mirage? Has he upset them to make them better or worse? Biblical quotations suggest that he is sent by God, but who is this God who wants to destroy people? Commenting on this film, Pasolini said that 'each thing represents another'. Spectators had to find personally what denoted what, or to conclude that parables defy interpretation. The looseness of the plot, the lack of precise indications, the absence of final elucidation induced contrasting responses in the public. Viewers could forget the narrative to focus on the images themselves. The protagonists of *L'avventura* and *The Eclipse*, Totò in *The Hawks and the Sparrows*, roam at length in uncharacteristic surroundings. It is tempting to forget them and to let one's mind wander for a few minutes. But there is also, in these seemingly empty sequences, a profusion of stylistic marks likely to catch the spectator's attention. In *L'avventura*, a man, who is courting a young woman, begins to pet her and put his hand on her thigh. This shot is briskly interrupted by another shot of Monica Vitti looking at the couple; although the actress does not manifest any feeling, this second shot is rather long; then, the film goes back to the shot of the couple; both actors are exactly where they were at the end of the initial shot, as if the scene had not been interrupted by the picture of Monica Vitti. Here, one might be tempted to say that the timing is 'wrong', at least from a purely narrative point of view. The long shot of Monica Vitti has annulled the sexual tension created by the gestures of the man; it has also frozen the couple, whom spectators now see through the expressionless gaze of the actress. In another sequence in the same film, the male protagonist kisses Monica Vitti; the public sees her laughing, but there is no noise and it is only after a lengthy silent pause that the laughter can be heard. I do not want to give too many examples, I merely want to stress the distance between the unfolding of the fiction and its representation. Extended, attentive takes which imposed concentration and underplaying on the actors' part, abrupt breaks in the editing process, hazardous synchronization between images and sound seem to imply a dry, immeasurable distance from the characters. Spectators had to face what Noami Green has called a 'hermeneutic impulse . . . demanding a process of interpretation',[17] they were reminded that the actors play a role, that the noises are not real noises but recorded ones, put on the soundtrack to create an impression in their minds, and that it was up to them to decide whether they wanted to immerse themselves in the story or to take the fiction for what it is, that is to say merely a gripping, enjoyable fantasy.

VULNERABLE FATHERS, DANGEROUS WOMEN

In *L'avventura* and *The Eclipse*, Monica Vitti, playing the role of an independent woman, was the main character and that in itself was a novelty. Before the 1960s, women were seldom, if ever, given the leading role in Italian cinema. Films portrayed two distinct kinds of women which, separately and together, fulfilled a symbolic role. The first category, by far the most important, was the mother who carried the weight of continuity in family life. Women as mothers helped maintain men's sense of virility by enabling them to become fathers. A second group was made of *femmes fatales*, pleasure-loving and harmful. They were the image of the betrayal that men feared and the ones who usually ended up punished. Italian films had much to tell about men, women and relations between the sexes. But they did it in the framework of traditional family relations and they did not make gender an essential element for the development of their plot since women were always depicted in relation to men.

On the other hand, looking at the comedies, historical or mythological epics and westerns offered to the fourth generation of cinema-goers, we have found a different, rather critical vision of independent women involved in business and politics. We have noted that these stories, be they amusing, thrilling or melodramatic, accord little mercy to any female character cast in a role beyond that of obedient wife, tender mother or innocent daughter. Comedies often refer to situations, places and people of which spectators are more or less knowledgeable, and it could be claimed that, in the 1960s, amusing films mirrored some aspects of the emancipation of women. But epics or westerns, which were entirely fictional, could not bear any similarity to the social context. The perfectly autonomous woman, such as portrayed by Claudia Cardinale in *Once Upon a Time in the West* or Monica Vitti in *The Eclipse* – that is to say, the woman who lives on her own, bargains with men, runs her business very effectively, was an invention of the 1960s. Obstinate and tough, she was sometimes an object of desire (Claudia Cardinale or Monica Vitti) but more often of fear, which gave her an ambiguous status. In Dino Risi's comedy *The Widower* (1959) the wife, a tenacious businesswoman, does not conceal her dislike for her husband. Instead of playing the part of a relaxed winner, Alberto Sordi has the role of a miserable loser. *Last Tango in Paris* is about an ageing man who, having long been henpecked by his wife, falls for a younger woman; they have an affair, but she jilts and then kills him. The tragedy in the background of Visconti's *Of a Thousand Delights* (1967) was that, during the war, a man had been denounced to the Germans by his wife.

All these images, which were fairly commonplace, contained with them a violent tension. Why? It is always impossible fully to account for representations and what I am going to suggest is based more on assumption than on evidence. A first notable issue was the strong influence of Freudian psychoanalysis in Italian social and cultural life during the 1960s. Freud was translated much later into Italian than into other European languages but, within a decade, his vocabulary and most simple concepts were accepted even by people not interested in mental disorders. Journalism,[18] daily talks, art works were filled with Freudian ideas. Pasolini's *Oedipus Rex* (1967) explored a myth revisited by Freud. Instead of telling the myth as it is exposed in Greek tragedies, the filmmaker started from psychoanalysis; the sphinx, in his film, is a metaphor of Oedipus's unconscious that the protagonist censures by killing him; Oedipus is in fact aware of his own incestuous drive – so much so that, unlike the mythical hero, he is able to make love to his mother after learning who she is. *Medea* (1969), another film directed by Pasolini, evoked, according to Noami Green, Freud's exploration of 'the primal collective consequences of the Oedipus complex'.[19] Visconti's *The Damned* and *Death in Venice*, Bertolucci's *The Spider's Stratagem* and *The Conformist* pointed clearly to psychoanalysis. In the last-named a tormented intellectual offers his services as an assassin to Mussolini's secret police to overcome his Oedipus complex and assuage the guilt induced by his latent homosexuality. *8½* can be interpreted as a light-hearted homage to Freud. In this movie, Guido's dreams and fantasies have something of a mausoleum devoted to the commemoration of his infancy since the memory of his absent parents is always present on the screen. Behaving like a child, treating others as children, the character is looking for an ideal mother who will care for him and tell him what to do. His carnal thoughts are deliciously cut short by his mother, or by religious figures who seem to look upon him accusingly. Furthermore he has built up in his fantasies an incestuous relationship with his wife to such an extent that when kissing the latter's lips he imagines he is bending over his mother.

For two decades, playing with Freud was a fashion. Cinema was not alone in making psychoanalysis one of the most appreciated intellectual gadgets of the time, but it made a substantial contribution to it. There was, obviously, something more urgent and concrete than a mere fancy behind this infatuation with the unconscious and its operations. Athos Magnani, the protagonist of Bertolucci's *The Spider's Stratagem*, arrives in the village where his father was killed during the Fascist era. The father is regarded as a local hero, his name is to be found everywhere, in the streets and on buildings, but his murderer has never been unmasked. One night, Athos goes to the cemetery and destroys the inscription engraved in honour of his father. An 'Oedipal' attempt to eliminate the parent of the same sex? Presumably. But it soon transpires that the hero was in fact a traitor and that his political friends, having killed him, made his death into that of a martyr. What is striking, here, is the distance and the conflict between two generations. Past and present overlap in many films of the decade: kitsch or art deco were used not merely for the pleasure of re-creating the Italy of the late nineteenth century or of the 1930s, they helped to emphasize the inadequacy, the hopelessness of the previous age-group, especially of the fathers. Mastroianni witnesses the degradation of his fictional father in *La dolce vita* and buries him alive in *8½*. There is a defective father in *L'avventura*, a deficient mother in *The Eclipse* and unsound older characters in a good many movies.[20] Freud called the stories children tell themselves to modify imaginarily their ties with their environment 'family romances',[21] an expression which is relevant to many films of the 1960s. A simplistic version of psychoanalysis was an opportunity for a *mise-en-scène* of phantasies that viewers could accept or not, according to their own wishes. When watching *8½* or *The Spider's Stratagem*, spectators either tried to establish a chronological order in the constant inter-cutting of different periods, or found pleasure in oedipal conflicts consonant with their own mental structures.

In many cases, the invented fathers had failed because they were betrayed by women. An air of diffidence is perceptible in many films;

while it may not be found in Antonioni's, it is very common in other directors. Its most obvious function was to show that independent women were
likely to destabilize a gendered equilibrium rooted in male domination.
However, I do not think that we should link this up to the autonomy
recently won by female workers since few women carried any great responsibilities in their jobs. The roles attributed to Monica Vitti or Claudia
Cardinale in the above-mentioned movies were fanciful and did not reflect
the social division of tasks. Weak fathers and unruly women were inven-
tions, mirages which helped men define themselves by contrast. Now, this
is merely a hypothesis which cannot be proved. Historians can analyse
the ideological message of an art work, but they cannot describe ade-
quately how spectators felt and responded to these messages at the time.
And yet, they have to take into account images as recurrent as the ones
we have just studied.

WHERE IS ITALY TO BE FOUND?

Another theory might be that the filmmakers were settling old scores with
Mussolini. Apart from Francesco Rosi, whom we shall meet shortly,
Italian directors, not being politically committed, combined Fascism, the
period in which they had grown up, with their own family story. Fellini's
Amarcord (1973) was a nostalgic evocation of the Mussolini era in which
the protagonist's father, an anti-Fascist, was as ineffectual as the Fascist
leaders. Meanwhile Bertolucci, in *The Spider's Stratagem*, challenged by
implication all the members of the preceding generation. 'What have we
inherited? What do we look like today? How has Italy changed since we
were born?' might be the questions that cinematographers attempted to
answer.

   The assumption is supported by the fact that, from 1955 to 1975, filmmakers were motivated to an unusual degree by place. Previously, the
cinematic vision of Italy did not matter very much, it was used mostly as
a background. Films made after the middle of the 1950s, instead of being
grouped into themes or chronological clusters, could be divided into
locations. There are for instance, in Antonioni's films, the northern, rainy
movies (*The Cry*, *The Red Desert*) and the southern, sunny ones
(*L'avventura*, *The Eclipse*). The idea of looking at the scenery was a hall-
mark of the fourth generation of cinema-goers. Cinematic society was
described in terms of movement, and also of resistance to that movement.

   However, Italian directors did not made tourist films. Some of them
went so far as to show that Italy did not exist.[22] In *La strada*, Fellini
opened a window upon the land that lay behind the official face of the
country, the face usually presented to foreign visitors. An athlete,
Zampano, and his helpmate, Gelsomina, travel from village to village,

Plate 24 La strada (1954, Federico Fellini)

performing pathetic stunts for miserable audiences. They are both victims, incapable of understanding the conditions that have shaped them; Zampano is a brute concerned only with wine and fast women, Gelsomina is simple-minded. The film captures superlatively the simple things which interest them, the efforts and brief pleasures of a dull life. But the characters, who have lost touch with any form of culture and have failed to become assimilated into the universe of fairground entertainers, have no environment, in the proper sense of the word. They settle on waste ground and wander on noisy, potholed roads. Pasolini was even more critical, since his films nullified Rome itself. Exploring the shanty-towns on the edge of the Italian capital city, *Accatone* (1961) shows how their ugliness and neglected state cut the inhabitants off from other Italians. *The Hawks and the Sparrows* covers an ill-defined journey, a random wandering in an urban wasteland. Totò and Ninetto Davoli, playing a father and his son, make an engaging, bizarre pair, both naive and sardonic, who stroll through a fantasy desert made up of pictures taken in a real world, the outskirts of Rome. They meet various people who live apparently isolated, contingent lives and the purposelessness of their peregrinations illustrates the utter emptiness of the Eternal City.

Cinematic landscapes were not sets likely to enliven film plots, they were signs used because of their expressive value. The fact that panoramas were never shot for themselves is exemplified by the contrast between Antonioni

Plate 25 The Hawks and the Sparrows (1966, Pier Paolo Pasolini)

and Bertolucci who worked in the same area, the Po valley. For the former, this was the realm of dampness, of water dripping everywhere, of fog. The latter depicted the same region as the country of sun where the main danger was water, which prevented people from moving freely and in which they drowned (*Before the Revolution, 1900*). Bertolucci's radiant landscape was a symbol of timelessness. The world depicted by this film-maker was mostly rural, but his was a countryside without workers, a land where crops seemed to grow by themselves. It was therefore antitheti-cal to Antonioni's universe. *The Cry* and *The Red Desert* pictured a plain devoured by industrial wastes, marred by chimneys and derricks, over-shadowed by smoke. Antonioni's plain was as flat as Bertolucci's, but its uniformity was a threat, in the fog the least unevenness became a trap.

Films shot in actual locations, and intent on respecting the characteris-tics of the filmed areas, offered highly contrasting interpretations of Italian landscapes. On the one hand, there was the desert, urban or industrial, a Nature ruined by modernism. On the other, there was idyllic scenery. This is seldom as obvious as in *The Leopard*. One of delights of the film was the rich visual poetry of the dusty, the earthy and the sun-burnt. Making the shimmering heat, blinding light and stifling powder of the island palpable, Visconti did not seek to explain anything. The incandes-cence of the day was not a painful metaphor for the immobility of Sicily, it was merely an impression that the brightness of the screen was able to translate. The delicately lit interiors were occasionally offset by explosions of sunlit radiance in outdoor scenes where the wonderful, silent palaces

Plate 26 The Leopard (1963, Luchino Visconti)

were surrounded in an expanse of summer fields, or in vistas of beautiful gardens. If this film in which so little happens is rather long, it is because many shots were taken solely to celebrate, capture and enhance the beauty of nature – in other words to give pleasure. This film is one of the Italian cinema mourning glamourously the world that industry had destroyed.

I have lingered over *The Leopard* because it idealized Sicily. During their short Neorealist experience, Germi and Visconti gave a much more critical vision of southern Italy. In the 1960s, Francesco Rosi was almost the only director who continued in the same vein, which makes his works a special case. Some of his films produce the effect of documentaries. *Hands over the City* (1963) deals with speculation in housing in Naples. A building contractor, who fails to evict tenants from a district which might be a profitable housing estate, knocks down an empty building, thus causing adjoining structures to collapse. Involving bankers, industrialists, politicians, the media and even the Church, the action moves immediately from the housing estate, where demolition had already started, to the town hall where corrupt politicians are backing the contractor.

This was a courageous work but Rosi was more original in *Salvatore Giuliano* (1962) where he did not draw such a crude distinction between the criminals and the victims. Giuliano, a Sicilian bandit, was killed in 1950; since he was paid by the autonomists to murder policemen and by

Plate 27 Salvatore Giuliano (1962, Franceso Rosi)

the landlords to murder leftist country people, there were many people
who wanted him dead. Beginning with the discovery of the corpse, Rosi's
film shows that it is impossible to account for the murder, since the
whole structure of Sicilian rural society is more or less involved in it.
Modernist film codes, taken in this regard as a sense of indecisiveness,
are effectively used in this film. Many sequences are interrupted briskly,
as if it were impossible to conclude them. The film emphasizes its own
ambiguity by refusing to offer a clear explanation of events. Taking advantage of what was merely an incident, Rosi suggests that Sicily cannot be
understood on the basis of the simple opposition between backwardness
and modernization and that it is not easy to disentangle a complex
system where kinship and patronage prevail over class-based relationships.
His concerns were close to Germi's, but his radically different style reveals
how old-fashioned Neorealism had become for the younger generation of
Italian film buffs.

*

Italian audiences were offered many more domestic films and fewer American ones in the 1960s than in any other period in Italian film history. Their interest in film decreased slowly and steadily during that period, but that was part of a general shift towards other forms of amusement – sport, music, tourism, betting – which developed quickly as Italians had more money to spend. This was perfectly consonant with the widespread image of a sweet life. Politicians, be they Marxist or liberal, were optimistic about the effects of the 'miracle'. It was contended that most problems would be solved by modernization, with the expansion of a strong industrial sector and an affluent middle class, and by political democratization. Few people acknowledged the symptoms of social discontent apparent even in the economically active and affluent northern provinces. Collective unrest differed from that in many other European countries because it was more dispersed and easily camouflaged. For instance, the mass protest in 1968–9 had nothing to do with the French events of 1968 which were violent but short-lived. The effects of social uneasiness were felt for a long time, more than a decade in Italy. Open violence began late but it lasted longer and was more traumatic than in any neighbouring country.

It is important to stress the social context of the time, because it emphasizes the discrepancy between films and people's ongoing concerns. The mainstream cinema pictured a perfectly affluent world, even though it is true that it was extremely critical of it, but only from a moral point of view. Nobody is redeemed in *La dolce vita* and other contemporary films. Fellini's protagonist, Marcello, an uninspiring, unlovable man, is lost in an absurd world where money is the universal criterion. The final message is a lay version of Catholicism: having got too much wealth and comfort, we have lost our sense of values. Comedies, built on classical patterns, and 'modernist' films expanded upon the same themes. The evocation of beautiful old landscapes, the condemnation of ambitious women, were part of the same mourning of traditional ethical principles. However, apart from Rosi, nobody admitted that, whereas both its nature and its location had changed, poverty had not disappeared. In this respect, and whatever their aesthetic quality, films contributed to connecting the urban population with the standards of the market. The bulk of their public was a social group, the product of growing literacy, middle-class comfort and a booming entertainment industry, which was gratified to see its way of life represented on the silver screen and enjoyed the critical portrayal of the very rich given in the movies.

And yet, at a time when movies were very remote from the most urgent issues, a group of Italian filmmakers from the late-1950s to the mid-1970s took an active part in the radical changes to the codes and conventions of narrative cinema and was in the vanguard of modernist films. Although there was a plot and a few characters (however modified) in their pictures, there was now also an 'excess' which was not justified by the unfolding of the story. Many sequences looked purposeless. This did not, however, mean that they were boring, for spectators could either ignore them, or integrate them into their personal fantasies and mental associations. Themes or subjects were not dismissed but formal elements were more or less divorced from content. In the wake of these experiments, even 'popular' genres, like Eurowesterns, indulged in the same process and offered their viewers images and sounds which they could arrange in their own minds. Film magazines and exhibitors' publicity, which stressed the sophistication of these 'quality' movies, suggested a growing distance between the typical mainstream film, based on old models, and modernist works. There was a difference, but it was not as great as critics suggested. With rare exceptions, modernist films reached a large audience in cities. They contributed to making the public familiar with a different conception of the moving image. To put it another way, they introduced them to television.

Fifth generation
The world in the box

Italy is the only country where a businessman, Silvio Berlusconi, a television tycoon, was appointed Prime Minister because he was the owner of a widespread broadcasting network. Having set up local television stations in the late 1970s, Berlusconi managed to transform them into a powerful company, Fininvest. He organized his own publicity agency, he seduced the most famous announcers working for other companies, but his master stroke was to broadcast, albeit illegally, all over Italy. When the authorities reacted, much too late, and blackened the screens, there was a rebellion in the country. Since Italians had become used to the new network and did not want to give it up, the government was obliged to grant private companies the right to broadcast nationally. Local or national elections soon revealed a profound evolution in the electorate. While the old parties were stagnating, Berlusconi, who was new in politics, transformed Fininvest into a party machine and, within a few weeks, won over not simply naive citizens but also a large section of the most dynamic entrepreneurs, white- and blue-collar workers.[1]

A HUNDRED TELEVISION CHANNELS

Berlusconi was much more a symptom than a cause. The crisis, political as much as moral and economic, was largely responsible for the shift described above, but television played an important part. The fifth generation of cinema-goers, which reached its twenties in the 1970s, was born with television. When they were still in their infancy television broadcasting hours were at a minimum and television followed cinema's model. Evening schedules were planned around drama programmes which were, in fact, more like films so that spectators, in front of television sets watched more or less what they would have seen in a picture theatre. Broadcasting was then entirely controlled by the government. The RAI, the official network, received enough money to make reasonably good transmissions but avoided any topic likely to upset the authorities. The end of the public monopoly in 1975, the proliferation of local and national private companies (there were, in some periods, more than one hundred channels) from 1976 onwards, brought about far-reaching innovations. Broadcasting deregulation extended to most developed countries in the 1980s but nowhere was it as rapid and unsupervised as in Italy. The extension of transmission time to twenty-four hours a day, coupled with competition between channels, offered viewers a wide range of comedies, soaps, documentaries, musicals and talk-shows. This was part of what pessimists then called the 'commercialization of culture' which was also characterized by the diffusion of 'bin ends' – books which the publishers had difficulty in disposing of, made available at bargain prices – and cheap records, pressed in their thousands, paid for by the copies initially marketed, with the remainder sold off. In the 1980s, while radio and television transmitting stations were burgeoning throughout the peninsula, a dense network of bargain book and record shops covered all the major cities. Pop music had been around in Italy for two decades, but the fact that almost everyone, and especially the young, could listen to it was largely due to the spread of records and to the systematic broadcasting of video musicals.

Television was involved in a general process of profit-making. It was also directly implicated in the social and political evolution of the country. The late 1970s and the 1980s have been labelled 'the leaden years', the years during which there seemed to be no prospect for anyone. There was the economic recession and accompanying unemployment. But above all, there was the permanent threat created by terrorism. Coming from both Left and Right, violence is said to have claimed more than one thousand victims. It culminated with the kidnapping and murder of Aldo Moro, leader of the Christian Democrats (1978), and the bombing of the Bologna railway station which left eighty-five people dead (1980). Thanks to television Italians witnessed events while they were happening. The cameras were there when Moro's corpse was found in a car boot, and when the wounded were being evacuated from Bologna station. Terrorists cleverly used the potential offered by television. By broadcasting messages written by Moro and by issuing ultimatums to the state, they made people believe that they were much more powerful than they really were.[2]

Television was often castigated for its growing influence. It was argued that sometimes the television set stayed on the whole day, that television and video cassettes made available violent films characterized by extreme cruelty and that, because of the programmes on offer, lots of viewers, notably the less educated, were becoming keen on watching brutality in ways which were simultaneously shocking and entertaining. As had already happened with films, alarmists forecast a wave of crimes and other misdemeanours sparked off by images seen on the screens. A few filmmakers were also critical, in a less exaggerated manner. Exploring the backstage of a television show, Fellini's *Ginger and Fred* (1986) demonstrated that it was a world of barely controlled anarchy where anchormen were deficient, singers had no voice and jokes were so bad that they had to be telegraphed. A younger director and actor, Maurizio Nichetti, specialized in deriding television. The protagonist of one of his films, *The Bi and the Ba* (1986), knew only the language of television and was thus unable to talk sensibly. Another film, *The Icicle Thief* (1989), depicted a family enslaved by its TV who habitually mistook pictures for life and vice versa. In this film, by unexpectedly broadcasting a black-and-white film interlaced with commercials, a TV channel causes panic in this family of couch-potatoes. To make matters worse, the son continually channel hops, preventing his mother from following the story and his father from gazing hungrily at the advertising models.

The Icicle Thief was praised for its wit and its clever tricks, as for instance when the father, having entered by mistake into the black-and-white film shown on television, rescues a drowning woman who has fallen from a commercial and, helping her to get undressed, strips her of her colours. However, there was considerable disagreement about the pessimism of the film. Were there only passive spectators? Switched-on television sets, it was said, often attracted brief and intermittent attention, as was made clear in many films, for instance in Silvio Soldini's *The Quiet Air of the West* (1990) which opens and closes with televisual information on major events (for instance the students' revolt in China, the fall of the Berlin Wall) which the characters do not even notice. It was also noted, in the 1980s, that obscene words peppered the dialogue of many television programmes, because announcers were giving their audience what they thought it wanted. In this respect, it was not television which influenced its public but rather the opposite. Television was often accused of triggering violence, which was paradoxical since Italy has a long tradition of social and political unrest, stretching back to the Middle Ages. Far from being fascinated, people used to watching images are more inclined to prove sceptical and discerning. The media has helped investigating magistrates to expose Mafia power in political collusion. And when accused politicians were interviewed on television, in the early 1990s, their talks were attended to avidly by viewers who soon realized how they distorted or camouflaged their responsibility. It is not my task, here, to adjudicate between two incompatible opinions. All I want to recall is that technical innovations in the media have been accompanied by tremendous changes in public and even private life but that no one is in a position to evaluate the impact of the broadcast image on the public.

'A GIANT FILM SOCIETY, OPERATING 365 DAYS A YEAR'

Assessing the influence of television and video on cinema seems less haphazard. It is obvious that, in the 1980s, this combination of media swept

aside such monolithic channels of information as the press and modified
every type of communication. Producers and filmmakers bitterly accused
television of stealing their clientele. In the early 1990s, all Italian families
had at least one television set and, depending on the region where they
lived, could pick up twenty or thirty channels. At the same time, cinema
attendance decreased from 500 million tickets sold in the mid-1960s to
100 million in the 1990s. Several thousand small picture theatres closed
down in suburban, working-class areas (where there were a greater
number of television watchers); the 800 cinemas still running were concentrated in the biggest cities.

Film production had decreased since the 1960s, but not in the same proportion as attendance since Italy still made, on average, 100 films every
year. The main problem that the studios had to solve was how to sell
their work. Distribution was dominated by American companies, which
supplied 60 per cent of the exhibitors and favoured American films.
A third of Italian movies were never released and a third were only presented in down-town cinemas for a few days. Producers and filmmakers
contended that the television networks, which offered their public up to
100 films a week, were killing the cinema. However, their claim proved
that they did not understand the important sociological changes under-
gone by the cinema buff between the 1960s and the 1980s. Spectators, in
the fifth generation, belonged in the main to the middle class and were
mostly young and had a secondary school education. They did not despise
television, they bought or hired video cassettes and CD, and felt at home
in the 'commercialized' culture. Unlike the members of the fourth generation, they were neither highly interested in the history or theory of
cinema nor fond of intellectual, sophisticated films. What they liked most
were American spectaculars, *Jurassic Park*, *Forrest Gump* and *Batman
Forever*, whose marketing was carefully prepared by the American distri-
buting companies, down to the colour of the posters and the merchandis-
ing (plastic dinosaurs, Batman bubble baths, Batman T-shirts) that went
with it and which often brought as much profit as the films themselves.
In the 1960s, Italian films took much more money, on the domestic
market, than their American counterparts. But in the 1990s, 70 per cent
of the gross box-office takings went to Hollywood. However, when watching a film on television, spectators, be they cinema-goers or not, preferred
Italian productions. Engaged in fierce competition, the various channels
filled their schedules with not only American sit-coms but also old,
previously forgotten, Italian films or 'classics'. Gian Piero Brunetta once
said that Italy had become 'a giant film society, operating 365 days a
year'[3] and it is true that, thanks to the small screen and cassettes, spectators who did not conceive of themselves as cinema buffs were much
more acquainted with the past and the evolution of the cinema than any
previous generation. Without television, most studios would have been

obliged to close down. It was first the intervention of the RAI and then the rise of independent networks, unable to produce their own pro-grammes, which gave cinema a second chance.[4] In 1990, to take but one example, a third of the films shot in Italy were financed, partly or in whole, by a television channel. Antonioni, who wanted to experiment with colour, was offered an opportunity by the RAI to shoot *The Mystery of Oberwald* (1980). Money did not go only to famous directors: television channels enabled newcomers like Maurizio Nichetti or Gabriele Salvatores to make their first film. What is more, the enormous increase in domestic consumption of films through home video created a new market for the films.

Thus, the birth of another kind of demand, unconnected with picture theatres, at first sight seems to explain this large number of new films issued every year. The situation was, in fact, more complicated. Television channels were extremely cautious and did not back a project unless its success was assured. The RAI refused Daniele Luchetti's *The Footman* (1991),[5] the story of a corrupt politician, because it was likely to create problems at a time when magistrates were investigating crooked MPs. It also rejected Bertolucci's *The Last Emperor* (1987) on the ground that it would be too expensive: however, Bertolucci easily found an American producer. Luchetti had recourse to Sacher, a firm created by Nani Moretti, although, given the success of his film, he might just as well have founded his own company as did Silvio Soldini who financed some of his own films. However, while Luchetti's *The Footman* did very well, many other films were never distributed. How was it possible to meet the cost of a film, however poor its reception? A law, passed in 1965, granted a state subsidy of 30 per cent of the budget of a film made by profit-sharing asso-ciations. Producers were quick to take advantage of these arrangements. By presenting to the authorities statements which included actors' and technicians' salaries which in fact had not been paid, they got enough money to pay for the film stock, equipment and developing. In exchange, the copies were deposited in a public office which was unable to make use of them. Practically speaking, they were lost for ever. The system was alternately praised because it prevented the Italian cinema from sinking and criticized because it enabled anybody to shoot unmarketable products.

I am not in a position to decide between these judgements. But it must be made clear that it was the small coterie of those involved in filmmaking which helped to maintain a high level of production and that this con-tributed to strengthening the links between directors, technicians and actors. We have seen that, in the 1960s, many films questioned the very nature of cinema and asked questions about why and how movies were made. In the 1980s, films still talked about films but, for them, shooting was nothing more than the daily routine of the studio. Antonioni's *Identification of a Woman* (1982) was released two decades after Fellini's

8½. In Fellini's film, a director, who is about to shoot a science-fiction movie, is invaded by doubts about himself and his work and gives up. In Antonioni's movie, a filmmaker, who has received an offer from a producer to make whatever pleases him, tells his scriptwriter: 'I don't know yet what it's going to be, but the protagonist will be a woman.' Not having found the woman he needs he opts, after quite a long wait, for a work of science fiction. Like Antonioni's protagonist, cinematographers had no crisis of conscience in the 1980s. In their view, filmmaking was a job, not a mission. They felt all the less anxious because they worked in a narrow sphere of people all involved in the same business. Actor–director Maurizio Nichetti had the role of a film director in his *Icicle Thief*, Nani Moretti was himself, that is to say a film director and an ordinary citizen, in *Dear Diary* (1993) and he played the main part in Luchetti's *The Footman*. Playwrights like Nino Marino or Gabriele Salvatores transposed their plays for the silver screen. Stage actors such as Roberto Benigni or Massimo Troisi adapted their shows for the cinema. The opinion of their peers was what mattered most for those who worked in the film studios.

Unlike their predecessors, actors and filmmakers in this period, eclipsed by sportsmen and pop stars, were seldom famous. Only two, Roberto Benigni and Nani Moretti, made a great reputation for themselves. Undoubtedly they were excellent actors. Resourceful and witty, Roberto Benigni won international acclaim thanks to his performance in Jim Jarmusch's *Down by Law* (1989); spectators were impressed not so much by what he was or what he said as by how he said it. His humour and comic sensibility were not a matter of making puns, they were more akin to nonsense or surrealism as, for instance, when he broke from a walk into seemingly insane gesticulation. The words he utters were often incomprehensible, his speech, delivered in a rush, sounded like a strange, musical incantation. As for Moretti, he conveyed his characters as much by the apparent insensitivity of his face as by his talk. Exploiting the audience's attentiveness triggered by close-ups, he murmured, or even simply mouthed the words, thus creating a bizarre rhetoric of silence. Such inventiveness made the most predictable situations look singular and slightly frightening. But that was not enough to confer on Benigni or Moretti an exceptional stature, there were other good actors in the 1980s, and the filmmakers of that generation often produced films that relied on voicing, inflection and tonality rather than on action. What made these two men so representative of their generation was their multifarious activities in the performing arts. We have already met Moretti and his numerous enterprises. Benigni was above all an inventive performer who succeeded in making films like *Weeping Is All We Have Left* (1984), where slapstick mixed with television and stage with cinema. Combining the functions of actor and director, both cinematographers aroused curiosity and even sympathy among people no longer interested in films and contributed to maintaining a positive image of the cinema in an era of television.

THE POWER OF SPEECH

Film producers soon understood that they had to compromise with television and, willy-nilly, they began to work with this situation always at the back of their minds. In its first two decades, television broadcast exclusively programmes shot with film cameras and tended to emulate the cinema. Lightweight video equipment opened up new possibilities that the technicians were quick to explore. In their wake, filmmakers had to adapt to the particularities of the medium. The spread of domestic video equipment also had a direct impact on television. Individuals were invited to create their own sound and pictures, which modified their relationship with their television set and accustomed them to watching more familiar, less elaborate images. Television companies and authors tended to issue films to satisfy this new kind of competent audience so that traces of domestic video could be observed in countless movies. In the first part of *Dear Diary*, Moretti shows a collection of pictures apparently taken at random (in fact immensely sophisticated) by an amateur riding around a deserted midsummer Rome on his Vespa. The middle of Gianni Amelio's *The Stolen Children* (1982) is filled with a family celebration which resembles a video made by the eldest brother; and the director purposely introduced in his film short scenes made with passers-by. Daniele Luchetti shot *The Week of the Sphinx* (1991) like a layman who films directly, without any prospect of editing his takes. Figuring in many films, where it was merely a piece of scenery, television influenced Italian filmmakers in four main ways: the pre-eminence of words over images, the insistence on close-ups, the choice of bright colours, and the adoption of a reporterage style of shooting.

Television, with its endless talk-shows, compels viewers to reflect on the importance of speech, but there is much more than that in the cinematic interrogations about language and its functions. Introducing a proliferation of words derived from English, slang and neologisms into the daily vocabulary of the young, pop culture has created a tension in the spoken word itself, and in the attention that listeners pay to it.[6] This has resulted in violence towards standard Italian which, in turn, has reopened the old debate about regional dialects. This is why in the 1980s some directors, taking their characters from different parts of the peninsula, were keen to use local idioms, while others attempted to question the very power of speech. The Taviani brothers were the first to define clearly the problem with their *Father and Master* (1977). A young Sardinian boy wants to go to school but his father obliges him to look after his sheep in the mountains, partly because he cannot afford a shepherd, but mostly because he thinks that an educated child will be less obedient. The film movingly depicts the fight of a loving, respectful son to free himself from both his family and his island by learning Italian. What was impressive in the Tavianis' film was the straight connection between power and language, a theme that other contemporary filmmakers attentive to far-reaching issues, political and social, explored on a much wider scale, but none more convincingly, accepting the uncertainty with which words overlay events. 'What do we know?' was a recurring query of the 1970s and 1980s. Re-examining an old case such as that of Lucky Luciano, Francesco Rosi, in a film of the same name (*Lucky Luciano*, 1973), played with the contradictory statements made about this mysterious man. A police superintendent, protagonist of another of his films, *Illustrious Corpses* (1976), investigates the death of a group of magistrates in Sicily and finds that everybody, even those who hate the Mafia, abides by the law of silence. Social conflicts were at stake here, but also individual choices and personal concerns. Having gathered at the death of their mother, the main characters of Rosi's *Three Brothers* (1981), however fond they are of each other, admit that they are miles apart in their manner of making sense of the world.

Fascism offered an ideal field for exploring the relationship between discourse and authority. While Rome was mobilized to welcome Hitler and celebrate *A Special Day* (1977), Scola imagined that two outcasts, a housewife and an homosexual, have a brief encounter. Rosi's *Christ Stopped at Eboli* (1979) follows a political exile sent to a distant township of southern Italy. What about speech in these films of the late 1970s? It is at the same time weak and overwhelming. Weak because people are not interested in Mussolini and because the characters do not seem concerned about the ceremonies of Fascism. Cinematic devices emphasize the extraneousness of discourse. A loudspeaker comments upon the parade in Scola's film, but it is inaudible. While one of Mussolini's talks is transmitted by radio in Rosi's movie, the camera moves down a hill, from a point of view which could be that of none of the inhabitants, telling us that Il Duce's voice fills a deserted space. Still, however empty they are, Mussolini's words have a strong impact on people's lives. They are used by those who want to exert authority, by the husband of Scola's housewife to justify his machismo, by the police to send the homosexual into exile, by leading citizens to justify and legitimize their social influence. At a time when television's audience was booming, filmmakers were keen on pointing out that speech is a major instrument of power.

THE GAZE OF A VIDEO CAMERA

Cinematic dialogue generally goes with pictures taken near the subject and thus is large in scale. However, the commonest framing, in film, is 'from

Plate 28 Interview (1987, Federico Fellini): a television close-up on the silver screen

the knees up'. Close-ups look uncanny because we are used to perceiving any form against a background and seldom see an object deprived of context. Close-ups are therefore exceptional in cinema, they are either a single vastly enlarged detail in which one face comes forward to underline a state of mind or a magnified object which stresses the importance of one point in comparison with the rest. On the other hand, close-up is the standard format on television. The usual framing is of a part of the human body, especially a face, shot by a camera set as close to the head as possible, which introduces a radical change in the representation of living beings. This device is justified by the social use of television, a domestic appliance which, like radio, must be perceived by people who cannot stay in front of it; it is conceived as a talking medium, even in its most fictional programmes. Television stories seem akin to cinematic fictions in which the meaning is conveyed by dialogue but on closer examination the difference becomes obvious. Since most television programmes are long-lasting chats, what people do does not really matter. But, when spectators take a glance at their set, it is essential to give them an impression of authenticity. For that purpose, operators do their best to catch a face and keep it within the frame. This kind of inquisitive glance gives spectators a special feeling, the larger the image, the more they believe themselves to be directly involved. The intrusive, and falsely confidential nature of close-ups, as they are shot on television, was perfectly understood by Daniele Luchetti. His film *The Footman* deals with a naive young man (the part was played by Nani Moretti) who assists a Minister devotedly until he realizes how corrupt this man is. The film was a success as much for its clever, challenging framing as for its political innuendo. In the opening sequences, medium-distance shots give the politician a kind of dignity, the young man feels comfortable when contemplating his good-looking boss. Later, the camera gets closer and closer to the face of the Minister. He goes on telling lies but, irrespective of what is said, the pictures expose his dishonesty. Since keeping a face in the centre of a frame is difficult, the screen becomes a surface of fragmentation and recomposition. As a result, the politician is decomposed by the actions of shooting.

Luchetti exploited his framing to trap the Minister, but other directors used close-ups to give their actors more freedom. The paradox of television is that its long-lasting shots may either lock up people or liberate them. The camera attempts to fix and scrutinize those who are interviewed but these people, being unaware of the limits of the frame, constantly move and tend to escape. This permanent chase, which makes television unpredictable and prevents it from becoming boring, was imported into the film studios in the 1980s. In *Giulia in October* (1985), Silvio Soldini, following Giulia, who has just broken with her lover, separates his dialogues, dense and coherent, from his split-up, fragmented images. The character seems blocked by her talk, which harks back to the past, while her body is longing for a still indistinct future. Benigni's comedies, whose plot was usually rather banal, delighted their public because the ever-present flow of words appeared to be searching for the actor's unstable, vanishing mouth. In these movies, directors succeeded in presenting limbs, or fragments of faces, as qualities of life. Any countenance was, obviously, a battlefield for emotions but the camera could also suggest passing feelings by transcribing the folds of a cheek or a wink. Taking advantage of what was, initially, a drawback, cinematographers shifted from the traditional representation of fictional characters to unpredictable insights into human bodies.

The end of the state monopoly on broadcasting (1975) was immediately followed, on the one hand, by the introduction of colour on television, and, on the other, by the proliferation of private networks financed by advertisements. Pepino Ortoleva has rightly suggested that the division black-and-white/colour, far from being purely technical, became then the symbol of a strong opposition between highbrows and lowbrows.[7] We have seen how many famous directors reluctantly adopted colour film in the 1960s. These people thought that this was a question of taste but there was much more to it: black and white symbolized austerity, colour

Plate 29 Roberto Benigni in *The Voice of the Moon* (1990, Federico Fellini)

was seen as equivalent to affluence, it was emblematic of the kind of consumption represented in adverts. From 1976 on, it became impossible not to shoot in colour. Sooner or later, young cinematographers working alternately for television and cinema would have made experiments in the use of colour, but it was a veteran, who had built his reputation on the rigour of his takes, Michelangelo Antonioni, who, at the very beginning of the 1980s, dared base one of his last movies on the artificiality of video colours. The choice, for *The Mystery of Oberwald*, of an hackneyed story, the impossible love between a queen and an anarchist, liberated Antonioni from the necessity of relating an anecdote. Shooting on video (the tape was then transferred onto film) he literally composed in colours. His frames were living pictures where motions transformed the relationship between tints. It was for instance an ochre halo, generated by the brown dress of the queen, which, spreading through a room, enlivened the body of the anarchist but, stopping against the chalky grey of another wall, created an illusion of volume on a flat surface. Antonioni's boldness shocked many spectators; they made fun of a few details, particularly of the passage where the traitor offered a rose, which suddenly blackened. Since everybody knew from the outset that this man was the baddy, the device was not a sign but a way of modifying the balance of colours. The red rose matched the pink wall in the background and contrasted with the dark brown suit of the traitor. When it blackened, the same rose divided the frame into two parts, the dark one (suit and furniture) and the light one (pink wall).

How far is it possible to search for new procedures and when does investigation turn into repetition? Antonioni's was a unique attempt. Ninchetti explored another solution when he matched two kinds of visual artefacts, black and white and video colours in *The Icicle Thief*. He was less happy when he combined cartoons and living actors. However astute it was, his *Volere volare* (1993), in which he himself seduced a pretty actress by becoming a cartoon character, looked too much like a late imitation of *Who Framed Roger Rabbit?* to enthuse spectators.

Italy was not capable of emulating the United States in the creation of special effects. The limited success of *Volere volare* induced producers rather to play with the very peculiar range of tints offered by the video camera. Cinematic colours are artificial and never reproduce natural colours. Television, whose spectrum is limited because it is merely a combination of the three primary colours, exaggerates this falsity. There is a specificity of the small screen built on bright, contrasting, excessive tints which provide television programmes with part of their dynamism. Film-makers who appropriated video shot their movies as they would have shot commercials. Organizing several sequences, and even entire movies, around one coloration, Moretti built *Small Red Dove* (1989), the beginning of *The Mass Is Over* (1985), and the second episode of *Dear Diary* (1993) on an intense blue which made water and sky look like postcards. The device was very effective in the first of these films where an electric blue, akin to those used in adverts, was the backcloth for a funeral oration about the fading of the red (read: of communism). As was the rule in commercials or video musicals, discordant tints were assembled and then briskly separated so that, for a few seconds, the shifting of colours substituted for the action or dialogue of the characters. In contrast with commercials, colour films had a plot-line, but the visual tricks borrowed from advertising, particularly the lighting and colour effects, immersed spectators in the familiar realm of posters, magazines and promotion.

MEN, YEARS, LIFE

As its name makes clear, cinematography was the art of writing with motions, of transcribing motions, its narrative put together a series of gestures ordered according to a spatial and temporal logic. On the other hand, the small screen, because it is small, offers no depth of field. It is not fit for quick, extended action such as horse chases, which it tends to blur, it has neither breadth nor volume. Classical films did not merely attempt to suggest imaginary distances by linking each shot to those which came before and after, they also created a mental world thanks to fictional characters who told, or participated in, the events, and they seldom departed from a model long ago described by Aristotle: initial situation, crisis, resolution. The main television categories cannot follow these patterns. Serials, which must go on endlessly, never come to a conclusion. Documentaries do not need an imaginary witness to explain what is displayed on the screen because they claim that they offer an outsider's neutral glance at a problem or event. Broadcast live or hastily edited before being transmitted, factual films line up different, loosely connected pictures that the public will associate according to its own mood. Serials and documentaries embody what Francesco Casetti has called the 'magnification of daily life'; both stress the importance of small details, of customs and routines, of the context people have created around themselves.[8]

It is no wonder that in the 1980s young filmmakers, who knew that their work would be broadcast, willingly accepted this kind of immediacy. But even older directors found it stimulating. In the 1960s, Ermanno Olmi and Michelangelo Antonioni were poles apart in their conception of cinema. The former tried to maintain the inheritance of Neorealism in his close study of social situations, the latter explored the limits of audiovisual story-telling. Their receptiveness to stylistic innovations is all the more remarkable in that they did not need it to acquire a reputation. Olmi's *The Tree of the Wooden Clogs* (1978) was an attempt to make a report on traditional rural life in the Po valley, at the end of the nineteenth century. As in most documented accounts, there was practically no story.

Plate 30 Identification of a Woman (1982, Michelangelo Antonioni)

Olmi shot on location, in natural light, and he was content to provide glimpses of the activities of five families, of their hard work and their festivities. Antonioni chose debutant actors for *Identification of a Woman*. Accompanying them in casual wanderings through different places and social circles, he often let them ad-lib and he cared neither when their rendering was awkward, or when they made gestures or said things which seemed inappropriate. The directness, the informality of the film made a striking contrast with Antonioni's previous works in which every line of dialogue was carefully calculated.

Whatever the respective qualities of their film, which were fairly different, Olmi and Antonioni help us delineate the main characteristics of television-style films. The narrative pretext around which these films developed was rather weak. Vague denominations, *The Family*, *The School*, *The Church*, *The Station* were so common that lots of films could have borrowed the evasive title chosen by a small Milan producer, Gianikan, for one of his quickies: *Men, Years, Life*. Let us take just a few of the above-mentioned films. Ettore Scola's *The Family* (1987) randomly follows the life of a middle-class Roman from his childhood to his old age; Daniele Luchetti's *The School* (1995) depicts a handful of adolescents, both sexually mature and socially immature, looking for individual support from their teachers but collectively refusing to learn anything. What matters is the community: the group of relatives in Scola's film, the class in Luchetti's; individuals are of little importance. Moretti's *The Mass Is Over* recreates the lives of a group of neighbours or friends in a suburban district of Rome, with the kind of domestic detail that is necessarily captured by a camera following the characters around an inhabited house. Starting from an anecdote about Italian adventurers operating in Albania, Gianni Amelio's *Lamerica* (1994) is a report on that country after the fall of Communism. A series of brief shots, filled with violent gestures and backed by a cacophonous soundtrack, evokes a ruined place, where people survive by cheating or killing. The narrative of *The Quiet Air of the West* (1990) describes the life of four different people over a few days without trying to establish any relationship between them. Its field of observation encompasses separate entities only, on which it provides unconnected details.

However, television films were not naive documentaries. They tried to win over their public by introducing elements of fiction in their narration. There is a story – four stories – in *The Quiet Air of the West* and there is even a trace of suspense, since all characters are offered a chance to modify something in their lives. But the film, in a documentary manner, only proposes elements of these people's concerns and activities, intercut with unmotivated shots of the surroundings that suggest an atmosphere, a place and a time (Milan in 1989). None of these shots is related to the four men and women who give the film its main thread. *The School* deals mostly with the problems of teenagers but, at times, devotes a sequence to Professor Vivaldi, a middle-aged bachelor, caught between his fondness for his pupils and his silent, hopeless love for his colleague, Professor Maiello, an unhappily married woman. There are shocks and turns, violent or start-ling shots in *Identification of a Woman* or Moretti's *Bianca* (1984). In both films, threats, anonymous phone calls, mysterious disappearances, give some sequences the flavour of a thriller, but death happens off screen, beyond the confines of the film: there is no dramatic effect in this. *Dear Diary* comprises three episodes, the third of which perfectly exemplifies this combination of personal involvement and documentary coldness. Starting from his own experience, Moretti satirizes the pharmaceutical industry and medical profession as he goes from specialist to specialist and is given contradictory opinions and expensive prescriptions, before his real illness is diagnosed.

While mocking doctors, Moretti also makes fun of himself. His is the story of a man whose health gets worse and worse but who is unable to make himself heard. However, despite the tragic theme, the plot devices with their misunderstandings seem to have been lifted from some light comedy. A touch of humour, a smile rather than a laugh make the charac-ters slightly ridiculous and prevent the public from taking them too seriously. Vivaldi, the small, clumsy professor in *The School*, challenges a tall, strong young man who refuses to let his girlfriend go to school. The girl finally complies, to avoid a clash, and Vivaldi goes back into the school to the enthusiastic applause of his pupils, as if he had knocked out the boyfriend.

Strolling on a beach, Michele (Moretti himself), the protagonist of *Bianca*, sees myriads of couples, and only couples, lying on the sand; he notices a woman who is alone and lies on top of her, thus arousing every-body's indignation. Michele could have been tragic or moving, like any people with inadequate personalities. He turns out, at the end of the film, to be a serial killer, but the film takes no interest in his motives and only stresses his self-centredness. The narrative drive is produced by the con-trolled release of bits of information which do nothing to help form an image of the psychology of the character. Films like that one, shot in documentary manner, aspire to look like circumstantial accounts; they treat their spectators as watchers who can observe but do not get involved in what is being presented on the screen. In *Bianca*, Michele is used to scrutinizing the world from his window or from his balcony, which frames the scenery like the border of a TV screen. If the film is often tense, tension is generated not by dramatic events but by this endless, obsessional contemplation. Close-ups are the ideal medium for such work since they give no scope for spectators to imagine a spatial relationship between objects and people, and limit the film's horizon to scattered elements. The absence of interaction, the disconnection, makes it difficult to get fully involved in the story.

However, stylistic devices always stress the fact that these films were fictions, not documentaries. A couple of seconds of slow motion, the unhurried pace of a sequence, make a moment distinct. Unexpected transitions from one place to another, infrequent but effective musical sounds, remind spectators of the artificial, or artistic character of the films. Most films made in the 1980s and early 1990s were intended to be suitable for television, partly because broadcasting was the best way of finding an audience but mostly because many directors, long used to watching television programmes, had learnt something from the small screen. Television, then, had a strong impact on the cinema; it induced filmmakers to care more for aspects of daily life, filmed at length, without haste, than for elaborate, carefully planned stories. New ways of framing, of using colours changed the look of films, blurring the distinction between film and television fictions.

THE FILM SHOW IS OVER

The opening credits of *The Mass Is Over* are followed by a few shots of a handsome young man swimming at a Sicilian beach. Then, accompanying the protagonist to Rome, spectators realize that he is an idealist priest who conceives of his role as part social-worker, part soul psychiatrist. They discover also how limited his resources are in the face of the apathy and indifference of his parishioners. This was a film of ferocious confrontation. What role was left to a priest in a predominantly secular culture? Such pessimism was in tune with the mood of many contemporary films. *Small Red Dove* might have been titled *A Farewell to Communism* but it was too late when Moretti shot it in 1989. Five years earlier Enrico Berlinguer, the Communist leader who attempted to integrate his party into the political life of the country, died and forty directors contributed to *Farewell to Enrico Berlinguer*, a curious collection of moving testimonies and grandiloquent eulogies. In his *Small Red Dove*, Moretti plays the part of a Communist who, having lost the key to something, wonders who he is, who his comrades are and whether they are like other Italians, or somehow different. Moretti's films illuminated the changing meaning of religious or political affiliation in a period of far-reaching transformations. It is necessary to compare them, briefly, with *The Hawks and the Sparrows*. In Pasolini's film, the protagonists, Totò and Ninetto, meet a raven, who is a fierce Marxist theoretician, and a group of Franciscans. The former invites all sparrows to unite against the hawks, the latter wants the hawks to fraternize with the sparrows. Spectators understood, at the time of the film's release, that these were not realistic ways of improving human relationships, but the film was more ironical than providing a message that was disillusioned or resigned. In the 1980s, there were no strong political convictions and therefore no speeches to ridicule. The discourse of the corrupt politician in *The Footman* did not rest on any principle, it was merely an act of seduction, a series of empty words which did not try to convey any message. Luchetti's film was rather cynical; others, like Moretti, were more passionate, but there was agreement among film-makers: ideologies were dead, films could no longer debate ideas.

Filmmakers who deplored the end of strong convictions were not content with depicting individuals striving to live in a society of lost causes; they mourned the cinema as well. A good many films of the 1980s could be gathered under the general heading of 'Requiem for the Cinema'. The glamour of the studios, as depicted in these films, is unsurpassed. The Taviani brothers' *Good Morning, Babylon* (1987) brought back to life, around the mythical figure of D.W. Griffith, the prodigious excitement aroused by the birth of the cinema, while Fellini's *Interview* (1987) sumptuously evoked Cinecittà in its glorious years. Filmmakers assumed that what had made such a miracle possible was the passion of myriads of film buffs. Tornatore's *Cinema Paradiso* (1987) and Scola's *Splendor* (1989) recall how happy spectators were when, every week, they chose their programmes and then flocked into their favourite picture theatre. All these films consciously depict the cinema as a dream-machine full of mystery and enthusiasm, kindness and illusion, which in the past had offered prodigious vistas, and let strange animals stroll beneath evergreen trees. By contrast, television, as it was presented in *Ginger and Fred*, is all chaos, a row of corridors where nasty people ridicule and destroy one another. Fellini was exceptionally good in featuring a colourful, paradisical cinema studio as well as mocking a mean, grey, noisy broadcasting station. Tornatore and Scola were more interested in the reverse side of cinema, public display; they portrayed the close relationship between exhibitors and clients, and explained why the cinemas had been a shelter and a wonderland for three successive generations.

Filmed nostalgia was not limited to the fading cinema, it was a dominant trend of Italian films in the 1980s. When *The Tree of the Wooden Clogs* won a series of awards, critics who acknowledged its formal qualities protested because, far from accurately documenting traditional rural life, the film glorified a mythical, idyllic community which had never existed. Other directors were less ambiguous when they openly admitted that theirs was a fanciful vision of an idealized past. In Fellini's *And the Ship Sails On* (1983) the crowned heads and celebrities of 1914 Europe are embarked on a cruise that is a modern version of the Flying Dutchman. Cars and factories do not mar Pupi Avati's Emilia in *Story of Boys and Girls* (1989), the film features a city and a countryside not yet standardized where rituals still help everybody to identify the social group to which he or she belongs.

It is always chancy to interpret recurring tendencies like this sentimental depiction of the good old days, so what I am going to suggest is highly arguable. We have noted that, in the 1960s, film screens were overwhelmed by sexuality, not to say pornography, and that films portrayed flamboyant, dangerous women. Sex was virtually excluded for the next two decades. There were also few women, and even so they were merely a vanishing image or a sexual object.[9] Often, in films dealing with contemporary themes, those of Amelio, Moretti, Luchetti for instance, the male protagonist is simply not very interested in sentimental relationships. Love intervenes mostly in films whose action takes place in a bygone age and it is depicted in a romantic, dreamlike manner. Attending the engagement of their son and brother in a far-away village, the two middle-class women of *Story of Boys and Girls* have fantasies about short, intense affairs with countrymen: their fancies are harmless and only incidental to the story. The impact of the dominant (American) cinema must not be underrated in this matter. Female stars, at that time, came low on Hollywood's scale; the highest paid actors were action heroes: what appealed more to Italian audiences was one-man-army and lone-rebel films.

Did Italian cinema, unwittingly, adapt to the prevailing pattern? Or was there a concomitant evolution on both sides of the Atlantic? The question cannot be answered unless we take into account one of the most important trends of film criticism at the end of the twentieth century, namely feminism. Developed first in Britain and the United States, feminism reached Italy rather late, in the mid-1980s but, thanks to the permanent exchanges between Italian-Americans and their country of origin, it expanded quickly in the peninsula, was extensively debated in cultural circles or workshops organized by local authorities and prompted Italian women to criticize the classical cinematic pattern centred on male characters whose gaze literally produced the female body.[10] The spread of feminism swept offensive exhibitions of female nudity from the silver screen. It contributed also to questioning the pre-eminence traditionally given in films to the love quest culminating in the wedding. It is a point the previous generation had already tackled, but in a purely cynical, derisive way. The fifth generation did not conceal sex, it even mentioned it bluntly, when for instance Amelio built up *The Stolen Children* (1982) around the case of an eleven-year-old girl forced into prostitution by her mother, but the scabrous things were only spoken of, not shown, and were got through as quickly as possible.

The cinema of the 1980s was serious and moralizing. It did not offer solutions, but it attempted to make spectators look at the shortcomings of the period. Unlike its predecessor of the 1960s, which portrayed a carefree society, it stressed the problems that contemporaries had to face. Banal though it was, *The School* illustrated the failure of the educational system. Adopting a seemingly neutral, objective manner, *The Stolen Children* followed its eleven-year-old girl and her brother all over Italy, from Milan to Sicily, and showed that sending them to a reformatory did not compensate for a childhood totally deprived of parental care.[11] Both movies tried to ease the panic felt by many adults faced with anxious, sometimes hostile adolescents. Exploring faces, clothes, seemingly insignificant gestures, in a television-like fashion, these films induced their spectators to care more about the motivations of the young and their state of mind than about their misdeeds.

Starting from individual experiences, the ethical reflexion developed in movies wavered between the representation of actual events and the construction of imaginary ones. The Taviani brothers opened the way when their *Father and Master* transformed the memoirs of a Sardinian writer into a parable about speech and domination. They went farther with *The Night of San Lorenzo* (1982). Here, the destruction of a Tuscan village by the Germans in 1944 offered a chance to ponder personal choices in war-time. The two directors imagined that, having been told that the Germans would destroy their houses but spare the church, the villagers split up, some of them departing, others remaining. What made people join one or the other of the conflicting camps? Traditional answers are ideology or interest. In the film, there is no political debate and both options turn out to be equally hazardous. The filmmakers were mostly concerned with the schisms that occur within a community during a period of unrest and stressed the fact that irrational factors were as influential as mature reflection. Yet the film was not a lecture on collective attitudes but rather a story told, many years later, by a woman who, a small girl in 1944, did not see or understand everything that was happening. The Tavianis were not content to jumble up assessments of power, obedience and self-determination, they also tested the accuracy of images and proved how unreliable they are. The nostalgia we have noted in many films including this one may have originated in that lack of confidence in images: making films had been much simpler when it was possible to recount stories from one privileged, well-defined perspective, but that was no longer the case in the 1980s.

*

Instead of sinking during the 1980s, as many other European national cinematographies did, Italian cinema was able to produce a significant number of films every year. Its situation was somewhat contradictory and most cinematographers felt uneasy about it. Thanks to the money granted by the state, actors and directors did not stop working, but their movies were not released or, at the most, were seen by a tiny group of fans. The only way to reach a wider public was to collaborate with television, which implied the adoption of techniques and standards alien to the traditions of the studios. The pessimism which prevailed in films expressed the reluctance of filmmakers who were perfectly able to create an original style well fitted to the small screen, but who mourned the glorious years of Cinecittà.

Television was accused of completely altering the originality of cinema. In fact what happened was something much more important, a great change in the conception of culture and education. Most industrial societies followed the same trend but it evolved differently according to the country. However opposed they were on political issues, Italian Catholics and Communists were and always had been equally willing to use institutions of education to accelerate social mobility. For two generations of young Italians, from the 1930s to the 1960s, learning had been the best way of acquiring knowledge and finding a profession. Films were numbered among the didactic tools, they entered classrooms and university lectures. The sophistication introduced with them by modernism, in the 1960s, made them fit for refined, scholarly analysis. The agreement between Italian society and its education system was seriously breached, however, by the economic crisis which began in the 1970s. It became clear that diplomas no longer led automatically to jobs; unemployment separated the school from the public and provoked a strain of anti-intellectualism in which films were included. Conversely, television was more and more valued, not only because it was entertaining but also because it was a source of information. Sit-coms told the young how to dress, how to behave with their friends, what kind of music was up-to-date. Documentaries, reports, even adverts spoke about current issues, work, cars, travel, as well as about more theoretical, scientific questions. The obvious ineffectiveness of education was balanced by the apparent utility of television.

By the 1980s and early 1990s, the cinematic culture, that is to say the manner of seeing films, of appreciating them and of making them an object of debate, was deeply affected by the undervaluing of school and the excessive praise of television. The 1980s witnessed the transition from a television which emulated the cinema to a television which incorporated most performing arts (theatre, music, dance, cinema), which widened their audience and provided them with enough financial and technical means to survive. A cinematic production sponsored by broadcasting networks and destined to be released on the small screen was necessarily more akin to television than to the kind of films made only for the silver screen. Since the beginning of the 1990s, the most popular films have been those which resemble television programmes, not because they call for less mental effort, as is often argued by film buffs, but because they seem to tackle problems which are of concern for most people and because they are well adapted to the habits of viewers. If films for television may at times be gripping and of considerable aesthetic value, they are no longer cinematic works, and it took some time for spectators used to attending picture theatres to get fully familiar with the pervasiveness of television. This is what the fifth generation of cinema-goers had to experience.

Conclusion

Although it ends with the hundredth anniversary of the first film-show in Italy, this book is not aimed at celebrating the centenary of film. The cinema, as it developed and then declined, was a very specific variety of performing art, distinct from those which preceded or followed it. Its fate depended upon the existence of picture theatres where people would gather at scheduled times to watch and hear, in darkness, recorded shows, of a limited duration, mostly fictional, and played by well-known actors. There have been and there will be many other kinds of moving pictures but all those which can be seen individually, at home, or which are transmitted all day long no longer belong to the category of cinema. Films are the most characteristic cultural production of the twentieth century, especially of its first two thirds. It is not by chance that a volume published at the end of the century is in a position to deal with the complete history of the medium, for its birth to its old age.

The cinema being first and foremost an art of images, it would not be artificial to illustrate its progression by means of a series of images. Let us picture three graphs representing the evolution of, respectively, cinema attendance, the production of domestic films, and interest in domestic movies in the peninsula. The first curve would be exactly what statisticians call bell-shaped, perfectly regular in its ascending phase, which was the age of the first generations of cinema-goers, culminating in the mid-1950s, at the time of the third generation, then decreasing again uniformly, as the fourth and fifth generations reached their twenties. The other two charts, which would be rather erratic, would not evolve in a parallel way. The graph denoting production would show an impressive flowering at the beginning of the century, a sudden fading after the First World War, a slow renaissance and a lively advance from the late 1930s to the end of the century. As for the impact of domestic films at home, one would note an alternation of interest and indifference, with a peak in curiosity during the 1950s.

There is much to be learnt from these curves. The first lesson is so obvious that it does not deserve much comment: Italian studios were effective in attracting people to the picture theatres but they did not contribute much to maintaining spectators' dedication. The downturn in domestic production, after two decades of brilliant prosperity, did not put off the public. Viewers who had soon got used to seeing American as well as Italian movies, without even clearly identifying their origin, began in the 1920s to connect the words cinema and Hollywood. As could be worked out from the elegant shape of the first chart, the behaviour of the Italian public was perfectly rational: its commitment did not slacken, and it consumed whatever was available, American or domestic, until it was offered other forms of entertainment. Compared to this graph, the curve of domestic production looks illogical. It is often said that filmmaking is a business, which should imply some consideration for the demand, but the Italian studios were not governed by the market. Having reached an optimal level of production before the First World War, in quantity as well as quality, they gave up at a time when audiences were booming. They managed to meet the increase in attendances in the 1950s and 1960s but then went on making movies that would not be released. Private sponsorship being unusual in Italy, the money necessary to shoot came from the state, whose intervention was decisive in some instances, especially when the Venice Festival, the first event of that sort in the world, helped to advertise Italian films and when the building of Cinecittà provided Italian cinematographers with one of the best European production plants. However, this did not engender a marriage of state and filmmaking. The authorities attempted, every now and then, to advertise their policy through films but they were much keener on controlling radio and television than cinema. What is more, since it did not want to displease Washington, the government was reluctant to actively promote Italian film production. If it ended up handing over quite a lot of money, this was due solely to the pressure exerted on it by producers, technicians, actors and directors.

Lobbying succeeded because it was backed by public opinion. This was one of the many paradoxes of Italian cinema. Audiences which were not particularly anxious to see domestic films, were extremely proud of the international fame won by Italian cinema. At this point, we should introduce a fourth graph representing the circulation of cinema magazines in the peninsula. Differing in size, price and scope, these periodicals sold extremely well throughout the century. Italians, who read them assiduously, acquired and perpetuated a very lively film culture, which implied a good knowledge of what was going on in world studios, of what was released, of the names of actors and titles of films. Cinema was popular not only because spectators liked it, but because they were fond of talking about it, and that was true even when domestic studios had to close or, at the end of the century, when people no longer attended picture theatres. Written or spoken comments on cinema are not something surrounding films like a border or a backdrop but a force that influences the choice of actors, screenwriters and composers, and even such apparently technical aspects as the framing of a background or the colour of costumes.

Film magazines trigger debates, they are important because of their capacity to generate alternative readings and divergent narratives, but people would not read them if they were not curious about the cinema and it is their curiosity which has to be questioned. The flexibility and openness of Italian cultural life is perhaps one of its most striking features, but adaptability does not necessarily result in compliance. Italians, who are intent on knowing what fashions are in other countries, are anxious at the same time to maintain many of the habits and forms of thought useful in their own environment. Hollywood's productions were praised as dreamlike fantasies, as images of a possible future, rather than as models. Films played an important part in introducing people to new ideas and new modes of consumption but they were not alone in so doing. Film history has often been seen as an intrinsic and essential part of the intelligence of filmmaking, likely to help us discover the very essence of the cinema. But films were watched by people who had many other concerns: they were very powerful in so far as they were associated with other means of communication – newspapers, radio programmes, songs and records. It is this network of media and amusements which made Italian society adopt new economic, political and emotional norms in tune with the contemporary world. From a statistical point of view, the degree of influence of cinema and other modern media is well documented but deciding how Italians responded to these challenges is another matter. Were they easily accepted, or did they produce unresolved conflicts? Were the sensations they aroused responses to feelings already present within the culture, or were they aimed at adapting behaviour to new social situations at work? It is one of the shortcomings of cultural studies that they have no way of answering questions of that kind, however essential they may be.

Some historians would argue that there is something to be learnt from the press in this area. Film magazines should be scrutinized to find illustrations of what the cinema meant for those who were in the habit of buying them. I have read a large number of weeklies, specialized and not, in preparing this book. They have told me a lot about the names of famous people, the ways of commenting upon films, the vocabulary in vogue but, obviously, little about spectators' deeper feelings. Up to the middle of the 1960s, the language of critics was an extension of everyday speech interspersed with references to ill-defined 'values' from which hierarchical structures could be evolved. Reviews seldom dealt with the content or technical qualities of films. Based on instinct and, when journalists were Catholic or Communist, on a transcendental ethical centre, they generally aimed to find traces of current issues and urgent problems in films, or to lament their absence. During the last third of the century, structuralism overran film criticism. We can guess that readers were disconcerted but, then, attendance was dropping and journalists knew they were addressing their peers much more than the general public.

Articles and reviews, which reflect the preoccupations of people who, identifying their feelings as the real ones, attempt to persuade their contemporaries that they are right, do not explain why Italians were enthusiastic about films for so long and, even after deserting the cinemas, continued to take an interest in what was happening in studios. However, together with memoirs and diaries, cinema magazines demonstrate that up to the fourth generation this excitement was common to everybody. There were divergences among viewers, intellectuals sometimes displayed an excessive admiration for foreign productions and compared American and Italian cinema to demonstrate how much better the former was. But, on the whole, all Italians were fond of films. It is only in the 1960s that a generation richer and more educated than previous ones tried to establish its intellectual superiority by distinguishing art-films from mainstream pictures. For about sixty years before that date, highbrows and lowbrows saw more or less the same programmes.

In the nineteenth century, theatre and opera were already appreciated equally by all social strata. But famous actors only performed in big cities; popular plays were given varying interpretations by each different theatre company, and in fact people never saw the same plays. In addition to that, every town, even the smallest, had its playhouse and used it to prove that it could surpass its neighbours. Theatres and operas helped to strengthen local communities in competition with other communities. Films could have become a weapon used in regional rivalries. Italian distributors were ready to create small circuits to circulate a limited number of films in a restricted area, but at the beginning of the century American companies established national networks which were soon the most powerful. Films were the first cultural artefacts shared not just by all classes in a given district, but by all inhabitants of the peninsula.

It would therefore be essential to figure out what Italians learnt from the silver screen. People cannot attend a performance without having ideas about the kind of entertainment they are going to watch, however simple these ideas are. What did Italian spectators expect, when they entered a cinema? Behaviour and feelings are not static but dynamic; those which at a given time seem normal are subsequently regarded in a totally different light. Films were certainly a decisive force in opening new prospects and creating new expectations which gave rise to debates and judgements. Given its impact on people, cinema should help us examine the culturally sanctioned emotions of a given time but, again, we are facing a riddle that nobody has yet solved: impressions and perceptions are not measurable. In this book, I have tried to observe spectators' changing attitudes, and to set them alongside the films which were then being shown. I believe we can go no further and I shall stick to this method in this Conclusion.

Film stars were famous everywhere, but it was Italy which contrived a new breed of stars, the *dive*. In traditional, pre-industrial Italian society, ranks and hierarchies were enormously diverse. A man's status was mostly local and was seldom perceived outside the region where it was defined. By contrast, an industrializing peninsula needed illustrious names which, known to everybody, would represent common reference-points. It is clear, for instance, that Mussolini rallied a great many Italians because his image was manifest, discernable, while most politicians and even the king were not visible. *Dive* and, subsequently, great actors had the same function, although obviously to a lesser extent. All Italians had seen Foolshead, Vittorio de Sica, Totò and Alberto Sordi, or had heard of them, their faces, their behaviour, their best jokes were familiar to everybody, an allusion to them was enough to make people who were otherwise strangers feel that they had something in common.

I have not chosen these names at random. I think that their case exemplifies the difficulties involved in any attempt to confront directly any series of films with the age in which they were produced. In the 1960s, Alberto Sordi was in close contact with his period. Alternately idealist and go-getter, sometimes heroic, sometimes a coward, much more interested in money, luxury cars and comfort than in women, he was not the typical man of the *dolce vita* decade, even assuming this man existed, which he probably did not, but rather the representation, the ideal type of this man. It would be impossible to comment in the same way about the three other actors. Both Foolshead and Totò belonged to an age before their appearance in films, they were survivors who, for a short time, kept alive out-dated forms of entertainment. It might be argued that, in periods when occupational structures were becoming unstable and physical work was declining in importance, people stood by old values, especially those attached to bodily skills, and loved actors who took them back to the past. Maybe, but such an assumption cannot be checked, it is merely a provocative hypothesis, based on guesses about viewers' reactions and not easy to tackle in a cultural study of movies. De Sica was another case, he was simultaneously ahead of his time and outside of it. While other actors stressed mostly their male strength, he introduced to the screen a fresher style made of casualness and elegance. He starred in films whose theme was not likely to alarm the authorities, but his graceful bearing, his smartness, were not consonant with the virile attitude advocated by Fascism. The films which he directed enthused lots of Italians but infuriated many more. It was his international fame which made him a figure in the peninsula, and his foreign reputation that prompted his fellow citizens to take his work seriously.

Actresses and actors played a crucial role in helping the Italians to construct not exactly an identity, but rather a repertory of images likely to be read as 'we are like that' or 'this is how others see us'. Of course, these images were not static, they were permanently reworked according to changes affecting the context. The evolution of community feelings is linked to the unstable, perpetually moving relationship between the social organization, the institutions, and the set of symbols (linguistic, visual and aural) which human beings use to make sense of the world that surrounds them. This process is itself determined by the existence of absence of a standardized, shared system of reference. The cinema was part of a cluster of tools which enabled the Italians to build a picture of themselves, both individually and as members of a group.

As films had to be sold to as many viewers as possible, in the peninsula and abroad, filmmakers opted for an extreme level of generalization and seldom paid attention to the differences between regions or social strata. The most obvious form of simplification was the systematic recourse, for the dialogues, to standard Italian. This is not an artificial idiom invented by intellectuals and civil servants, but an extremely formalized language which contrasts strikingly with the flexible, ever-changing dialects that many Italians spontaneously use. People who associated standard Italian with school and did not speak it enjoyed hearing it in films, maybe because it established a note of distance and artificiality, maintained throughout the narrative, which prevented them from taking the story too seriously. Together with radio and television, the cinema contributed actively to making standard Italian the peninsula's vehicular language.

In picture theatres, Italians learnt words which were not theirs but which could be uttered in their country. They discovered also a land called Italy. Tourists from Europe and the United States had long made this land a country of the imagination and transformed its past into a museum. Painters and photographers had become used to depicting it as a mythical, half-dreamed country. Cinema radically modified this idealistic vision. Right from its first days, it produced short films taken in various regions which circulated throughout the country. Later, the Light Institute, created to advertise the government's policy, shot and distributed excellent documentaries illustrating the diversity of Italian regions, thus inaugurating a tradition of investigations relative to all regions. Italian filmmakers were much keener than any of their European colleagues on working in different parts of their country. Visconti and Antonioni moved from Milan to Sicily via the Po valley and Rome. Blasetti, de Sica, Rosi and many others shot in at least three regions. Antonioni worked abroad for a decade but he was an exception; most Italian talent did not accept Hollywood's invitations. Long before the expression 'road-movie' had been contrived, Italian films followed people migrating from one area to another and, in quite a different way, Rossellini's *Paisa* and

Fellini's *La strada* were perfect 'travelogues'. All these movies created new clichés, but they charmed their public by appearing to discover them and by delivering them in a critical, seemingly unbiased manner. Antonioni's Milan, Fellini's outskirts of Rome, were not legendary places, they were cold, muddy and damp. Cinematic Italy could not seduce the tourists and, for that reason, it appealed to the natives, even if it was merely a collection of images, less enticing and no nearer the truth than travel agents' brochures.

Tourist vestiges were never totally eliminated. Those which were linked to the Roman past of the peninsula persisted tenaciously and gave birth, at the outset of the century, to one of the most famous series of Italian films, the colossal, fanciful reconstructions of the antique world. The stories were rather casual and at times illogical; they were interrupted by sub-plots and long visual or narrative digressions; but the films won universal praise for their technical achievement, their handling of myriads of extras and their fantasy. However, after the First World War, because of the closing down of domestic studios, spectators became accustomed to American films with their well-knit plots, their perfectly defined characters and their precise context. This model proved to be so powerful that Italian cinematographers adopted it when they resumed their production. There were then strong affiliations between Hollywood and Italy's literary imagination. Journalists, playwrights and novelists kept at the back of their minds a pattern borrowed partly from American books but mostly from films. Screenwriters and directors had the same inspiration; they structured their films as Americans would have done but they developed them against an Italian background. Critics will quarrel endlessly about the realism or lack of realism of these productions – theirs is a metaphysical debate based on incompatible definitions of reality. But the combination of a strict, well-ordered narrative with glimpses of Italian life was very effective. Italians felt at home when watching melodramas whose main characters looked like them, while foreigners sensed an aura of exoticism in Neorealist films.

The graphs introduced earlier show that, although they still showed an interest in domestic productions, the third generation of cinema-goers still preferred Hollywood. A shift occurred with the fourth generation: audiences began to decrease but the Italian films attracted more spectators than their American counterparts. The 1960s were also the years when Italian directors, departing from the classical, American-style formulae, were less interested in the logical unfolding of events than in the medium itself, cinema, with its combination of sounds and images, with a focus on the predominant function allotted to actors. But it was in the same decade that Italy on the one hand adopted and transformed the most typical Hollywood 'genre', the western and, on the other, signed contracts of co-operation with foreign companies.

How can we define the films Italian firms produced at that time? Were they international because of external participation or genuinely Italian because they departed from traditional patterns? The query is, I am afraid, meaningless. These were hybrid, heterogeneous films, so inter-related with other films or cultural artefacts as to beggar any unitary or simply delineated characterization of their individuality. An Italian novelist, Gianni Celati, who began to write in the early 1970s, has explained how interdependent in his mind were cinematic impressions and literary invention. Everything he saw on screen triggered his imagination and refreshed his memory, he never imitated what he had watched but any detail, any actor, inspired him to create other situations in which per-sonal ideas mingled with images borrowed from films. Celati's is a perfect example of cinematic reception and what he said is probably true of many of his fellow citizens, throughout the twentieth century. Four generations of cinema-goers built up an enormous palimpsest of different sounds and images, domestic as well as alien, and used it to organize their lives in the particular place where they were residing, Italy. The films they enjoyed were American as often as domestic, but the manner in which they assimilated and re-used this material was theirs and it is their appropriation of various cinematic sources which has made up Italian national cinema.

One of the most striking changes introduced during the 1960s was the modification of film endings. In Antonioni's films, nothing was settled when the story finished, the future remained ill-defined. In Fellini's, an episode was closed, with some display of nostalgia, but something new was announced and yet not screened. While ostensibly mourning the glorious decades of the Italian studios, *Interview* and *Ginger and Fred* pointed the way to another era. A certain form and quality of films were over but moving images still amused and interested large audiences – and these images would never have been produced, had it not been for the inheritance bequeathed by the cinema.

Notes

INTRODUCTION

1 David Bordwell, Janet Steiger and Kristin Thompson, *The Classical Hollywood Cinema: Film Style and Mode of Production to 1960* (London, Melbourne, 1985). Tom Gunning, *D.W. Griffith and the Origins of American Narrative Film* (Champaign–Urbana, 1991).
2 Gramsci was then drama critic for the socialist newspaper *Avanti*; his article on Borelli was published on 16 February 1917; it has been published in *Letteratura e vita nazionale* (Rome, 1975), pp. 335–6.
3 A question well explored, where Italy is concerned, by Gian Paolo Biasini, *The Flavour of Modernity* (Princeton, 1993).
4 Ernest Gellner, *Nations and Nationalism* (Ithaca, 1983) takes a close look (p. 43 ff.) at states such as Italy which, at their foundation, did not have the support of an imaginary construction of the nation. See also Benedict Anderson, *Imagined Communities. Reflections on the Origin and Spread of Nationalism* (London, 1983).
5 *Corriere della Sera*. 11 April 1969.
6 *The House that Nino Built* (Eng. trans., New York, 1953), pp. 40–3.
7 An extended review of papers can be found in Aldo Bernardini's 'L'Inferno della Milano Films', *Bianco e nero*, XLVI, 2, 1985, pp. 92–111.
8 Auro Bernardi, *Al cinema con Savinio* (Lanciana, 1992).
9 See Renzo Renzi, *Da Staracce a Antonioni* (Padua, 1966) and Calvino's foreword to Fellini's *Quattro film* (Turin, 1974).
10 Marcia Landy, *Fascism in Film: The Italian Commercial Cinema, 1931–1943* (Princeton, 1986); James Hay, *Popular Film Culture in Fascist Italy: The Passing of the Rex* (Bloomington, 1987).

1 FIRST GENERATION: THE WORLD IN A DARK ROOM

1 The mean price, in 1896, was the same as that of about one kilo of pasta. When attendance started slackening, exhibitors promptly lowered the charge. For a discussion of the figures, see Aldo Bernardini, *Cinema muto italiano*, vol. 1 *Ambiente, spettacoli e spettatori* (Rome/Bari, 1980), p. 217.
2 See a careful analysis of programmes and attendance in Andrea Veneri's 'Lo spettacolo cinematografico a Reggio Emilia, 1895–1906', in A. Costa, ed., *La meccanica del visibile* (Florence, 1983), pp. 129–38.
3 *Can della Scala*, Verona, 9 June 1907, quoted by Gian Piero Brunetta, *Buio in sala* (Venice, 1989), p. 71.

4 *Ohe . . . Hop*, 25 July 1905, quoted by Gianfranco Gori, 'Dal Cinematografo Edison a *Histoire d'un Pierro*', in A. Costa, ed., 1983, pp. 139–48. There is a good anthology of contemporary opinions on cinema in Enzo Lauretta, ed., *Pirandelle e il cinema* (Agrigento, 1978), pp. 32–41.

5 Gori, p. 144.

6 For the relationship between cinema and variety show, see Bernardini, *Cinema muto italiano*, I, pp. 65–107.

7 *Lanterna*, Naples, 9 February 1908, quoted by Aldo Bernardini, 'Lessico semiserio del cinema italiano delle origini', in A. Costa, ed., 1983, pp. 149–75.

8 For the relationship between urban sites, arcades and picture houses, see Giuliana Bruno, *Streetwalking on a Ruined Map* (Princeton and Oxford, 1993), p. 38 ff., and Sileno Salvagnini, 'Luoghi dello spettacolo e immaginario urbano tra Otto e Novecento in Italia', in A. Costa, ed., 1983, pp. 47–63.

9 It lasted twelve minutes and was only made of seven frames (three of which have disappeared); the final assault is well filmed, with an impressive crowd of extras breaking in through a breach in the wall of the city, but the other scenes are played rather clumsily. For an analysis, see Guido Cincotti, *The Italian Risorgimento in Theatre and Cinema* (Rome, 1962), pp. 226 ff.

10 R. Redi, *La Cines. Storia di una casa di produzione italiana* (Rome, 1991).

11 In addition to Bernardini's works already mentioned, see his *Cinema muto italiano*, II, *Industria e organizzazione dello spettacolo, 1905–1909* (Bari, 1981); III, *Arte, divismo e mercato 1910–1914* (Bari, 1982).

12 See 'Lessico semisserio . . .' pp. 149 ff.

13 *Cinema muto italiano*, II, 216–18. See also Roberta Maietti, 'Le manuffature cinematografiche', in R. de Berti and E. Mosconi, eds, *Il cinema delle origini a Milano, 1895–1920* (Milan, 1994), pp. 253–4.

14 See L. Cafagna, *Dualismo e sviluppo nella storia d'Italia* (Venice, 1992).

15 The George Kleine Archive, at the Library of Congress, keeps the contracts signed between the General Film Company, trading branch of the MPPC, and Cines. In 1911, the former contracts to buy yearly more than 1500 prints of shorts; according to a second contract signed the 23 July 1913, Cines promises to sell yearly at least five feature-length films and sixty shorts. See H. Harrisson and N. Mazzanti, 'La collezione George Kleine' in R. Renzi, ed., *Sperduto nel buio. Il cinema muto italiano e il suo tempo, 1905–1930* (Bologna, 1991), pp. 159–69 and *The George Kleine Collection of Motion Pictures in the Library of Congress: A Catalog* (Washington, 1980).

16 *Cent'anni di cinema italiano* (Rome/Bari, 1991), p. 35. On cinema production in Turin, see G. Rondolino, *Torino come Hollywood* (Bologna, 1980).

17 There is an accurate study of the technical problems in M. Bernardo, *La macchina del cinematografo* (Florence, 1984) and Bernardini, *Cinema muto italiano*, III, pp. 5–11.

18 An anthology of reviews published in American and British papers can be found in A. Bernardini and V. Martinelli, *Il cinema muto italiano, 1913* (Turin, 1994); for the articles quoted here see pp. 31, 106 and 151.

19 This was possible because the standard movie camera was equipped with a lens of 53 mm focal length. The preference given to that lens may explain why close-ups were seldom used in Italian pictures.

20 *The Moving Picture World*, 13 December 1913, in Bernardini and Martinelli, p. 172; see also pp. 31, 96, 196, 285, 301.

21 'Il cinema italiano dalla nascita alla Grande Guerra: un'analisi stilistica' in R. Renzi, ed. (1991), pp. 49–58.

22 I doubt that numbering is possible for silent films, which had many different versions; the length Salt gives for the films he has studied is far less than that of the original pictures, probably because he has looked at copies exported to Britain.

23 Anecdote borrowed from one of the most famous Italian children's books by Edmondo de Amicis, *Heart* (1884).

24 Letter to Martoglio, from *Morganafilm*, 17 May 1913.

25 For a general view on the actor system, see P. Bianchi, *La Bertini e le dive del cinema muto* (Turin, 1969) and A. Bernardini, *Cinema muto italiano*, III, *Arte, divismo e mercato* (Bari, 1981), pp. 192–211.

26 Her memoirs can be found in C. Costantini, *La diva imperiale. Ritratto di Francesca Bertini* (Milan, 1982).

27 A. Farassino and T. Sanguinetti, eds, *Gli uomini forti* (Milan, 1983).

28 P. Cherchi-Usai, ed., *Giovanni Pastrone. Gli anni d'oro del cinema a Torino* (Turin, 1986). Pastrone involved in the writing of the captions the greatest Italian poet, Gabrielle d'Annunzio, whose name helped advertise the film.

29 *The Body in the Mirror: Shapes of History in Italian Cinema* (Princeton, 1992), p. 30.

30 P. Carrano, *Malafemmina: La donna nel cinema italiano* (Florence, 1977).

31 Giulia Alberti, 'Conditions of illusion' in G. Bruno and M. Nadotti, eds., *Off Screen: Women and Film in Italy* (London and New York, 1988), pp. 48 and 53.

32 To be precise, the most famous tear-jerker is *Lost in Darkness* (1914), a film unanimously praised for having all the making of a realist story, although nobody can see it since the only print was destroyed during the war.

33 See 'I comici del muto', *Griffithiana*, 24–25 October 1985.

34 For a general description of comedies and a comparison with America, see W.D. Gehring, *Screwball Comedy: A Genre of Madcap Romance* (New York, 1986).

2   SECOND GENERATION: THEIR MASTER'S VOICE

1 Mino Argentieri, *La censura nel cinema italiano* (Rome, 1974).

2 Mario Isnenghi, 'L'imagine cinematografica della grande guerra', *Rivista di storia contemporanea*, 1978, iii, pp. 341–53.

3 Gian Piero Brunetta, *La guerra lontana* (Roveretto, 1985).

4 On the relationship between industrialists and Fascism, see David Forgasc, ed., *Rethinking Italian Fascism: Capitalism, Populism and Culture* (London, 1986).

5 In the Italian name 'Luce' was an abbreviation for 'Cinematic Union for Education'. On this experience, see: Gian Piero Brunetta, *Intelletuali, cinema e propaganda tra le due guerre* (Bologna, 1972); Gian Paolo Bernagozzi, ed., *Propaganda di regime e giudizio della storia* (Bologna, 1973); D. Biondi, *La fabbrica del Duce* (Florence, 1973); Gian Paolo Bernagozzi, ed., *Vincere, vinceremo* (Bologna, 1975); Mino Argentieri, *L'occhio del regime. Informazione e propaganda nel cinema del Fascismo* (Florence, 1979); Massimo Cardillo, *Il Duce in moviola. Politica e divismo nei cinegiornali e documentari 'Luce'* (Bari, 1983).

6 Italy's economic problems are clearly explored in Douglas J. Forsyth's *The Crisis of Liberal Italy: Monetary and Financial Policy, 1914–1922* (Cambridge, 1993), which, notwithstanding its modest title, is a complete, penetrating analysis of the situation in Italy before Fascism.

7 See the figures in Gian Piero Brunetta's *Storia del cinema italiano*, I, *Il cinema muto* (Rome 1993), pp. 54–5.

8 Two attempts were made to create a centralized, well capitalized film company. The Italian Cinematic Union (UCI) founded in 1919, collapsed four years later. In 1930, Pittaluga, a film distributor who owned a chain of cinemas, bought Cines which went bankrupt in 1933. The last episode is well documented in Elaine Mancini's *The Struggle of the Italian Film Industry during Fascism, 1930–35* (Ann Arbor, 1985) pp. 57–98.

9 *Streetwalking on a Ruined Map*, (Princeton, 1993), pp. 24–6 and 137–44.

10 For a close study of the 'transition to sound' see Mancini, *The Struggle of the Italian Film Industry*, pp. 33–56.

11 On radio, see A. Monticone, *Il fascismo al microfono. Radio e politica in Italia, 1924–1945* (Rome, 1978); Gianni Isola, *Abbassa la tua radio per favor. Storia dell'ascolto radiofonico nell'Italia fascista* (Florence, 1990); and Franco Monteleone, *Storia della radio e della televisione in Italia, 1922–1992* (Venice, 1993).

12 However critical it was, Pirandello's paper in the *Corriere della sera* (16 June 1929) offered a positive, optimistic image of the talkies: 'The cinema should free itself from the word, I mean from literature, and immerse itself in music. That is the point: pure music and pure vision. The most aesthetic of our senses, the eye and the ear, united in a single pleasure; the eye that sees, the ear that hears and the heart that feels . . .'

13 *La vita dello spettacolo in Italia nel decennio 1924–1933* (Rome, 1934). In the picture houses of Rome, money was spent as follows:

	Italian films	American films	other countries
1932	5,900,000 lire	23,000,000 lire	8,500,000 lire
1933	7,100,000 lire	25,000,000 lire	8,000,000 lire

14 MGM, Paramount, Fox, United Artists.

15 Pittaluga, for instance, had a monopoly of Warner until the American company organised its own distribution.

16 On this aspect of Mussolini's dictatorship, see Philipp Cannistraro, *La fabbrica del consenso* (Rome, 1975), pp. 287 ff.

17 *Christ Stopped at Eboli* (New York, 1947), p. 131.

18 N. Carducci, *Gli intelletuali e l'ideologia americana nell'Italia letteraria degli anni trenta* (Manduria, 1973); G. Spini, G. Migone and M. Teodori, eds, *Italia e America dalla grande guerra a oggi* (Turin, 1976); Guido Fink, 'All American Boys' in David E. Ellwood and Gian Piero Brunetta, eds, *Hollywood in Europa: industria, politica, pubblico del cinema* (Florence, 1991), pp. 149–58.

19 Leo Longanesi, *L'Italiano*, January 1933. There is an anthology of deprecating texts in Brunetta, *Spari nel buio* (Rome, 1992), pp. 71–97.

20 *Rivista del cinema*, 1926, 10. This text and the following one can be found in Francesco Casetti and Raffaela de Berti, eds, *Il cinema a Milano tra le due guerre* (Milan, 1988).

21 *Stelle* [= Stars], 19 August 1933.

22 Called *Gialli* (= Yellows) because of their yellow cover, they were launched in 1929 and immediately became immensely popular.

23 We find here a problem already tackled in the Introduction. Dubbing was very efficient, most characters were renamed, Mickey became Topolino (Mouse in Italian), Jungle Jim became Geo, records of popular tunes were sold in Italian versions. And yet people realized that these were non-Italian films, comic-strips or songs. See Gino Frezza, *La macchina del mito. Tra film e fumetti* (Florence, 1995).

24 Written in 1927; see *The Second Life of Art* (New York, 1982), pp. 218–19.

25 Five, if we take into account *The Cry of the Eagle*, made at the beginning of Mussolini's dictatorship (1924), and *Redemption*, made at its end (1941).

26 F. Freddi, *Il cinema. Miti, esperienze e realtà di un regime totalitario* (Rome, 1949).
27 This is, at least, what can be inferred from the prompt, and enthusiastic response of the press, for we have no figures about the number of admissions in that period.
28 *Cinema illustrazione*, 19 October 1932.
29 An original German script was shot in four versions, English, French, German and Italian; the English version, *Sunshine Susie*, was directed by Victor Saville.
30 *The Struggles of the Italian Film Industry*, p. 64.
31 On the variability of programmes, see Elena Mosconi, 'Nascita e evoluzione dell'esercizio cinematografico' in de Berti, R. and Mosconi, E., eds, *Il cinema delle origini a Milano, 1895–1920* (Milan, 1994), pp. 355–6.

3   THIRD GENERATION: THE MOST POPULAR FORM OF ENTERTAINMENT

1 The only available figures concern the population; between 1931 and 1940, there was a population increase of 7 per cent but the number of workers decreased by 3 per cent, which implies a high level of unemployment.
2 In 1935, the Light Institute was instructed by the government to buy Pitaluga's chain of cinemas and distribution company and to create a National Office of Italian Cinematic Industries (ENIC); a law, passed in 1938, established state aid to the producers.
3 'Emancipazione del cinema italiano', *Cinema*, 6, 25 September 1936, quoted in Carabba, C., *Il cinema del ventennio nero* (Florence, 1974), pp. 128–31.
4 M. Arosio, G. Cereda and F. Iseppi, *Cinema e cattolici in Italia* (Milan, 1974); G.P. Brunetta, 'Tattiche della negazione e del consenso nei giudizi del centro cattolico cinematografico, 1934–1945', in *Retorica e politica* (Padua, 1977), pp. 245–70); G. Gori, ed., *Cinema e parrocchia. Materiali per una rassegna* (Rimini, 1980); G. Gori and S. Pivato, eds, *Gli anni del cinema di parrocchia* (Rimini, 1980).
5 *The Culture of Consent: Mass Organization of Leisure in Fascist Italy* (Cambridge, 1981), p. 128.
6 This magazine was published by the Experimental Centre for Cinema.
7 This autobiography can be found in *The Road to San Giovanni* (London, 1993); see pp. 37–8
8 G.P. Brunetta, *Buio in sala* (Venice, 1989), pp. 127 and 185.
9 Unfortunately, we lack important evidence: the level and rise in prices on the black market; it is therefore difficult to tell whether cinema audiences comprised those who had some 'excess' over what they could actually spend for their daily life, or whether they visited cinemas from other motives.
10 English translation, Manchester, 1968; see pp. 89–93.
11 *I zii di Sicilia* (Turin, 1964), p. 14.
12 Pier Paolo Luzzatto Fegiz, ed., *Il volto sconosciuto dell'Italia. Dieci anni di sondagi Doxa, 1946–1955* (Milan, 1956) pp. 335 ff.
13 For statistical data, see Alessandro Pavolini, *Rapporto sul cinema*, in *Cinema Italiano, Anno XIX* (Rome, 1941); L. Bizzari and L. Solaroli, *L'industria cinematografica italiana* (Florence, 1958); L. Solaroli, 'Storia economica dell'industria cinematografica italiana', in P. Bächlin, ed., *Il cinema come industria* (Milan, 1958); Lorenzo Quaglietti, *Storia economico-politica del cinema italiano, 1945–1980* (Rome, 1980).

14 'Poesia, solo affare del cinema italiano', *Film d'oggi*, 25 August 1945.
15 References in note 9 of the Introduction.
16 *White Squadron* (1936) and *Bronze Sentries* (1937) for Africa, *The Siege of the Alcazar* (1940) for Spain.
17 F. Bolzoni, *Il progetto imperiale* (Venice, 1976).
18 Gramsci, *Note sul Machiavelli* (Turin, 1972), pp. 123 ff. and *Letters from Prison* (New York, 1994), II, pp. 169–72. See also Richard Bellamy and D. Schecter, *Gramsci and the Italian State* (Manchester, 1993), pp. 122–4 and 137–48.
19 *Popular Film Culture in Fascist Italy* (Bloomington, 1987), p. 60; see also pp. 40–7.
20 The most complete series was published by the association of producers, ANICA: *Venti anni dell'ANICA per il cinema italiano, 1944–1964* (Rome, 1964). It often lacks consistency; for instance, p. 14, the figures given in the third column for the period 1948–1958 have been established by arbitrarily doubling the figures of the second column.
21 See Gian Piero Brunetta, *Fifty Years of ANICA: An Outline History of ANICA* (Rome, 1994).
22 'The Place of Neorealism in Italian Cinema from 1945 to 1954', in Nicholas Hewitt, ed., *The Culture of Reconstruction: European Literature, Thought and Film, 1945–50* (Basingstoke and London, 1989), p. 74.
23 Carlo Ginzburg, 'Mondo cattolico e vita politica dalla Resistenza a oggi', in *Storia d'Italia. I caratteri originali* (Turin, 1972) pp. 673–4.
24 See Nicola Tranfaglia, ed., *Il 1948 in Italia. La storia e i film* (Florence, 1991).
25 Quoted by Brunetta, *Fifty Years of ANICA*, pp. 26–7.
26 *Libertas*, 24 February 1952.
27 In addition to Brunetta's 'Tattiche della negazione e del concenso' mentioned above, see Bruno P.F. Wanrooij, 'Dollars and Decency: Italian Catholics and Hollywood, 1945–1960', in David W. Ellwood and Gian Piero Brunetta, eds, *Hollywood in Europe: Experiences of a Cultural Hegemony* (Amsterdam, 1994), pp. 247–65.
28 Quoted by Gian Piero Brunetta, 'Mondo cattolico e organisazione del consenso: la politica cinematografica', in S. Lanaro, ed., *La democrazia cristiana dal fascismo al 18 aprile* (Venice, 1978), pp. 425–34.
29 'The Making and Unmaking of Neorealism in Postwar Italy', in N. Hewitt, ed., *The Culture of Reconstruction*, op. cit., p. 51.
30 'Neorealismo: alle fonti di un mito', in *Intelletuali, cinema e propaganda tra le due guerre* (Milan, 1988), p. 130.
31 The most important documents in the debate can be found in Carlo Carotti, *Alla ricerca del Paradiso. L'operaio nel cinema italiano, 1945–1990* (Genoa, 1992).
32 4 September 1948.
33 20 May 1955.
34 'Some Ideas on the Cinema', in R. Dyer, ed., *Film: A Montage of Theories* (New York, 1966), pp. 216–28.
35 Introduction to *The Pass to the Nest of Spiders* (English trans., New York, 1976), p. vii.
36 *Italian Film in the Light of Neorealism* (Princeton, 1986), p. 23.
37 *Storia dell'Italia repubblicana* (Venice, 1992) pp. 5 ff.
38 See Lino Miccichè, ed., *Visconti e il neorealismo* (Venice, 1990).
39 'The Place of Neorealism in Italian Cinema', p. 72.

40 On the film, see Lino Micciché, ed., *La Terra trema di Luchino Visconti. Analisi di un capolavoro* (Turin, 1993).
41 Not to be mistaken for the Roman daily *Il Tempo*.
42 *The Road to San Giovanni*, p. 47.
43 On the attitude of the Communists, see Stephen Gundle, *I comunisti italiani tra Hollywood e Mosca. La sfida della cultura di massa* (Florence, 1995), pp. 105–49.
44 Aldo Bernardini and Vittorio Martinelli, *Titanus* (Milan, 1987).
45 *Neorealismo d'appendice. Per un dibattito sul cinema popolare: il caso Matarazzo* (Florence, 1976).
46 An approximation for 'minaccia a spalla armata'. Most puns, based on homonyms which have no equivalent in English, cannot be translated. There is a good sample of Totò's puns in Totò, *Parli come badi* (Milan, 1994).

4 FOURTH GENERATION: THE SWEET LIFE

1 George H. Hildebrand, *Growth and Structure in the Economy of Modern Italy* (Cambridge, Mass., 1965).
2 Massimo Paci, *Mercato del lavoro e classi sociali in Italia. Ricerche sulla composizione del proletariato* (Bologna, 1976); A. de Donato, ed., *I giovani e il lavoro* (Bari, 1978).
3 Figures regarding cinema attendance during the two decades under consideration are to be found in Istituto Doxa, *Il pubblico del cinema* (Rome, 1976).
4 Franco Monteleone, *Storia della radio e della televisione in Italia* (Venice, 1993) pp. 275 ff.
5 On the important issue of sport in television, see Giorgio Simonelli, 'Come le televisioni trasformano lo sport', in G. Bettetini and A. Grasso, eds, *Lo specchio sporco della televisione* (Turin, 1988), pp. 283 ff.
6 'A Forkful of Westerns: Industry, Audiences and the Italian Western', in R. Dyer and G. Vincendeau, eds, *Popular European Cinema* (London, 1992), pp. 254–61).
7 Op. cit., pp. 252–4.
8 'Italian Cinema since 1945: The Social Costs of Industrialization', *Historical Journal of Film, Radio and Television*, xv, 3, Fall 1995, pp. 387–92.
9 In the last sequence of the film, Silvio decides to go away, but only because he has been humiliated in public by the boss, not because he disagrees with him.
10 *L'Italia del pizzo. Fenomenologia della tangente quotidiana* (Turin, 1993).
11 See Michèle Lagny, 'Popular Taste: The Peplum', in Dyer and Vincendeau, *Popular European Cinema*, pp. 163–80.
12 See Stephen Gundle, *I comunisti italiani tra Hollywood e Mosca. La sfida della cultura di massa* (Florence, 1995), pp. 319 ff.
13 Thomas Weisser, *Spaghetti Westerns: The Good, the Bad and the Violent. 558 Eurowesterns and Their Personnel, 1961–1977* (Jefferson and London, 1992).
14 *The Road to San Giovanni* (London, 1993), p. 63.
15 See T. Bentley Hammer, *International Film Prizes* (New York, 1991).
16 *Forma e parola nel cinema* (Padua, 1979), p. 113.
17 *Pier Paolo Pasolini: Cinema as Heresy* (Princeton University Press, 1990), p. 140.
18 There is abundant proof. I shall be content with quoting a banal article in a newspaper: 'Only son of a barrister, spoiled by an excessively loving mother who had developed his Oedipus complex, Marino Vulcano was a jack-of-all-trades' (*Corriere della sera*, 6 April 1972).

19 *Pier Paolo Pasolini*, op. cit., p. 165.
20 On the rebellion against the authority of fathers, especially in films, see Angela delle Vacche, *The Body in the Mirror: Shapes of History in Italian Cinema*, (Princeton, 1992), pp. 219 ff.
21 *The Standard Edition of the Complete Works of Sigmund Freud*, ix (London, 1944), p. 237.
22 See F. Ferzetti, 'Città e cinema. La periferia urbana nella filmografia italiana', in F. Fiorentini, ed., *Città come* (Rome, 1988).

5 FIFTH GENERATION: THE WORLD IN THE BOX

1 Gabriele Calvi and Andrea Vannucci, *L'elettore sconosciuto* (Bologna, 1995).
2 David Moss, *The Politics of Left-wing Violence in Italy, 1969–1985* (London, 1990); Robert C. Meade, *Red Brigades: The Story of Italian Terrorism* (London, 1990).
3 *Cent'anni di cinema italiano* (Bari, 1991), p. 443.
4 F. Fiorentini, *1500 film e sceneggiati prodotti dalla RAI: 1954–1986* (Turin, 1988).
5 *Il portaborse. Portaborsi* prove so servile that they carry the bag (*borsa*) of the people upon whom they fawn.
6 Sergio Rafaelli, *La lingua filmata. Didascalie e dialoghi nel cinema italiano* (Florence, 1992).
7 *Un ventennio a colori. Televisione privata e società in Italia, 1975–1995* (Florence, 1995), pp. 12–13. The government delayed the introduction of colour for four years. Both the Christian Democrat majority and the Communists found that colour was too expensive and not fit for serious themes. It is not by chance that, in most people's minds, moralism and black and white were associated.
8 *Tra me e te. Strategie di coinvolgimento della spettatore nei programmi della neotelevisione* (Turin, 1988), p. 24.
9 G. Grazziani, *Eva dopo Eva. La donna nel cinema italiano dagli anni sessanta a oggi* (Bari, 1980).
10 Giuliana Bruno and Maria Nadotti, eds, *Off Screen: Women and Film in Italy* (London and New York, 1988).
11 See Fabiola Brugiamolini, ed., *La fine del gioco. La rappresentazione dell'infanzia nel cinema di Gianni Amelio* (Ancona, 1993).

Filmography

This filmography lists all the Italian films mentioned in the book. It gives:

- The title of the version distributed in English-speaking countries, or, when the film has not been distributed, a translation of the title in square brackets [ ];
- The Italian title in parentheses ( );
- The year of the first release;
- p: the corporate name of the producer;
- d: the name of the director;
- page references within this volume.

Accattone! (id.), 1961, p: Arco Film, d: Pier Paolo Pasolini, 7, 138.

[*Adventure of Salvator Rosa, An*] (*Un' avventura di Salvator Rosa*] 1939, p: Stella Film, d: Alessandro Blasetti, 80.

Adventurer's Love, An (*Amore di apache*), 1912, p: Cines, 39.

Agnes Visconti (id.), 1910, p: Itala Film, d: Giovanni Pastrone, 26.

Amarcord (id.), 1973, p: FC Produzioni, d: Federico Fellini, 137.

And the Ship Sails on (*E la nave va*), 1983, p: RAI 1/Vides, d: Federico Fellini, 160.

Antony and Cleopatra (*Marcantonio e Cleopatra*), 1913, p: Cines, d: Enrico Guazzoni, 36.

[*Assunta Spina*] (id.), 1915, p: Caesar Film, d: Gustavo Serena, 38, 39, 40.

L'avventura (id.), 1960, p: del Duca/Lyre, d: Michelangelo Antonioni, 125, 127, 133, 134, 136, 137.

Bandits at Orgosolo (*Banditi a Orgosolo*), 1961, p: de Seta, d: Vittorio de Seta, 7.

Before the Revolution (*Prima della rivoluzione*), 1964, p: Iride Cinematografica, d: Bernardo Bertolucci, 139.

Bellissima (id.), 1951, p: Film Bellissima, d: Luchino Visconti, 89, 92.

[*Bianca*] (*Bianca*), 1984, p: Faso Film, d: Nani Moretti, 158.

[*Bi and the Ba, The*] (*Il Bi e il Ba*), 1986, p: New Team/RAI 1, d: Maurizio Nichetti, 146.

Bicycle Thieves (*Ladri di biciclette*), 1947, p: Produzioni de Sica, d: Vittorio de Sica, 90, 91, 102, 103, 119.

Bitter Rice (*Riso amaro*), 1948, p: Lux, d: Giuseppe de Santis, 76, 88, 90, 94, 96, 97, 98, 101, 113.

[*Black Shirt*] (*Camicia nera*), 1933, p: Istituto Luce, d: Giovacchino Forzano, 62.

Bread, Love and Dreams (*Pane, amore e fantasia*), 1953, p: Titanus, d: Luigi Comencini, 122.

[*Bronze Sentries*] (*Sentinelle di bronzo*), 1937, p: Fono Roma, d: Romolo Marcellini, 178.

Cabiria (id.), 1914, p: Itala Film, d: Giovanni Pastrone, 26, 28, 29, 31, 34, 35, 37, 38, 42, 43, 45, 48.

[*Chains*] (*Catene*), 1949, p: Titanus, d: Raffaello Matarazzo, 107, 108, 109, 110.

Christ Stopped at Eboli, (*Cristo si è fermato a Eboli*), 1979, p: Vides, d: Francesco Rosi, 151.

[*Church, The*] (*La chiesa*), 1989, p: ADC, d: Michele Soavi, 157.

Cinema Paradiso (*Nuovo Cinema Paradiso*), 1987, p: Cristaldifilm/RAI 3, d: Giuseppe Tornatore, 160.

Colonial Romance (*Una avventura coloniale*), 1911, p: Cines, 30.

Condemned of Altona, The (*I sequestrati di Altona*), 1962, p: Titanus, d: Vittorio de Sica, 7.

[*Condottieri*] (id.), 1937, p: ENIC, d: Luis Trenker, 78, 79.

Conformist, The (*Il conformista*), 1970, p: Green Film, d: Bernardo Bertolucci, 135.

Conjugal Bed, The (*Ape regina*), 1963, p: Sancro Film, d: Marco Ferreri, 124.

Constantine and the Cross (*Costantino il Grande*), 1961, p: Jonia Film, d: Lionello de Felice, 7.

Cry, The (*Il Grido*), 1957; p: SPA Cinematgografica, d: Michelangelo Antonioni, 13, 132, 137, 139.

[*Cry of the Eagle, The*] (*Il grido dell'aquila*), 1924, p: Istituto Fascista di Propaganda, d: Mario Volpe, 176.

Damned, The (*La caduta degli dei*), 1969, p: Ital Noleggio, d: Luchino Visconti, 128, 130, 135.

Dante's Inferno (*L'inferno*), 1911, p: Milano Films, d: Adolfo Padovan, 14, 31.

[*Dawn over the Sea*] (*Aurora sul mare*), 1935, p: Manenti, d: Giorgio Simonelli, 63.

Dear Diary (*Caro diario*), 1993, p: Sacher Film, d: Nani Moretti (three episodes), 149, 150, 155, 158.

Death in Venice (*Morte a Venezia*), 1971, p: Alfa Cinematografica, d: Luchino Visconti, 135.

[*Decameron, The*] (*Il Decameron*), 1971, p: Produzioni Europee, d: Pier Paolo Pasolini, 126.

Divorce Italian Style (*Divorzio all'Italiana*), 1961, p: Galatea/Lux/Vides, d: Pietro Germi, 123.

Dolce vita, La (id.), 1960, p: Riama Film, d: Federico Fellini, 115, 116, 117, 127, 130, 132, 136, 142.

Don Camillo's Last Round (*Don Camillo e l'onorevole Peppone*), 1955, p: Rizzoli Film, d: Carmine Gallone, 121.

[*Down with Misery*] (*Abbasso la miseria*), 1945, p: Lux, d: Gennaro Righelli, 111.

Earth Quakes, The (*La terra trema*), 1948, p: Universalia, d: Luchino Visconti, 90, 92, 93, 94, 101, 102.

Eclipse, The (*L'eclisse*), 1962, p: Cineriz/Interop, d: Michelangelo Antonioni, 125, 131, 133, 134, 135, 136, 137.

8½ (id.), 1963, p: Cineriz, d: Federico Fellini, 119, 127, 131, 132, 133, 136, 149.

[*1860*] (id.), 1934, p: Cines, d: Alessandro Blasetti, 63, 64, 80.

[*Ettore Fieramosca*] (id.), 1938, p: Nembo Film, d: Alessandro Blasetti, 80.

[*Fabiola*] (id.), 1918, p: Palatino, d: Enrico Guazzoni, 36.

Fall of Rome, The (*La presa di Roma*), 1905, p: Alberini & Santoni, d: Filoteo Alberini, 20.

[*Family, The*] (*La famiglia*), 1987, p: Cinecittà/RAI 1, d: Ettore Scola, 157.

[*Old Guard*] (*Vecchia Guardia*), 1935, p: Fauno Film, d: Alessandro Blasetti, 61, 62.

Once Upon a Time in the West (*C'era una volta il West*), 1968, p: Finanziaria San Marco, d: Sergio Leone, 126, 135.

Open City (*Roma città aperta*), 1945, p: Excelsa, d: Roberto Rosselini, 88, 89, 90, 92, 94, 97, 98, 99, 101, 111.

Ossessione (id.), 1943, p: ICI, d: Luchino Visconti, 95, 101.

Paisa (*Paisà*), 1946, p: OFI, d: Roberto Rossellini, 98, 100. 101. 106, 110.

Persons Unknown (*I soliti ignoti*), 1958, p: Vides/Lux, d: Mario Monicelli, 122.

Poisoned Barrel, The (*La botte avvelenata*), 1911, p: Pasquali, 31.

[*Private Secretary, The*] (*La segretaria privata*), 1931, p: Cines, d: Goffredo Alessandrini, 65, 66.

[*Quiet Air of the West, The*] (*L'aria serena dell'ovest*), 1990, p: Pic Film/RTSI, d: Silvio Soldini, 146, 157.

Quo Vadis? (id.), 1913, p: Cines, d: Enrico Guazzoni, 26, 27, 36, 42.

[*Rebellion of the Gladiators, The*] (*La rivolta dei galdiatori*), 1958, p: Alexandra, d: Vittorio Cottafavi, 125.

Red Desert, The (*Deserto rosso*), 1964, p: Film Duemila/Francoriz, d: Michelangelo Antonioni, 128, 129, 130, 133, 137, 139.

Redeeming Angel, The (*L'angello redentore*), 1911, p: Ambrosio, 39.

[*Redemption*] (*Redenzione*), 1941, p: Andros Film, d: Marcello Albani, 176.

Road, The (*La strada*), 1954, p: Ponti-de Laurentiis, d: Federico Fellini: see *La Strada*.

Rocco and His Brothers (*Rocco e i suoi fratelli*), 1960, p: Titanus, d: Luchino Visconti, 116, 117, 120, 127, 132.

Rome, Eleven O'clock (*Roma, ore undici*), 1952, p: Titanus, d: Giuseppe De Santis, 96.

Romeo and Juliet (*Romeo e Giulietta*), 1968, p: Dino de Laurentiis, d: Franco Zeffirelli, 7.

Salvatore Giuliano (id.), 1962, p: Galatea, d: Francesco Rosi, 140, 141.

Sardinian Drummer Boy (*Il tamburino sardo*), 1915, p: Film Gloria, d: Vittorio Rossi Pianelli, 28, 31, 36.

[*Satanic Rhapsody*] (*Rapsodia satanica*), 1917, p: Cines, d: Nino Oxilia, 25, 26.

[*School, The*] (*La scuola*), 1995, p: Cecchi Gori Group, d: Daniele Luchetti, 157, 158, 162.

[*Scipio the African*] (*Scipione l'Africano*), 1937, p: ENIC, d: Carmine Gallone, 70, 78, 79.

Senso (id.), 1954, p: Lux, d: Luchino Visconti, 88, 120, 128.

Shoeshine (*Sciuscià*), 1946, p: Alfa Cinematografica, d: Vittorio de Sica, 94, 102, 103, 106, 113.

[*Siege of the Alcazar, The*] (*L'assedio dell'Alcazar*), 1940, p: Film Bassoli, d: Augusto Genina, 125.

[*Sister, The*] (*La sorella*), 1920, p: Tacita, d: Orlando Vassallo, 45.

[*Small Red Dove*] (*Palombella rossa*), 1989, p: Sacher, d: Nani Moretti, 155, 159.

Special Day, A (*Una giornata particolare*), 1977, p: Champion, d: Ettore Scola, 151.

Spider's Stratagem, The (*La strategia del ragno*), 1970, p: RAI/Red Film, d: Bernardo Bertolucci, 135, 136, 137.

Spivs (*I vitelloni*), 1953, p: Lorenzo Pegoraro, d: Federico Fellini, 15.

Splendor (id.), 1989, p: Cecchi Gori Group, d: Ettore Scola, 160.

Station, The (*La stazione*), 1990, p: Fandango, d: Sergio Rubini, 157.

Stolen Children, The (*Il ladro di bambini*), 1982, p: Erre/RAI 2, d: Gianni Amelio, 150, 161, 162.

Story of Boys and Girls (*Storia di ragazzi e di ragazze*), 1989, p: Duea Film, d: Pupi Avati, 160, 161.

Strada, La (id.), 1954, p: Ponti-de Laurentiis, d: Federico Fellini.

Sweet Life, The (*La dolce vita*), 1960, p: Riama Film, d: Federico Fellini: see *La dolce vita*.

Swindlers, The (*Il Bidone*), 1955, p: Titanus, d: Federico Fellini, 132.

Taming of the Shrew, The (*La bisbetica domata*), 1967, p: FAI, d: Franco Zeffirelli, 7.

Tempestuous Love (*Un amore selvaggio*), 1912, p: Cines, 39.

Theorem (*Teorema*), p: Aetos Film, d: Pier Paolo Pasolini, 132, 133.

Three Brothers (*Tre fratelli*), 1981, p: Iter Film, d: Francesco Rosi, 151.

To Bed . . . or Not To Bed (*Il diavolo*), 1962, p: Dino De Laurentiis, d: Gian Luigi Polidoro, 7.

[*Totò and Caroline*] (*Totò e Carolina*), 1956, p: Rosa Film, d: Mario Monicelli, 112.

[*Totò Third Man*] (*Totò terzo uomo*), 1951, p: Golden Films, d: Mario Mattòli, 112.

Tragic Pursuit, The (*Caccia tragica*), 1947, p: ANPI, d: Giuseppe de Santis, 96.

Tree of the Wooden Clogs, The (*L'albero degli zoccoli*), 1978, p: GPC/RAI 1, d: Ermanno Olmi, 156, 160.

True till Death (*Attilio Regolo*), 1911, p: Cines, 31.

Two Women (*La Ciociara*), 1960, p: Champion, d: Vittorio de Sica, 7.

Umberto D (id.), 1952, p: Films de Sica/Rizzoli, d: Vittorio de Sica, 87, 89, 91, 94, 102, 103, 104, 113.

[*Voice of the Moon, The*] (*La voce della luna*), 1990, p: Cecchi Gori Group, d: Federico Fellini, 154.

Volere volare (id.), 1993, p: Bambu Cinema, d: Maurizio Nichetti, 155.

Way to Hope, The (*Il cammino della speranza*), 1950, p: Lux, d: Pietro Germi, 88, 94, 96, 113.

[*Week of the Sphinx, The*] (*La settimana della sfinge*), 1991, p: Erre/Berlusconi Communications, d: Daniele Luchetti, 150.

[*Weeping Is All We Have Left*] (*Non ci resta che piangere*), 1984, p: Best International Films, d: Roberto Benigni and Massimo Troisi, 149.

[*We, Sinners*] (*Noi peccatori*), 1953, p: Titanus, d: Guido Brignone, 109.

[*What Rascals Men Are!*] (*Gli uomini, che mascalzoni!*), 1932, p: Cines, d: Mario Camerini, 65, 66.

[*White Angel*] (*Angelo bianco*), 1954, p: Titanus, d: Raffaello Matarazzo, 108, 110.

[*White Squadron, The*] (*Lo squadrone bianco*), 1936, p: Roma Film, d: Augusto Genina, 178.

[*Widower, The*] (*Il vedovo*), 1959, p: Paneuropa, d: Dino Risi, 123, 135.

[*Yes Madam*] (*Sissignora*), 1941, p: ATA/ICI, d: Ferdinando Poggioli, 81, 82, 92, 94, 95, 101.

Yesterday, Today and Tomorrow (*Ieri, oggi, domani*), 1963, p: Champion, d: Vittorio de Sica, 7.

Select bibliography

GUIDES AND CATALOGUES

Bernardini, A., *Archivio del cinema italiano* (Rome):
—— *Il cinema muto, 1905–1931* (1991).
—— *Il cinema sonoro, 1930–1969* (1992).
—— *Il cinema sonoro, 1970–1990* (1993).
—— *Il cinema sonoro, 1930–1990. Indici* (1993).
Cardullo, B., *What is Neorealism? A Critical English-language Bibliography of Italian Cinematic Neorealism* (Lanham and London, 1991).
di Giammatteo, F., *Nuovo dizionario universale del cinema* (Rome):
—— I, *I film* (2 vols, 1995).
—— II, *Tecnica, generi, istituzioni, autori* (1985).
Dizionario gremese del cinema italiano (Rome):
—— Chiti, R. and Lancia, E., *Dal 1930 al 1944* (1993).
—— Chiti, R. and Poppi, R., *Dal 1945 al 1959* (1991).
—— Poppi, R. and Pecorari, M., *Dal 1960 al 1969* (1992).
ISTAT, *Sommario di statistiche storiche italiane* (Rome, periodically updated).
Martinelli, V., *Il cinema muto italiano. I film del dopoguerra* (4 vols, Rome, 1980–1).
Redi, R., ed., *Cinema scritto. Il catalogo delle riviste italiane di cinema, 1907–1944* (Rome, 1992).
Rondolino, G., *Catalogo Bolaffi del cinema italiano dal dopoguerra a oggi* (Turin, 1964, periodically updated).
—— *Dizionario del cinema italiano, 1945–1969* (Rome, 1969).
Savio, F., *Ma l'amore no. Realismo, formalismo, propaganda e telefoni bianchi nel cinema di regime* (Milan, 1975).

ITALIAN CULTURE AND SOCIETY

Brera, G., *Storia del calcio italiano* (Milan, 1975).
Cadioli, A., *L'industria del romanzo. L'editoria letteraria in Italia dal 1945 agli anni ottanta* (Rome, 1981).
Caesar, M. and Hainsworth, P., eds, *Writers and Society in Contemporary Italy: A Collection of Essays* (Lemington Spa, 1984).
Castronovo, V. and Tranfaglia, N., eds, *Storia della stampa italiana* (6 vols, Rome, 1976).

Falaschi, G., *La resistanza armata nella narrativa italiana* (Turin, 1976).

Furlong, P., *Modern Italy: Politics and Policy-Making* (London, 1994).

Ginsborg, P., *A History of Contemporary Italy: Society and Politics, 1943–1988* (London, 1990).

Gundle, S., *I comunisti italiani tra Hollywood e Mosca. La sfida della cultura di massa* (Florence, 1995).

Lanaro, S., *Storia dell'Italia repubblicana. Dalla fine della guerra agli anni novanta* (Venice, 1992).

Murialdi, P., *La stampa italiana del dopoguerra, 1943–1972* (Bari, 1973).

Sassoon, D., *Contemporary Italy: Politics, Economy and Society since 1945* (London and New York, 1986).

ITALIAN CINEMA

Adams Sitney, P., *Vital Crises in Italian Cinema* (Austin, 1995).

Argentieri, M., *La censura nel cinema italiano* (Rome, 1974).

Argentieri, M. and Turchino, A., *Cinema e vita contadina* (Bari, 1984).

Aristarco, G., *Miti e realtà nel cinema italiano* (Milan, 1961).

Attolini, V., *Dal romanzo al Set. Cinema italiano delle origini a oggi* (Bari, 1988).

Baccolini, R., Bollettieri Bosinelli, R.M. and Gavioli, L., eds, *Il doppiaggio. Trasposizioni linguistiche e culturali* (Bologna, 1994).

Bertieri, C., Giannarelli, A. and Rossi, U., *L'ultimo schermo: Cinema di guera, cinema di pace* (Bari, 1984).

Bizzari, L. and Solaroli, L., *L'industria cinematografica italiana* (Florence, 1958).

Bondanella, P., *Italian Cinema: From Neorealism to the Present* (New York, 1983).

Bragaglia, C., *Il piacere del raconto. Narrativa italiana e cinema, 1895–1990* (Florence, 1993).

Brunetta, G.P., *Buio in sala. Cent'anni di passioni dello spettatore cinematografico* (Venice, 1989).

—— *Cent'anni di cinema italiano* (Rome/Bari, 1991).

—— *Storia del cinema italiano* (Rome, 1993):

—— I, *Il cinema muto, 1895–1929.*

—— II, *Il cinema del regime, 1929–1943.*

—— III, *Dal neorealismo al miracolo economico, 1943–1959.*

—— IV, *Dal miracolo economico agli anni novanta, 1960–1993.*

Bruno, G. and Nadotti, M., eds, *Off Screen: Women and Film in Italy* (London and New York, 1988).

Calandoli, G., *Materiali per una storia del cinema italiano* (Parma, 1967).

Caldiron, O., *La paura del buio. Studi sulla cultura cinematografica in Italia* (Rome, 1980).

Campari, R., *Hollywood – Cinecittà. Il raconto che cambia* (Milan, 1980).

Carotti, C., *Alla ricerca del Paradiso. L'operaio nel cinema italiano, 1945–1990* (Genoa, 1992).

Carrano, P., *Malafemmina. La donna nel cinema italiano* (Florence, 1977).

Comune di Roma, Assessorato alla cultura, *La città del cinema. Produzione e lavoro nel cinema italiano, 1930–1970* (Rome, 1979).

di Giammatteo, F., *Lo sguardo inquieto. Storia del cinema italiano, 1940–1990* (Florence, 1994).

Faldini, F. and Foffi, G., *L'avventurosa storia del cinema italiano racontata dai i suoi protagonisti, 1935–1959* (Milan, 1976).
Gambetti, G., *Cinema e censura in Italia* (Rome, 1972).
Gromo, M., *Cinema italiano, 1903–1953* (Milan, 1954).
Jarrat, V., *The Italian Cinema* (London, 1951).
Lawton, B.R., ed., *Literary and Socio-political Trends in Italian Cinema* (Los Angeles, 1975).
Liehm, M., *Passion and Defiance: Films in Italy from 1942 to the Present* (Berkeley, Los Angeles, and London, 1984).
Lizzani, C., *Il cinema italiano dalle origini agli anni ottanta* (Rome, 1982).
Malerba, L. and Siniscalco, C., *Fifty Years of Italian Cinema* (Rome, 1954).
Marcus, M., *Italian Film in the Light of Neorealism* (Princeton, 1986).
—— *Filmmaking by the Book: Italian Cinema and Literary Adaptation* (New York, 1993).
Marinucci, V., *Tendenze del cinema italiano* (Rome, 1959).
Napolitano, R., *La commedia all'italiana* (2 vols, Rome, 1986).
Quaglietti, L., *Storia economico-politica del cinema italiano, 1945–1980* (Rome, 1980).
Raffaelli, S., *La lingua filmata. Didascalie e dialoghi nel cinema italiano* (Florence, 1992).

MONOGRAPHS

Aristarco, G., *Sotto il segno dello scorpione. Il cinema dei fratelli Taviani* (Messina, 1978).
Bettetini, G. and De Berti, R., *L'attività cinematografica a Milano nel novecento* (Milan, 1990).
Blasetti, A., *Il cinema che ho visuto* (Bari, 1982).
Bondanella, P., *The Cinema of Federico Fellini* (Princeton, 1992).
—— *The Films of Roberto Rossellini* (New York, 1993).
Bondanella P. and Degli-Esposti, C., *Perspectives on Federico Fellini* (London, 1993).
Brunette, P., *Roberto Rossellini* (New York, 1987).
Capraro, V., ed., *Mordi e fuggi. La commedia secondo Dino Risi* (Venice, 1993).
Daretta, J., *Vittorio de Sica: A Guide to References and Resources* (Boston, 1983).
Gori, G.M., *Blasetti* (Florence, 1984).
Green, N., *Pier Paolo Pasolini: Cinema as Heresy* (Princeton, 1990).
Mancini, E., *Luchino Visconti: A Guide to References and Resources* (Boston, 1986).
Micciché, L., *Visconti e il neorealismo* (Venice, 1990).
—— ed., *De Sica: autore, regista, attore* (Venice, 1992).
Novell-Smith, G., *Luchino Visconti* (London, 1973).
Perry, P. and Prieto, R., *Michelangelo Antonioni: A Guide to References and Resources* (Boston, 1986).
Rifkin, N., *Antonioni's Visual Language* (Ann Arbor, 1977).
Stirling, M., *A Screen of Time: A Study of Luchino Visconti* (London, 1979).
Tonetti, C., *Luchino Visconti* (London, 1983).
Ugo, P. and Floris, A., eds, *Facciamoci del male. Il cinema di Nani Moretti* (Cagliari, 1992).
Willemen, P., ed., *Pier Paolo Pasolini* (London, 1977).

CHAPTER 1

Bernardini, A., *Cinema muto italiano* Bari):
—— I, *Ambiente, spettacoli e spettatori, 1896–1904* (1980).
—— II, *Industria e organizzazione dello spettacolo, 1905–1909* (1981).
—— III, *Arte, divismo e mercato, 1910–1914* (1981).
Bruno, G., *Streetwalking on a Ruined Map: Cultural Theory and the City Films of Elvira Notari* (Princeton and Oxford, 1993).
Camerini, C. and Redi, R., eds, *Tra una film e l'altra. Materiali sul cinema muto italiano, 1907–1920* (Venice, 1980).
Costa, A., ed., *La meccanica del visible. Il cinema delle origini in Europa* (Florence, 1983).
de Berti, R. and Mosconi, E., eds, *Il cinema delle origini a Milano, 1895–1920* (Milan, 1994).
Miccichè, L., ed., *Tra una film e l'altra. Materiali sul cinema muto italiano, 1902–1920* (Venice, 1980).
Prolo, M.A., *Storia del cinema muto italiano* (Milan, 1951).
Renzi, R., ed., *Sperduto nel buio. Il cinema muto italiano e il suo tempo 1905–1930* (Bologna, 1991).
Rondolino, G., *Torino come Hollywood. Capitale del cinema italiano, 1896–1916* (Bologna, 1980).

CHAPTER 2

Argentieri, M., *Risate di regime. La commedia italiana, 1930–1944* (Venice, 1991).
Bernardini, A. and Martinelli, V., *Il cinema italiano degli anni venti* (Rome, 1979).
Brunetta, G.P., *Intelletuali, cinema e propaganda tra le due guerre* (Bologna, 1973).
—— *Spari nel buio* (Rome, 1992).
Cannistraro, P.V., *La fabbrica del consenso. Fascismo e mas-media* (Rome, 1975).
Cardillo, M., *Il Duce in moviola. Politica e divismo nei cinegiornali e documentari 'Luce'* (Bari, 1983).
—— *Tra le quinte del cinematografo. Cinema, cultura e società in Italia, 1900–1937* (Bari, 1987).
Casetti, F. and De Berti R., eds, *Il cinema a Milano tra le due guerre* (Milan, 1988).
Ghigi, G., ed., *Venezia 1932. Il cinema diventa arte* (Venice, 1992).
Gori, G., ed., *Cinema e parrocchia* (Rimini, 1980).
Gori, G., and Pivato, S., eds, *Gli anni del cinema di parrocchia* (Rimini, 1980).
Hay, J., *Popular Film Culture in Fascist Italy: The Passing of the Rex* (Bloomington, 1987).
Landy, M., *Fascism in Italy: The Italian Commercial Cinema, 1931–1943* (Princeton, 1986).
Mancini, E., *Struggles of the Italian Film Industry during Fascism, 1930–1935* (Ann Arbor, 1981).
Martinelli, V., *Il cinema muto italiano. I film della grande guerra, 1916–1918* (Rome).
—— *1916* (2 vols, 1991).
—— *1917* (2 vols, 1992).
Pividori, B., ed., *Critica italiana, primo tempo: 1926–1934* (Rome, 1973).

CHAPTER 3

Aiello, G., *Il cinema italiano negli ultimi vent'anni* (Cremona, 1965).

Apra, A. and Carabba, C., *Neorealismo d'appendice. Per un dibattito sul cinema popolare: il caso Matarazzo* (Florence, 1976).

Apra, A. and Pistanesi, P., *The Fabulous Thirties: Italian Cinema, 1929–1944* (Milan, 1979).

Aristarco, G., *Neorealismo e nuova critica cinematografica* (Florence, 1980).

Armes, R., *Patterns of Realism* (South Brunswick, 1971).

Baldelli, P., *Cinema dell'ambiguità* (Rome, 1969).

Brunetta, G.P. and Gili, J., *L'ora d'Africa del cinema italiano* (Rovereto, 1989).

Calderon, O., *Il lungo viaggio del cinema italiano, antologia di 'Cinema', 1936–1943* (Padua, 1965).

Canziani, A., *Gli anni del neorealismo* (Florence, 1977).

Carabba, C., *Il cinema del ventennio nero* (Florence, 1974).

Carpi, F., *Cinema italiano del dopoguerra* (Milan, 1958).

Chamoux, E., ed., *Cinema, storia, resistenza* (Milan, 1987).

Ferrara, G., *Il nuovo cinema italiano* (Florence, 1957).

Gili, J., *Stato fascista e cinematografia. Repressione e promozione* (Rome, 1981).

Livolsi, M., ed., *Schermi e ombre. Gli italiani e il cinema nel dopoguerra* (Florence, 1988).

Malerba, L., *Italian Cinema, 1945–1951* (Rome, 1951).

Micciché, L., ed., *Il neorealismo cinematografico italiano* (Venice, 1975).

Overby, D., ed., *Springtime in Italy: A Reader on Neorealism* (London, 1978).

Pintus, P., *Storia e film. Trent'anni di cinema, 1945–1975* (Rome, 1980).

Redi, R., *Cinema italiano sotto il fascismo* (Venice, 1979).

Rondi, B., *Il neorealismo italiano* (Parma, 1956).

Savio, F., *Cinecittà anni trenta. Parlano 116 protagonisti del secondo cinema italiano, 1930–1943* (3 vols, Rome, 1979).

Silverman, M., 'Italian Film and American Capital, 1947–1951', in Mellencamp, P. and Rosen, P., eds, *Cinema Histories, Cinema Practices* (Los Angeles, 1984).

Tinazzi, G., ed., *Il cinema italiano dal fascismo all'antifascismo* (Padua, 1966).

Ugoletti, L., *Il cinema italiano, 1945–1952* (Rome, 1952).

Vento, G. and Mida, M., *Cinema e resistenza* (Florence, 1954).

Verdone, M. and Autera, L., *Antologia di 'Bianco e Nero', 1937–1943* (Rome, 1964).

Zavattini, C., *Sequences from a Cinematic Life* (Englewood Cliffs, 1977).

CHAPTER 4

Amico M. d', *La commedia all'Italiana. Il cinema comico in Italia dal 1945 al 1975* (Milan, 1985).

Apra, A. and Pistagnesi, P., *Comedy Italian Style, 1950–1980* (Rome, 1986).

Arosio, M., Cereda, G. and Iseppi, F., *Cinema e cattolici in Italia* (Milan, 1974).

de Berti, R., ed., *Il cinema a Milano dal secondo dopoguerra ai primi anni sessanta* (Milan, 1991).

Ferrero, A., Grignaffini, G. and Quaresima, L., *Il cinema italiano degli anni' 50* (Florence, 1977).

Fofi, G., *Il cinema italiano: servi e padroni* (Milan, 1971).

Grande, M., *Abiti nuziali e biglietti di banca. La società della commedia nel cinema italiano* (Rome, 1986).

Grazzini, G., *Eva dopo Eva. La donna nel cinema italiano dagli anni sessanta a oggi* (Bari, 1980).

May, R., *Angoscia e solitudine nel cinema italiano contemporaneo* (Fessano, 1968).

Micciché, L., *Il cinema italiano degli anni '60 e oltre* (Venice, 1995).

Moscati, M., *Western all'Italiana* (Milan, 1978).

Rondi, G.L., *Cinema italiano oggi, 1952–1965* (Rome, 1966).

Salizzato, C., ed., *Prima della rivoluzione, schermi italiani, 1960–1969* (Venice, 1989).

Spinazzola, V., *Cinema e pubblico. Lo spettacolo filmico in Italia, 1945–1965* (Milan, 1975).

Tinazzi, G., ed., *Il cinema italiano degli anni '50* (Venice, 1979).

——, ed., *Il 'nuovo' cinema italiano* (Padua, 1963).

Torri, B., *Cinema italiano. Della realtà alla metafora* (Palermo, 1973).

Weiser, T., *Spaghetti Westerns: The Good, the Bad and the Violent. 558 Euro-westerns and Their Personnel, 1961–1977* (Jefferson and London, 1992).

CHAPTER 5

Bechelloni, G., ed., *Il mutamento culturale in Italia* (Naples, 1989).

Brosio, G. and Santaga, W., *Rapporto sull'economia delle arti e dello spettacolo in Italia* (Turin, 1992).

Casetti, F., *Tra me e te. Strategia di coinvolgimento dello spettatore nei programmi della neotelevisione* (Turin, 1988).

Forgacs, D., *L'industrializzazione della cultura italiana* (Bologna, 1992).

Gieri, M., *Italian Contemporary Filmmaking: Strategies of Subversion* (Toronto, 1994).

Magrelli, F., ed., *Sull'industria cinematografica italiana* (Venice, 1986).

Montini, F., *I novissimi, Gli esordienti nel cinema italiano degli anni '80* (Turin, 1988).

Ortoleva, P., *Un ventennio a colori. Televisione privata e società in Italia, 1975–1995* (Florence, 1995).

Witcombe, R.T., *The New Italian Cinema: Studies in Dance and Despair* (London, 1982).

Zagarrio, V., ed., *Dietro lo schermo. Ragionamenti sui modi di produzione cinemato-grafici in Italia* (Venice, 1988).

Index of films

Index of names

Subject index

actors and acting: cinema 28, 32–5, 92, 100, 122, 130, 149, 153, 169–70; *divismo* 32–4, 169; radio 55, 107; star-system 32–5, 169; television 153; theatre 32, 149
advertisement: cinema as 4; on television 153
amateurism 30
Ambrosio 21, 29–30
American Motion Picture Patents Company 53
architecture 20
Arcitrezza 92
Argentina 22
artistic quality: government assessment of 88; modernism and 127–34
audience 9, 12, 13, 165, 166, 168–9, 171; in 'economic miracle' years 118, 119, 142; Fascist propaganda and 52; in inter-war years 55–6, 58, 60–1, 67, 72–6, 84, 114; neorealism and 105–7; in post-war years 114; pre-1914 16–17, 30, 40, 42–3; in television age 147

Bianco e nero (White and Black) (magazine) 73
Bologna railway station bomb 145
book shops 145
Brazil 22
bribery and corruption 122, 123, 127, 146, 148, 153

cameramen 30
captions in silent films 18
cars 119
cartoons 155

Catholic Centre for Cinema 71, 87
Catholic Church *see* Roman Catholic Church
Celio Film 32
censorship 44–5, 78, 87
Christian Democrats 74, 85, 88
Cine-forums 120
Cinecittà 13, 70, 160, 166
Cinema (magazine) 73
cinemas (picture-houses): architecture of 20; in 'economic miracle' years 120; in inter-war years 56, 71, 72; in post-war years 74–5; pre-1914 17–18, 20; sound pictures and 56; in television age 147
Cinematic Information (magazine) 71, 87
cinematography: internationalism of 2–4; national character and 4–7, 8–12, *see also* Italian cinema
Cines 20, 21, 30, 36, 54, 55, 63, 64
civil service 73, 87
class: cinema-going and 17, 73, 75–6, 125; conflict and 49, 81–2, 142
classical cinema 2–3
classicism 31, 127
close-ups 152–3
colonialism 37, 69
colour: in films 120, 153–5; on television 153, 155
comedies: in 'economic miracle' years 119, 121–4, 127, 135, 142; in inter-war years 64–5, 80–1, 83; in post-war years 111–13; pre-1914 41–2
communalism, Italian 5–6
Communist Party 50, 58, 74, 86, 90–1, 107, 159, 163
consensus 79–80